"GENTLEMEN OF

PROPERTY AND STANDING"

Anti-Abolition Mobs in Jacksonian America

"GENTLEMEN OF

PROPERTY AND STANDING"

Anti-Abolition Mobs in Jacksonian America

LEONARD L. RICHARDS

New York · *Oxford University Press* · *1970*

FOR THERESA

Preface

This book is about white Northerners who attacked abolitionists and blacks. Since it first began taking shape about five years ago, events have brought a new urgency to the question of violence in American society. Why was Detroit burned? Martin Luther King murdered? Robert Kennedy assassinated? One campus after another disrupted? We have been deluged with "answers" to these questions and dozens of similar ones. Yet, as George Sorel put it sixty years ago, "the problems of violence still remain very obscure." [1]

Some commentators assume that our present state of domestic disorder is the product of some mysterious defect in the American character. Others point to the sadism of motion pictures and comic books, or to the unsettledness of American life, or to our youthfulness as a nation, or to white racism, or to our frontier tradition, or to rising expectations. Many claim that "black rage" and "student unrest" represent the birth pangs of a new order or the righteous wrath of the desperate and the downtrodden. Some remember that mob violence has often been the last spasm of a dying order and the age-old remedy of those who felt that power was

[1] *Reflections on Violence* (Collier Books edition; New York, 1961), 60.

vii

slipping from their hands. But few have any clear notion of how, when, and why mob violence erupted and ebbed in our past.

Unfortunately, there is very little in our history books that is likely to help either the specialist or the intelligent layman, and there is much in many books that is apt to mislead them. Indeed, it has been my experience that intelligent people of all descriptions—black and white, young and old, radical and conservative— are dumbfounded when confronted with some of the history of ante-bellum violence. It seems that most people have formed their opinions on the basis of half-truths and distorted historical information, and that many of our leading sociological theories rest upon shaky historical foundations.

I hope that this book will shed a little light on violence in one period of our history. And I hope that it will cause scholars to pause—and perhaps even take a second look—before dashing off glib references to America's bloody heritage or to the long, hot summers of the past. For our present passion for self-denunciations and familiar generalities only conceals our ignorance. We need to admit our ignorance, clear the air of half-truths, and concede that broad beams of light will have to wait upon further research and investigation. I hope that this study will prove to be a step in the right direction.

Since the book deals with several problems that have never been adequately investigated, it is rather inevitable that I have made some mistakes. I would have made more mistakes, however, if it had not been for many generous and obliging scholars who have read and criticized the manuscript. I owe most to Wilson Smith. His kindness and counsel were invaluable at every step of the way. I am also heavily indebted to Daniel H. Calhoun. Whenever I had the wit to follow his inventive comments, I profited immensely. Special thanks are also due to Paul Goodman and Thomas Bickman for their cordial aid and timely suggestions.

In my research I received assistance from the staffs of many libraries and depositories. I am particularly indebted to Mrs. Vera Loomis and the Inter-Library Loan Service of the University of California at Davis for securing countless books, pamphlets, and microfilms and saving me the expense of additional time and travel. Special thanks are also due to the personnel of the Boston Public Library, the Cincinnati Historical Society, the Cincinnati Public Library, the Hall of Records of the City of New York, the Municipal Archives of the City of New York, the New-York Historical Society, the New York Public Library, the Library of Congress, the National Archives, the Oneida Historical Society, and the Utica Public Library.

Finally, the book is dedicated to my wife, Theresa, whose encouragement and calm confidence that I would finish made it a labor of love from the beginning.

L. L. R.

Amherst, Massachusetts
September, 1969

Contents

"GENTLEMEN OF

PROPERTY AND STANDING"

Anti-Abolition Mobs in Jacksonian America

1

Introduction

Why were Northerners so hostile to organized antislavery? This remains a major problem in the history of the American antislavery movement. For over a century historians have been telling us that Northerners dragged the antislavery agitator William Lloyd Garrison through the streets of Boston in 1835; broke up a convention of the New York State Anti-Slavery Society at Utica on the same day; petitioned in 1835 and 1836 for legislation to make the propagation of abolitionist sentiments a criminal offense; supplied the necessary votes to pass the famous gag rule which was renewed at each session of Congress between 1836 and 1844; established the Connecticut gag law in 1836 to bar abolitionist lecturers from Congregational pulpits; murdered the abolitionist editor Elijah Lovejoy at Alton, Illinois, in 1837; burned down Pennsylvania Hall in Philadelphia in 1838. But why? How are we to account for these and dozens of similar incidents?

It no longer seems possible for historians to dismiss these happenings as simply aberrations in an otherwise healthy and enlightened society. Too many scholars have uncovered evidence indicating that Northern anti-abolitionism was both a pervasive and an intensive component of Northern life. Ever since Adelaide Avery

Lyons demonstrated in 1919 that slavery had many staunch defenders in the North, "particularly in the colleges and the
churches," it has become increasingly clear that the traditional
view of the "antislavery North" is largely a myth. Even in those alleged strongholds of antislavery, the Congregational churches of
New England and the Presbyterian churches of the West, there
are strong indications that anti-abolitionism, rather than abolitionism, prevailed. And, as Lorman Ratner's recent study indicates, it
appears that "the New England conscience," the holy of holies in
antislavery literature, included as much anti-abolitionism as the
ethical guideposts of supposedly less scrupulous Americans. It is
clear, then, that anti-abolitionism permeated much of Northern
life.[1]

Historians will be deeply indebted to these scholars, for their
studies have undermined myths whose persistence has been alarming. But perhaps they have raised as many questions as they have
answered. For anti-abolitionism had a selective influence in the
North. Thousands of Northerners were alarmed by the pronounce-

---

[1] Adelaide Avery Lyons, "Religious Defense of Slavery in the North,"
Trinity College Historical Society, Historical Papers, XIII (1919), 5–34;
Henry Clyde Hubbart, " 'Pro-Southern' Influence in the Free West, 1840–
1865," *Mississippi Valley Historical Review* 20 (June 1933), 45–62; Irving
Stoddard Kull, "Presbyterian Attitudes toward Slavery," *Church History* 7
(1938), 101–14; Philip S. Foner, *Business and Slavery* (Chapel Hill, 1940);
Howard C. Perkins, "The Defense of Slavery in the Northern Press on the
Eve of the Civil War," *Journal of Southern History* 9 (November 1943),
501–31; Madeleine Hook Rice, *American Catholic Opinion in the Slavery
Controversy* (New York, 1944); Russel B. Nye, *Fettered Freedom* (East
Lansing, Michigan, 1949); Robert C. Senior, "New England Congrega-
tionalists and the Anti-Slavery Movement, 1830–1860" (Unpub. Ph.D. disser-
tation, Yale University, 1954); Joel H. Silbey, "Pro-Slavery Sentiment in
Iowa, 1838–1861," *Iowa Journal of History* 55 (October 1957), 289–318;
Victor Howard, "The Anti-Slavery Movement in the Presbyterian Church,
1835–1861" (Unpub. Ph.D. dissertation, Ohio State University, 1961);
Donald G. Mathews, *Slavery and Methodism* (Princeton, 1965), Chapter 6;
William Dusinberre, *Civil War Issues in Philadelphia, 1856–1865* (Philadel-
phia, 1965); Lorman A. Ratner, "Northern Opposition to the Anti-Slavery
Movement, 1831–1840" (Unpub. Ph.D. dissertation, Cornell University, 1961),
"Northern Concern for Social Order as Cause of Rejecting Anti-Slavery,
1831–1840," *The Historian* 28 (November 1965), 1–18, and *Powder Keg:
Northern Opposition to the Anti-Slavery Movement, 1831–1840* (New York,
1968).

ments of Garrison and Lovejoy, and millions heard and repeated commonplaces about the danger of disunion and civil war. Yet only certain men tried to silence the "incendiaries." Why should some Northerners remain passive, and still others damage homes and churches and hurl eggs and stones when abolition meetings were in progress? Who were the more zealous anti-abolitionists, and what motivated them?

I believe that the best way to answer this difficult question is to analyze the Northern anti-abolition mobs. By "mobs," I mean those situations where dozens, hundreds, or even thousands of persons temporarily assisted one another and in a violent or turbulent manner broke up meetings, assaulted abolitionists, damaged or destroyed property. Such incidents were frequent, well reported, and much discussed. To the casual observer they often seemed to be spontaneous outbursts, but in nine cases out of ten the mobs involved explicit planning and organization.[2] Their membership usually included many prominent and articulate men—doctors and lawyers, merchants and bankers, judges and Congressmen. These "gentlemen of property and standing," as contemporaries called them, had so little fear of indictment or public censure that they often made public pronouncements—and sometimes even permitted records of their meetings and membership to be published! The mobs therefore provide a convenient entry to the sources of Northern hostility to antislavery.

II

The anti-abolitionist mobs also furnish a medium for studying the problem of violence in ante-bellum America. It is one of the scandals of American historiography that there is no solid study of this important subject.

Historians, of course, will be quick to point out that ante-bellum

[2] Owing largely to conventional wisdom and partly to the influence of Gustav Le Bon's *The Crowd: A Study of the Popular Mind* (English translation, London, 1896), sociologists have generally assumed that mobs lack organization, planning, structure. Closer inspection, I suspect, would probably reveal that even slum mobs generally involve more coordination and design than scholars assume.

histories are filled with data about murders, lynchings, wars, and insurrections. The "revisionists" may blame the strife and disorder on "unrealistic and senseless misunderstandings," a "blundering generation," "irresponsible and blind" political operators, "hyper-emotionalism," or an "excess of democracy." Their critics may reassert the importance of moral disgust with slavery or the concomitant problem of race adjustment. But both sides agree that the period was one of increased hysteria, violence, and turbulence.[3] Thus a few minutes' browsing in almost any library will reveal such chapter titles as the "Turbulent Thirties" or "Fitful Fifties" or "Age of Passion."

Nevertheless I think that my generalization is valid. Historians have written about violent acts, but they have not investigated the question of violence itself.[4] As a result, when it comes to explain-

[3] Compare Avery Craven, *The Repressible Conflict* (Baton Rouge, 1939); James G. Randall, "The Blundering Generation," *Mississippi Valley Historical Review* 27 (June 1940), 3–28; Roy F. Nichols, *The Disruption of American Democracy* (New York, 1948); David Donald, *Lincoln Reconsidered* (2d ed.; New York, 1961), 209–35; with Arthur Schlesinger, Jr., "The Causes of the Civil War: A Note on Historical Sentimentalism," *The Partisan Review* 16 (1949), 469–81; Pieter Geyl, "The American Civil War and the Problem of Inevitability," *New England Quarterly* 24 (June 1951), 147–68; Harry V. Jaffa, *Crisis of the House Divided* (New York, 1959); Allan Nevins, *Ordeal of the Union* (2 vols.; New York, 1947), and *The Emergence of Lincoln* (2 vols.; New York, 1950).

[4] Among ante-bellum histories, David Brion Davis' *Homicide in American Fiction* (Ithaca, New York, 1957), Chapter 9, and John Hope Franklin's *The Militant South* (Cambridge, Massachusetts, 1956) come closest to dealing squarely with the problem.

To some extent the problem of human violence, as the reports of Brandeis' Conferences on Violence (1963 to date) clearly reveal, has eluded scholarly research. For a wide range of recent general references, see "Patterns of Violence," *The Annals of the American Academy of Political and Social Science* 364 (March 1966), entire issue; Elton B. McNeil, ed., *The Nature of Human Conflict* (Englewood Cliffs, New Jersey, 1965); Jules Masserman, ed., *Violence and War* (New York, 1963); "Anthropology of Conflict," *Journal of Conflict Resolution* 5 (1961), entire issue; Joseph S. Roucek, "The Sociology of Violence," *Journal of Human Relations* 5 (1957), 9–21; Jessie Bernard, "Some Current Conceptualizations in the Field of Conflict," *American Journal of Sociology* 70 (1965), 442–54; Charles Tilly and James Rule, *Measuring Political Upheaval* (Princeton, 1965); "Urban Violence and Disorder," *American Behavioral Scientist* II (March–April 1968), entire issue; Hugh Davis Graham and Ted Robert Gurr, eds., *Violence in America* (New York, 1969).

ing such matters as why mob violence was the hallmark of one decade but not of another, there is a real paucity of knowledge. An inference can be found here, a page or two there—but a solid study of this important subject has yet to be written.

Despite this neglect, historians periodically have called attention to a sharp increase of riot and turbulence in the Jacksonian period. Many have been rather vague about dates. Some have assumed that the rise came in the mid-1820's, either with the political advent of Andrew Jackson or with the "rise of the common man." Others have assumed that mob violence came in 1831 as a reaction to the initial publication of Garrison's *Liberator*. Still others have followed the lead of abolition polemics and placed the date in 1833, 1834, or 1835.[5]

Not only the abolitionists, but also their contemporaries were convinced that a spirit of riot descended on the country in the mid-1830's. Although there was anything but unanimity, most saw an upsurge of violence in 1833, 1834, or 1835.[6] Alexis de Tocqueville, it should be noted, recorded very little turmoil during his visit in the early 1830's, but subsequent travelers filled their note-

[5] Among the more specific references are John Bach McMaster, *A History of the People of the United States* (8 vols.; New York, 1883–1914), Vol. VI, pp. 86–87, 230–32, 271–98; William Graham Sumner, *Andrew Jackson* (Boston, 1882), 364–65, 428–29; Woodrow Wilson, *Division and Reunion, 1829–1889* (New York, 1893), 115–17; James Elbert Cutler, *Lynch-Law: An Investigation into the History of Lynching in the United States* (New York, 1905), Chapter 4; Clement Eaton, "Mob Violence in the Old South," *Mississippi Valley Historical Review* 29 (December 1942), 351–71; Nye, *Fettered Freedom*, Chapter 5; Davis, *Homicide in American Fiction*, 240–51, 272–76.

[6] In the mid-1830's, particularly in August and September 1835, every newspaper that I read (see bibliography) addressed itself repeatedly to the question of increasing violence. Through judicial asides it is possible to trace the growing awareness of widespread violence. Cf. *State v. Cole*, 2 McCord 117 (South Carolina, 1822); *Commonwealth v. Jenkins*, Thacher, Criminal Cases 118 (Massachusetts, 1825); *Commonwealth v. Dupuy*, 6 Pennsylvania Law Journal 223 (1831); *State v. Allison*, 11 Tennessee 428 (1832); *State v. Brooks*, 1 Hill 361 (South Carolina, 1833); *Douglas v. State*, 14 Tennessee 525 (1834); *United States v. Peaco*, 4 Cranch C. C. 601 (1835); *United States v. Fenwick*, 4 Cranch, C. C. 675 (1836); *State v. Bennett*, 20 North Carolina 170 (1838); *State v. Brazil*, Rice 257 (South Carolina, 1839).

books with clippings about knifings, shootings, riots, and internal wars. Using a barrage of such clippings, Thomas Brothers, an Englishman, presented a strong case that America was not a land of tranquil and friendly neighbors as Thomas Paine had promised; instead its citizens habitually lynched editors, burned convents, and tortured Negroes. With delight the *Montreal Herald* called attention to "'the strifes and hatreds,' which exist in that miscalled 'land of liberty' . . . No wonder that a British house of commons paused in its downward career! " [7]

Americans, though they would not accept the *Montreal Herald's* contention that democracy invariably leads to anarchy and murder, generally agreed that the United States was no longer a happy, peaceful land of friendly neighbors and modest desires. There was a time, wrote Hezekiah Niles from his Baltimore office in August, 1835, "when every citizen . . . would 'rally round the standard of the law, and unite in common efforts for the common good'—when a person, armed only with a small piece of paper, could proceed a thousand miles through the country, and bring the strongest man to answer to the law. . . . But is it so now? Alas, no!" Across the nation, a few years later, Abraham Lincoln explained to the Young Men's Lyceum of Springfield, Illinois, that "in this land so lately famed for law and order," violence and disorder had become "the everyday news of the times." [8]

What troubled Lincoln, Niles, and other Americans was not the sudden rise of violence itself. For years Americans had been told

[7] J. P. Mayer, ed., *Alexis de Tocqueville: Journey to America* (New Haven, 1960), 108–9, 269; Thomas Brothers, *The United States of North America as They Are; Not as They Are Generally Described* . . . (London, 1840), 8 and *passim*; *Montreal Herald*, October 22, 1835, as quoted in *Niles' Weekly Register* 49 (November 7, 1835), 157.

[8] *Niles' Weekly Register* 48 (August 8, 1835), 393; T. Harry Williams, ed., *Abraham Lincoln: Selected Speeches, Messages, and Letters* (New York, 1957), 7, 14. Hundreds of similar comments can be gleaned from contemporaries; among the more accessible are Allan Nevins, ed., *Diary of Philip Hone, 1828–1851* (New York, 1927), 167–69 [entries for August 2 and 11, 1835]; Theodore Sedgwick, Jr., *Political Writings of William Leggett* (2 vols.; New York, 1839), Vol. I, *passim*; *Southern Literary Messenger* II (May 1836), 389; *Atkinson's Saturday Evening Post* (Philadelphia), August 15, September 5, November 7, 1835; "The March of Anarchy," *New England Magazine* 7 (November 1834), 409.

that their urban crime rate was higher than England's, and that fisticuffs, eye gougings, knife and gunplay characterized the frontier. And America already had a history of "lawful" violence—of violence committed by civil, penal, and military authorities. Some Americans were more concerned about these matters than Europeans often thought.[9] But what really bothered thoughtful men in the 1830's was the sudden outbreak of mobs, the growing propensity of many Americans to "take the law into their own hands." "Many of the people," lamented Niles, ". . . are 'out of joint.' A spirit of riot . . . prevails in every quarter." Mobs, complained Lincoln, "have pervaded the country from New England to Louisiana; they are neither peculiar to the eternal snows of the former nor the burning suns of the latter. . . . Alike they spring up among the pleasure-hunting masters of Southern slaves, and the order-loving citizens of the land of steady habits. Whatever then their cause may be, it is common to the whole country." [10]

"What is the meaning of all this?" asked James Gordon Bennett, editor of the nation's fastest growing newspaper, the New York *Herald*. The nation, he continued, was obviously in a state of hysteria. But why? Why the nationwide tension? Why should Americans suddenly begin attacking abolitionist merchants in New York City, assailing nuns in Massachusetts, hanging gamblers in Vicksburg, burning the mail in Charleston, razing the dwellings of Negroes in Philadelphia? [11]

[9] For thoughtful appraisals of those Americans who did question "lawful" violence, see David Brion Davis, "The Movement to Abolish Capital Punishment in America, 1787–1861," *American Historical Review* 63 (October 1957), 23–46; John Demos, "The Antislavery Movement and the Problem of Violent 'Means,'" *New England Quarterly* 37 (December 1964), 501–26; and Merle Curti, *The American Peace Crusade, 1815–1860* (Durham, North Carolina, 1929).

For statistical comparison of American and British crime rates, see William Bradford, *An Enquiry How Far the Punishment of Death is Necessary in Pennsylvania* . . . (Philadelphia, 1793), 38–39; Edward Livingston, *A System of Penal Law for the State of Louisiana* . . . (Philadelphia, 1833), 30; Luther Hamilton, ed., *Memoirs* . . . *of Robert Rantoul* (Boston, 1854), 502–6.

[10] *Niles' Register* 48 (August 22, 1835), 439; Williams, *Lincoln's Selected Speeches*, 6–7.

[11] New York *Herald*, September 1, 1835.

Some Americans were frankly puzzled. Others blamed it on strong drink, poor upbringing, the "spirit of the times" in general, or "ultraism" in particular. Many connected it with some alien force such as "the" foreigners, "the" Catholics, "the" gamblers, or "the" bankers. But most men agreed that the upsurge of violence was the inevitable result of organized antislavery. The abolitionists, it was commonly assumed, not only directly provoked slave insurrections, race riots, and anti-abolitionist mobs, but also indirectly produced the tension that led to the mobbing of Mormons, Catholics, prostitutes, gamblers, and other outcasts. "The abolitionists," as Bennett put it in September, 1835, "a few thousand crazy-headed blockheads have actually frightened fifteen million people out of their senses. So terribly scared are these fifteen million that the ordinary operation of laws against evil doers are thrown aside as too slow." [12]

III

To what extent was it valid for Jacksonian Americans to insist that mobs were more prevalent in the 1830's than in the 1820's or the 1810's? For Lincoln to claim that mobs had pervaded all segments of the nation? For Bennett to say that fear of a few thousand abolitionists was the source of the turmoil?

To assess these questions, I assembled data on all the major and minor mobs, riots, disturbances, civil disorders, and the like that were reported in *Niles' Weekly Register* between 1812 and late 1849. The *Register*, despite its reputation for exhaustive detail and national coverage, obviously did not list every instance of public disorder; had others compiled its contents, some events doubtless would have been omitted, and others included. And, like all papers, its contents were undoubtedly influenced by the whims of its editor, who from time to time admittedly tried to manage the news, and by changes in newsgathering, technology, and communications.[13]

[12] *Ibid.*

[13] For the possible pitfalls, see Raoul Naroll, *Data Quality Control—A New*

Nevertheless I do not think that we need to be unduly worried about the effects of such matters as the editor's idiosyncrasies, the Transportation Revolution,[14] or the rise of the penny press. For the *Register* prided itself on being a traditional paper and to its own peril refused to adopt modern techniques.[15] Moreover, if an outbreak of rioting were due merely to news outreach, then one would expect a disproportionate rise of rural rioting; that is, one would expect the number of rural incidents to suddenly jump from, say, 50 per cent of the total to perhaps 65, 75, or 85 per cent. Actually the percentages of rural to urban disorders remained constant; in the ten years before the outburst, rural incidences composed 54 per cent of the total; in the three years of heavy rioting, 53 per cent; and in the year of the heaviest rioting, 57 per cent.[16] The *Register*, then, probably provides an excellent sampling of social disorder.

Data from the *Register* confirm, as the following table illustrates, the generalized belief of Jacksonian Americans that there was a sharp increase of mob violence in the 1830's: [17]

Research Technique (New York, 1962), and Nahum Z. Medalia and Otto N. Larsen, "Diffusion and Belief in a Collective Delusion: The Seattle Windshield Pitting Epidemic," *American Sociological Review* 23 (1958), 180–86.

[14] The reference here is to George Rogers Taylor's famous concept. In essence, Taylor argues that the great boom in canals, turnpikes, steamboats, and railroads was central to American development after 1815. By cheapening and facilitating the movement of people and goods, for example, it not only created markets and spurred producers but also stimulated specialization, the division of labor between sections and between town and country, the development of large corporations, the interchange of news, and the development of large metropolitan newspapers. For a full discussion, see *The Transportation Revolution, 1815–1860* (New York, 1951).

[15] The *Register* finally ceased operations partly because it refused to change its techniques to fit the dictates of the telegraph. For a full discussion of the *Register's* policies and methods, see N. N. Luxon, *Niles' Weekly Register, News Magazine of the Nineteenth Century* (Baton Rouge, 1947).

[16] Computed from data, *Niles' Register* Vols. 24–51 (1823–1836). From 1839 on, there was a sharp rise of rural incidents; in the 1840's, however, there were a number of very serious rural disturbances, stemming largely from the anti-rent "wars" in New York and the Mormon "wars" in Illinois.

[17] Computed from data, *Niles' Register* Vols. 1–75 (1812–1849). The figures that I present here and elsewhere tell us nothing about the "magnitude"

1812–1819	7 incidents reported
1820–1829	21
1830–1839	115
1840–1849	64

The data also help to explain why keen observers, such as Tocqueville, who visited the country in the early 1830's, had so little to say about the subject, while others who arrived later in the decade devoted page after page to the evils of mob rule. As the following table illustrates, the flood tide of mobs came in 1834, 1835, and 1836—several years after Tocqueville's visit: [18]

1830	1 incident reported
1831	3
1832	1
1833	4
1834	20
1835	53
1836	16
1837	3
1838	4

This table probably minimizes the sharp increase in 1835, for by August of that year Niles was receiving hundreds of articles a week on various mobs and riots throughout the country—so many that he decided to print only a "specimen" of the articles in his possession. "We cannot," he regretfully admitted, "consent to hold

of the incidents. This is unfortunate, but the accounts of most disturbances do not provide the data needed for such measurement. If one seriously intends to measure the amount of human energy expended in a riot, he has to consider such matters as the number of man-hours or man-days involved, the proportion of the community that participated, the geographical scope of the disturbance, the degree of violence, and the size and capacity of the resisting force. (For a full discussion, see Tilly and Rule, *Measuring Political Upheaval.*) The accounts almost always exaggerate the number of participants, the number killed, or the amount of damages, but the degree of exaggeration is never constant; one account, for example, might report ten deaths when there were only five, while another might report thirty deaths when there was only one. To make matters worse, almost every account fails to provide information about the size and capacity of the resisting force, and many omit information on one or more other items.

[18] Computed from data, *Niles' Register* Vols. 39–55 (1830–1838).

up our country to contempt and scorn of the old world, and shall, therefore, generally suppress them, though some cases of peculiar atrocity must be inserted." [19]

The increased violence of the 1830's affected all parts of the country. It was not primarily a Southern problem, stemming largely from a defective Southern personality and Southern way of life, as John Hope Franklin argues.[20] The lynching mob, to be sure, was largely a Southern phenomenon—or, to be more exact, a mode of the Old Southwest; but mob violence, as Lincoln pointed out, was neither peculiar to "the burning suns" of the South nor to "the eternal snows" of New England; it was, as the following table shows, increasing everywhere, in the North and in the South, in the older, well-established communities of the East as well as in the bustling, raucous, newer villages of the West: [21]

	1820's	1830's
New England	4 incidents reported	17 incidents reported
Middle Atlantic	10	33
South Atlantic	3	25
Southwest	3	30
Northwest	1	10

[19] *Niles' Register* 49 (September 5, 1835), 1. Due to the obvious implications of this statement, I tried to determine to what extent Niles suppressed minor disturbances after September 1835. After comparing the data from the *Register* with the older, more detailed histories of Portland, Boston, New York City, Philadelphia, Charleston, Mobile, New Orleans, St. Louis, Nashville, and Cincinnati, I concluded that if Niles did suppress such disturbances, either he did so over a very short time, or he only suppressed rural incidents. With the possible exception of two interior cities—Nashville and Cincinnati —I found that the *Register's* reporting was consistently more thorough than the urban histories, even those that seemingly specialized in local calamities. Between September 1, 1834, and September 1, 1835, 56 per cent of the 41 incidents reported were rural; between September 1, 1835, and September 1, 1836, 55 per cent of 29.

[20] *The Militant South.*

[21] Computed from data, *Niles' Register* Vols. 18–57 (1820–1839). In establishing regions, I followed the census of 1830—New England: Massachusetts, Maine, Vermont, New Hampshire, Rhode Island, and Connecticut; Middle Atlantic: New York, New Jersey, and Pennsylvania; South Atlantic: Maryland, Delaware, District of Columbia, Virginia, North Carolina, South Carolina, Georgia, Florida; Southwest: Mississippi, Tennessee, Alabama, Kentucky, Missouri, Louisiana, and the Arkansas Territory; Northwest: Ohio, Indiana, Michigan, Illinois, and the Wisconsin Territory.

The mobs, moreover, were both urban and rural. Despite evidence to the contrary, Jeffersonian Americans had generally assumed that mobs were an urban problem. After 1833, Jacksonian Americans learned, to their dismay, that sleepy, rural communities were not immune to mob violence. As the following chart indicates, rural mobs were prevalent in all parts of the country—except the Middle Atlantic states: [22]

Mobs: 1833–1838

	Urban	Rural
New England	5 incidents reported	10 incidents reported
Middle Atlantic	24	7
South Atlantic	9	13
Southwest	10	15
Northwest	1	6

In the 1830's, then, mob violence not only increased markedly but also became a feature of American life—not urban life, or Southern life, or Western life—but American life. The reader of the daily newspaper might associate the Nat Turner rebellion with Virginia, the burning of convents with Massachusetts, the lynching of gamblers with Mississippi, the burning of Negroes with St. Louis, the bank riot with Baltimore, the Flour Riot with New York City, the anti-rent wars with upstate New York, and the Mormon wars with either Missouri or Illinois; but a careful reader would have to agree with Lincoln's conclusion that mobs were a pervasive feature of American life.

It was in this atmosphere that most of the anti-abolitionist violence occurred. Of the nation's 48 anti-abolition and racial incidents that the *Register* reported in the 1830's and 1840's, 73 per cent took place between 1833 and 1838.[23] Similarly, of the 209 Northern mobs that the three leading antislavery newspapers—the *Liberator,* the *Emancipator,* and the *Philanthropist*—reported dur-

[22] Computed from data, *Niles' Register* Vols. 44–55. In establishing urbanization, I used the figure of 8,000 inhabitants and followed the data given in J. D. B. DeBow, *Statistical View of the United States . . . Being a Compendium of the Seventh Census* (Washington, D. C., 1854), 192–93.

[23] Computed from data, *Niles' Register* Vols. 44–55.

ing these two decades, 79 per cent occurred between 1833 and 1838.[24] It is obvious, then, that there were outbursts of violent anti-abolition and social violence in general during the same five-year period.

It is also clear that the incidence of both anti-abolitionist mobs and non-abolitionist mobs rose and fell almost simultaneously. As the following graph illustrates, both reached a peak during the late summer of 1835 and gradually subsided to "normal" by 1837: [25]

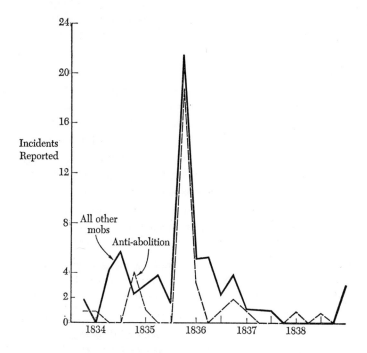

[24] Computed from data, the *Liberator* (Boston, 1831–1849), *Emancipator and Republican* (New York and Boston, 1833–1849; title varies), *Philanthropist* (Cincinnati, 1836–1847; title varies). Since the abolitionists often used the word "mob" indiscriminately, the diligent reader will find more incidents than I have listed. Again, as I define the word, a "mob" is characterized either by violence or by turbulence.

[25] Computed from data, *Niles' Register* Vols. 44–75 (1833–1849).

To some extent this synchronization of anti-abolition with other violence explains why so many Americans assumed that the nation's turmoil stemmed largely from the fear of organized anti-slavery. The two, as James Gordon Bennett pointed out in September, 1835, apparently went together.

It is particularly noteworthy, however, that the peak of both anti-abolition and other mobs came in the summer of 1835, for after June of that year, organized antislavery was unquestionably the paramount issue of the day. Almost every major city and town in the nation held anti-abolitionist rallies. From Maine to Missouri, from the Atlantic to the Gulf, crowds gathered to hear mayors and aldermen, bankers and lawyers, ministers and priests denounce the abolitionists as amalgamationists,[26] dupes, fanatics, foreign agents, and incendiaries.[27]

By mid-August, emotions had reached high tide. Fiery speeches and torchlight parades became everyday news. Citizens formed vigilance committees to patrol Negro quarters, to question strangers, and to search post offices, ships, and stages for antislavery literature. Southern vigilance committees offered rewards for leading abolitionists. In East Feliciana, Louisiana, citizens posted $50,000 for the delivery of Arthur Tappan, the president of the American

[26] "Amalgamation" was the ante-bellum equivalent of "miscegenation," which did not come into use until the Civil War. See Sidney Kaplan, "The Miscegenation Issue in the Election of 1864," *Journal of Negro History* 34 (July 1949), 274–343.

[27] For further commentary, see Nye, *Fettered Freedom*, Chapter V; Clement Eaton, "Censorship of the Southern Mails," *American Historical Review* 48 (January 1943), 266–80; Bertram Wyatt-Brown, "The Abolitionists' Postal Campaign of 1835," *Journal of Negro History* 50 (October 1965), 227–38; William Freehling, *Prelude to Civil War* (New York, 1966), Chapter 10; Charles M. Wiltse, *John C. Calhoun: Nullifier, 1829–1839* (Indianapolis, 1947), Chapter XX; Samuel Eliot Morison, *Life and Letters of Harrison Gray Otis* (2 vols.; Boston, 1913), Vol. II, Chapter XXXII; W. Sherman Savage, *The Controversy over the Distribution of Abolition Literature, 1830–1860* (n.p., 1938), 15–26, and *passim*; Thomas M. Owen, "An Alabama Protest Against Abolitionism in 1835," *Gulf States Historical Magazine* II (July 1903), 26–34; Edwin A. Miles, "The Mississippi Slave Insurrection Scare of 1835," *Journal of Negro History* 42 (January 1957), 48–61; N. Dwight Harris, *The History of Negro Servitude in Illinois* (Chicago, 1904), 69–71.

Anti-Slavery Society, dead or alive; in Mount Meigs, Alabama, $50,000 for Arthur Tappan or any other prominent abolitionist; in New Orleans, $100,000 for Tappan and LaRoy Sunderlund, the editor of *Zion's Watchman*. The grand jury of Tuscaloosa, Alabama, demanded that R. G. Williams, the publishing agent of the American Anti-Slavery Society, be sent south for trial. Forty angry citizens of Hinds County, Mississippi, promised Williams a taste of Kentucky hemp if he ever ventured south. And a Virginia grand jury indicted and demanded the extradition of all the key personnel of the Anti-Slavery Society.[28]

In New York City, the home base of Arthur Tappan, R. G. Williams, and the American Anti-Slavery Society, excitement became so intense by mid-August that Elizur Wright, the society's corresponding secretary, barricaded his doors with "bars and planks an inch thick." From sundown to sunup the Mayor of Brooklyn patrolled the neighborhood where Tappan lived, and a relay of men stood ready to carry his messages to the Brooklyn Navy Yard. The "least spark," merchant Philip Hone confided to his diary, "would create a flame in which the lives and property of Arthur Tappan and his associates would be endangered." Under the present circumstances, William Leggett, editor of the *Evening Post*, cautioned his readers, "a few inflammatory phrases might easily set men's minds on fire." "I have not ventured into the city," wrote abolitionist Lydia Maria Child, ". . . so great is the excitement here. . . . 'Tis like the times of the French Revolution, when no man dared to trust his neighbors." [29]

It seems plausible, therefore, that there was a direct relationship between fear of organized antislavery and the outbreak of mob

[28] Nye, *Fettered Freedom*, 180; *Alabama Senate Journal* (November 1835), 12; *New York Assembly Journal* (1836), 38–48; Charles Zebina Eastman, *Messages from the Governors* . . . (11 vols.; Albany, 1909), Vol. III, pp. 594–604; Thomas Harney and others to R. G. Williams, Clinton, Mississippi, August 28, 1835, quoted in Washington *United States Telegraph*, September 24, 1835; New York *Evening Post*, August 26, October 12, 1835.

[29] Lewis Tappan, *Arthur Tappan* (New York, 1870), 249–50; Nevins, *Diary of Philip Hone*, Vol. I, p. 173 [entry for August 26, 1835]; *Evening Post*, August 26, 1835; Lydia Maria Child to Mrs. Ellis Gray Loring, August 15, 1835, *Letters of Lydia Maria Child* (Boston, 1883), 15.

violence. This plausibility becomes even more reliable if we consider more closely the data from the *Register*. For during the summer of 1835, there was a close relationship between the rise of both anti-abolitionist and non-abolitionist tension. Both anti-abolitionist and other mobs reached their high points in August, 1835, and subsided thereafter. The following graph, presenting data for June through December, 1835, demonstrates this relationship: [30]

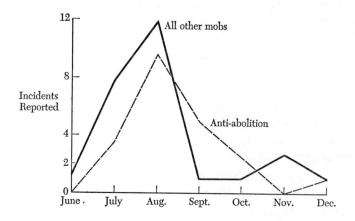

Despite this simultaneity, we should not push our conclusion too far. State-by-state analysis reveals a few localities—notably in Maryland—where the rise of social disorder had little or no connection with either slavery or race. Thus the American Anti-Slavery Society, with its thirteen agents and $25,000 budget, probably did not frighten "fifteen million people out of their senses" as Bennett claimed. But there is no doubt that it frightened millions. Antislavery was not the only target of the mobs that erupted in the country from New England to Louisiana. In Maryland, Irish workingmen repeatedly terrorized the countryside; in Missouri, mobs harassed Mormons; in the Old Southwest, vigilantes lynched gamblers and other outcasts; and in the Northeast, nativists attacked Catholics. Yet, only anti-abolition mobs sprang up in both East

[30] Computed from data, *Niles' Register* Vols. 48 and 49.

and West, in both North and South. They alone were neither peculiar to "the burning suns" of the South nor to "the eternal snows" of New England.

But why? What moved so many Americans to engineer mobs, to break up abolition meetings, to destroy antislavery presses, and to torture Negroes? What, precisely, did men see in the antislavery movement that made them afraid? Was it the threat of abolishing slavery, the message of "immediate abolition," the vivid epithets of William Lloyd Garrison and Stephen Symonds Foster, the fear of the free Negro, or the image of the antislavery organization itself that incited men to riot? Why did violence erupt in the mid-1830's, rather than in 1831, 1832, or 1833? And why did anti-abolition violence decline so rapidly in the late 1830's? Many of the answers, I submit, can be found through a close examination of the Northern anti-abolitionist mobs.

2

Generation of
Anti-Abolitionist Violence

Historians have rarely given much attention to the question of
what triggered violent anti-abolitionism, but the traditional historical argument—or, to be more exact, the traditional assumption—
is that the mobs were a reaction against "Garrisonism." Garrison's
children, for example, took it for granted that their father's moral
crusade touched the South where it hurt; and for this reason
Southern "man-stealers" and their Northern lackeys responded
with wrath and fury. Forty years later Gilbert Hobbes Barnes,
who clearly disliked Garrison and enjoyed debunking his "legend,"
reversed the tone of the argument: Garrison's vitriolic pen, his vi-
sionary and reckless agitation, and his notoriety fostered hatred
and violence not only toward himself and his "fanatics" but toward Theodore Dwight Weld and "moderate" antislavery men as
well. Thus Garrison's staunchest admirers and his foremost de-
bunker have agreed that anti-abolitionist violence was largely a response to "Garrisonism." [1]

[1] Wendell P. and Francis J. Garrison, *William Lloyd Garrison* (4 vols.;
New York, 1885–1889); Barnes, *The Antislavery Impulse, 1830–1844* (Har-
binger Books edition; New York, 1964).

There are ample grounds for partially accepting the traditional argument. The *Liberator* and its fiery editor undoubtedly contributed to tension in Northern society; the Garrisonians surely heightened the fears and anxieties that bred outbursts of anti-abolitionist violence. Any white friend of the Negro—any advocate of Negro uplift—probably would have inspired Northern racists to mob abolitionists and to terrorize Negroes. Yet neither Garrisonism nor Northern racism can account for the dramatic upsurge of anti-abolitionist violence in the summer of 1835.

II

Garrison's vehement denunciations of the South caused scarcely a ripple in the North. Even after the Nat Turner insurrection in Virginia in August, 1831, when Southerners became alarmed and demanded that Garrison be silenced, Northerners expressed little concern. Most, in fact, were unaware of the *Liberator's* existence. Even in Boston few men knew the *Liberator* or its editor. In October, 1831, the influential Washington *National Intelligencer* startled Boston's Mayor Harrison Gray Otis by demanding that he find some legal way of silencing the "incendiary" paper that was operating in his city. Otis made a few inquiries, but "no member of the city government, nor any person of my acquaintance, had ever heard of the publication." At Otis' orders city officers "ferreted out" Garrison in his "obscure hole" and reported that his only supporters were "a very few insignificant persons of all colors." The *Liberator*, concluded Otis, commanded "insignificant countenance and support." [2]

It was Garrison's attack against the American Colonization Society that eventually commanded attention. Since 1817 this society had been trying without much success to promote the migration of free Negroes to Africa. Staunch colonizationists insisted that African colonization would rid the country of the poor and despised

[2] Samuel Eliot Morison, *The Life and Letters of Harrison Gray Otis* (2 vols.; Boston, 1913), Vol. II, pp. 259–62; W. P. and F. J. Garrison, *Garrison,* Vol. I, pp. 242–46.

free blacks, encourage planters to emancipate their slaves, and provide a nucleus of black missionaries to carry the Gospel to the Dark Continent. Their plan had the support of such men as President James Monroe, Henry Clay, and Chief Justice John Marshall. Zealots claimed that it had the endorsement of God Himself. For years, however, Northern blacks had angrily denounced African colonization as forcible expulsion, and Garrison's *Liberator,* which was essentially a Negro newspaper, saved its sharpest barbs for the Colonization Society.

African colonization, said Garrison, was "a libel upon humanity and justice—a libel upon republicanism—a libel upon the Declaration of Independence—a libel upon Christianity." The colonizationists, said Garrison, were not simply misguided; they were evil, deceitful, hypocritical, anti-Christian, odious apologists for the crime of slavery. The American Colonization Society was a monster, a "creature without heart, without brains, eyeless, unnatural, hypocritical, relentless, unjust." It was essentially anti-Negro, rather than antislavery. It bolstered Southern slavery by the removal of free Negroes, by annually sending "hundreds of worn-out slaves . . . off to die, like old horses." Above all, its philanthropic façade dulled the nation's conscience concerning the sin of slavery and "shamefully duped" many men of good intention. It had to be destroyed. "I look upon the overthrow of the Colonization Society," Garrison told his future brother-in-law, "as the overthrow of slavery itself—they both stand or fall together." [3]

It would be a mistake to assume—as many have—that Northern sensibilities were outraged by these epithets. Obviously colonizationists objected, and some abolitionists pleaded with Garrison to tone down his language. But rancorous journalism prevailed in the 1830's. Almost every town and village in the nation had at least one editor who in vileness and vulgarity approached James Fenimore Cooper's Steadfast Dodge. Not only the penny presses, but also the more "respectable" presses used with abandon words such

---

[3] William Lloyd Garrison, *Thoughts on African Colonization* (Boston, 1832), 10–14, and *passim;* William Lloyd Garrison to Henry E. Benson, July 21, 1832, William Lloyd Garrison Papers, Boston Public Library.

as "cur," "fool," "knave," "scoundrel," "wretch." Newspaper editors, Tocqueville insisted, were generally vile and abusive, and American readers had conditioned themselves to read for facts, rather than for opinion. And at least one of Garrison's future enemies, a religious journal, even praised him for the "strength" of his language.[4]

Whatever effect the *Liberator's* denunciations had on Northern sensibilities, it is abundantly clear that Garrison's harangues did not drive men to violence. Some colonizationists fumed secretly, but outwardly they remained calm. It was not until Garrison and the New England Anti-Slavery Society proved that abolitionists had bite, as well as bark, that colonizationists became openly hostile.

From the beginning Garrison had been committed to organized agitation. Without a formal "concentration of moral strength," he insisted, little could be accomplished either for the slave or for the free Negro. In November, 1830, several months before the founding of the *Liberator*, he sought to establish an antislavery society. This attempt failed, but after numerous false starts and much constitutional quibbling, twelve men formed the New England Anti-Slavery Society in January, 1832.[5]

Almost immediately the new society launched a campaign to destroy the American Colonization Society. In May, Garrison's masterful polemic, *Thoughts on African Colonization*, came out. With a boost from Arthur Tappan's pocketbook it soon circulated widely. In June the New England Society instituted weekly anti-

---

[4] James Fenimore Cooper, *Home As Found* (Capricorn edition; New York, 1961); Marvin Meyers, *The Jacksonian Persuasion* (Vintage edition; New York, 1960), Chapter 4; Alexis de Tocqueville, *Democracy in America* (Vintage edition; New York, 1958), Vol. I, pp. 190–91, 194–95; *The Quarterly Christian Spectator*, IV (1832), 312–19.

[5] William Lloyd Garrison to Henry E. Benson, November 12, 1831, Garrison Papers; *Liberator*, January 1, March 26, July 30, December 17, 1831, January 3, 1835; Nina Tiffany, *Samuel Sewall, A Memoir* (Boston, 1898), 36–40; W. P. and F. J. Garrison, *Garrison*, Vol. I, pp. 272–79; Samuel J. May, *Recollections of Our Anti-Slavery Conflict* (Boston, 1869), 30–32; Roman J. Zorn, "The New England Anti-Slavery Society: Pioneer Abolition Organization," 43, *Journal of Negro History* (July 1957), 157–76.

colonization forums in Boston, sent lecturers to nearby cities and towns, and planned special Fourth of July meetings to compete with traditional colonizationist exercises. Taking excerpts from the *African Repository* and other colonization publications, the Garrisonians relentlessly hammered readers and audiences with the theme that the Colonization Society out of its "own mouth" condemned itself; it clearly showed itself to be a moral cancer, and thus it must be destroyed.[6]

Still colonizationists remained mute. The colonizationist press ignored Garrison's *Thoughts,* and colonizationist lecturers refused to rebut abolitionist attacks. So long as abolitionist audiences remained small or black and collections were meager, the Colonization Society held fast to its policy of not calling attention to the opposition. The society, after all, held a virtual monopoly in the antislavery field, and thus it had no reason to panic.

But reason was soon abandoned. As the New England Society's grass-roots operation expanded, as more whites began turning out to hear anticolonizationist arguments, as Providence and other cities showed signs of forming abolitionist societies, and as Garrison's *Thoughts* stunned colonizationists as far west as Hudson, Ohio, colonizationists became increasingly edgy. New England members, particularly, demanded action.[7] In August 1832, the Colonization

---

[6] Zorn, "New England Anti-Slavery Society," 162–63; W. P. and F. J. Garrison, *Garrison,* Vol. I, pp. 286–90, 312–13; New England Anti-Slavery Society Records, entries for April 30–June 25, 1832, Boston Public Library; William Lloyd Garrison to Robert Purvis, June 22, 1832, to Ebenezer Dole, June 9, 1832, and to Henry E. Benson, July 7, 1832, Garrison Papers.

[7] Complaints and demands for action to the Colonization Society's Washington office and to leading colonizationists read almost like a fever chart. Consider the location and the timing of the following: Gabriel P. Disosway to the society's secretary R. R. Gurley, New York, June 23, 1831; Charles Tappan to Gurley, Boston, August 18, 1831; Leonard Bacon to Gurley, Ellington, Connecticut, October 26, 1831; J. N. Danforth to Gurley, Boston, June 10, 1832; Levi H. Clarke to Gurley, Albany, July 14, 1832; J. K. Converse to Gurley, Burlington, Vermont, August 13, 1832; B. B. Thatcher to Gurley, Boston, September 10, 1832; Henry T. Tuckerman to Gurley, Boston, October 1, 1832; David O. Hudson and Horace C. Taylor to Gurley, Western Reserve College, Hudson, Ohio, October 29, 1832; H. C. Taylor, David O. Hudson, and T. H. Barr to Gurley, Western Reserve College,

Society's principal New England agent, the Reverend Joshua Danforth, pounded the abolitionists with abuse. Finally in October, the Colonization Society's official organ mentioned the New England Anti-Slavery Society, but only in a footnote: "A few men in Boston (chiefly young, and of course ardent), with A. Buffum a Quaker, for their President, and Garrison for their Secretary, have associated and assumed this larger title, than which none could be more inappropriate. New England disavows them." In November, the same journal mildly denounced Garrison's *Thoughts*. And then, as if in response to a signal, Eastern colonizationists erupted with tirades against "amalgamationists," "fanatics," "lunatics," "reckless incendiaries," "cut-throats," and "firebrands." The self-imposed silence was over; war had been declared.[8]

Declaring war on the Garrisonians did not bring the reversals that many colonizationists had expected. If 1832 had been a troublesome year for the Colonization Society, 1833 proved to be disastrous. From four local societies in two states, the antislavery movement expanded to forty-seven in ten states. Arthur Tappan, who had been secretly supplying the Garrisonians with funds, shocked colonizationist clergymen and temperance reformers by dramatically renouncing the Colonization Society and accusing it of drenching Africa with "liquid poison." [9] British abolitionists—using

December 10, 1832; Asa Cummings to J. N. Danforth, Portland, Maine, December 14, 1832; J. N. Danforth to Gurley, Boston, December 21, 1832; Cyril Pearl to Danforth, Dedham, Massachusetts, December 24, 1832; J. N. Danforth to Gurley, Boston, December 27, 1832; J. N. Danforth to Rev. Dr. James Laurie, Boston, December 28, 1832—all in American Colonization Society Papers, Library of Congress.

[8] *Liberator*, September 1, 1832; *African Repository*, VIII (October 1832), 247, (November 1832), 271–78; beginning in December 1832, the Boston *Recorder* and the New York *Commercial Advertiser* contained numerous articles attacking the Garrisonians; see also *The Quarterly Christian Spectator*, V (March 1833), 145–57, and *The Methodist Magazine and Quarterly Review*, XV (January 1833), 111–16. In *The African Colonization Movement, 1816–1865* (New York, 1961), 202–4, P. J. Staudenraus argues that the central office's rebuke of Garrison's *Thoughts* triggered the vehement denunciations.

[9] *First Annual Report . . . of the New England Anti-Slavery Society* (Boston, 1833), 43; *Second Annual Report of the New England Anti-Slavery*

Garrison as their main weapon—not only checkmated the Colonization Society's campaign for English largesse, but also maneu-
vered a large audience at Exeter Hall into censuring the Colonization Society and unanimously endorsing the New England abolitionists. Fortified with these victories and the famous "Wilberforce
Protest"—a document in which some of England's leading philanthropists formally denounced colonization—Garrison returned to
America in triumph.[10]

Meanwhile the Colonization Society developed serious—and
perhaps overwhelming—internal weaknesses. At the annual meeting in 1833 delegates became bitterly divided over a bold attempt
to depose five managers and give Northerners more control of the
society. The society's Fourth of July collections fell from $12,000 in
1832 to $4,000 in 1833; many donors failed to honor their pledges;
and by the end of 1833 the society faced a $46,000 deficit. Thus,
while the Garrisonians were apparently riding a wave of triumph,
once-confident colonizationists were fighting to stay alive.[11]

It was against this background that some colonizationists decided on mob action.[12] On the evening of October 1, 1833, a

Society (Boston, 1834), 11–12; Liberator, April 6, 1833; Joseph Tracy to
R. R. Gurley, May 16, 1833, American Colonization Society Papers; Staudenraus, African Colonization Movement, 212–13.

[10] In 1933, in The Antislavery Impulse, 52–53, 220–21, Gilbert Hobbes
Barnes insisted that Garrison played a minor role in the battle between
colonizationists and abolitionists in England—thus stirring up a minor, but
hot debate among historians. Solely on the basis of reading the reports of
Elliot Cresson, the Colonization Society's agent in England, I suspect that
Barnes was right. Cresson was an easy mark.

[11] Staudenraus, African Colonization Movement, Chapter XVI; Early Lee
Fox, The American Colonization Society, 1817–1840 (Baltimore, 1919), 94–
100, 125–26, 136–38; African Repository, VIII (1832), 115, 367; IX (1833),
199; X (1834), 8–17, 162–68.

[12] My account of the mob is based on bits and pieces—largely from the
following sources: the October 2–5, 1833, issues of these New York news-
papers—Courier and Enquirer, Gazette, Standard, Sun, Commercial, Adver-
tiser, Journal of Commerce, American, Evening Post, Evening Star; New
York Evangelist, October 5, 1833; Working Man's Advocate, October 5, 1833;
New York Emancipator, October 5, 12, 1833; Liberator, October 12, 19, 1833.
R. R. Gurley to P. R. Fendall, New York, October 2, 8, 1833; John Neal to
R. R. Gurley, New York, October 2, November 20, 1833—all in American

group of active colonizationists and their sympathizers met in the office of James Watson Webb, the thirty-one-year-old editor of New York City's influential *Courier and Enquirer*. There they planned to pose as "Friends of Immediate Abolition in the United States" and invade the initial meeting of the New York City Anti-Slavery Society, which had been called for seven-thirty the following evening at Clinton Hall. Their object, John Neal informed the Colonization Society's secretary, was to put a stop to Garrison's "calumnies" and "misrepresentations." "For my own part," explained the thirty-six-year-old Portland Yankee, who eagerly sought the Colonization Society's agency in England, "I am for mild, firm and effectual measures—but it is not so with most who are opposed to Garrison." [13]

Indeed not! Even the most naïve of Neal's Quaker relatives would not have expected that evening's proceedings to be limited to "kind and temperate, but manly resolutions." That morning, as Neal knew, both Webb's *Courier and Enquirer* and Solomon Lang's *Gazette* had issued thinly veiled calls for a mob. "Are we

Colonization Society Papers. Allan Nevins, *Diary of Philip Hone, 1828–1851* (New York, 1927), 102 [entry for October 3, 1833]; Lewis Tappan, *Arthur Tappan* (New York, 1870), 168–75; Edward S. Abdy, *Journal of a Residence and Tour in the United States* (3 vols., London, 1835), Vol. I, pp. 388–91; John Neal, *Wandering Recollections of a Somewhat Busy Life* (Boston, 1869), 401–2.

Neal's *Life* is somewhat misleading; he was not the innocent figure he pretends.

The abolitionists reprinted many of the pertinent articles on numerous occasions. These reprints are also somewhat misleading. Abolitionists invariably took some liberties with their opponents' articles—adding italics here, omitting a passage there, etc. The anti-abolitionists, I might add, generally engaged in the same abuses.

[13] John Neal to R. R. Gurley, New York, October 2, 1833, American Colonization Society Papers. I have been unable to ascertain whether Neal and his colleagues were acting on orders from the society's national office. New York colonizationists were so quick and so persistent in denying the existence of such orders that it makes one suspicious. And then, after the Colonization Society's officers decided that Neal was too notorious to be the agent in England, Neal made the curious remark that he was astonished at the board's "behavior toward me; considering *how* & *where* the plan originated. . . ." John Neal to R. R. Gurley, New York, November 20, 1833, American Colonization Society Papers.

tamely to look on," asked Webb, "and see this most dangerous species of fanaticism extending itself through society?" No, counseled
Webb, the safe and proper course was for everyone to meet outside Clinton Hall a half-hour before the scheduled meeting and
crush "this many-headed Hydra in the bud." Such fearless and
prompt action, said Webb, would "expose the weakness as well as
the folly, madness, and mischief of these bold and dangerous
men." [14] And that day posters were tacked up all over the city:

NOTICE
TO ALL PERSONS FROM THE SOUTH

All persons interested in the subject of a
meeting called by

J. Leavitt,   W. Goodell,
W. Green, Jr.,   J. Rankin,
Lewis Tappan,
At Clinton Hall,
This evening at 7 o'clock,
Are requested to attend at the same hour
and place.

MANY SOUTHERNERS

New-York, Oct. 2d, 1833.
N.B. All citizens who may feel disposed
to manifest the *true* feeling of the State on
this subject, are requested to attend.

That evening, as expected, some fifteen hundred New Yorkers—
and perhaps a handful of Southerners—stood outside Clinton Hall
yelling for the blood of Arthur Tappan and Garrison. Wandering
amongst them was Garrison himself, who had arrived early only to
find the hall locked. After learning of the proposed mob, the building's trustees had withdrawn permission to hold the meeting there;

[14] New York *Courier and Enquirer*, October 2, 1833.

and Tappan and his friends—without notifying Garrison—had decided to meet uptown at Chatham Street Chapel.

The crowd soon adjourned to Tammany Hall for a meeting of their own. In the chair, cautioning moderation, was General Robert Bogardus, a sixty-two-year-old veteran of the War of 1812, a former state senator, and one of the city's leading lawyers. At his side were the meeting's secretaries, M. C. Patterson and P. P. Parsells, with whom Neal had previously planned the night's events. Also on the platform were the aristocratic-looking Colonel Webb, his former associate James Gordon Bennett, the prominent Whig and next state senator Frederick Tallmadge, the future postmaster James Lorimer Graham, and the "literary genius" John Neal. All were men of some prominence. All except Bogardus were young men—in their twenties or thirties. All except the Scotsman Bennett were Northeastern-born. And all except Bennett openly identified with African colonization.[15]

The Tammany Hall audience had settled for speeches and resolutions, when suddenly news came that the abolitionists were meeting at Chatham Street Chapel. Quickly the crowd passed the resolutions and then proceeded to the chapel. Finding the iron gate locked, they milled about until a janitor came out and opened the gate. With a roar the mob stormed the chapel only to find it empty. The abolitionists had just slipped out the rear door after quickly organizing their society and electing Arthur Tappan president in a thirty-minute meeting. In frustration, the mob seized "a wretched looking old black," derisively dubbed him "Arthur Tappan," and forced him to preside over a mock meeting.[16] Laughing and shouting, the rioters cheerfully agreed to resolutions favoring

---

[15] Bennett maintained that the colonizationists were "species of abolitionists"; they differ "about as much as Thomas Tweedledum differs from Thomas Tweedledee." During the antislavery uproar of 1835, he was one of few Northerners who argued that slavery was a positive good. Usually—but not consistently—he opposed anti-abolition mobs, arguing that they only strengthened the antislavery movement. See New York *Herald*, September 5, 11, 25, 30, October 21, November 5, 28—all 1835.

[16] Abdy, *Journal*, Vol. I, pp. 388–91.

immediate emancipation and—significantly—"immediate amalgamation." An hour later, they dispersed. And thus, as the *Journal of
Commerce* quipped the next day:

> The King of France, with 80,000 men,
> Marched up the hill, and then marched down again.

In the next few years—when Arthur Tappan and his New York
associates took over the reins of the antislavery movement and expanded both its operations and its campaign against African colonization, when prominent colonizationists such as James Gillespie
Birney and Gerrit Smith defected to the American Anti-Slavery Society, when state and local auxiliaries openly or clandestinely
seceded from the American Colonization Society, when Colonization society funds dropped disastrously—still other colonizationists resorted to mob violence. The New York City rioters of July,
1834, shouted colonization vows in Chatham Street Chapel. The
Utica mob of October, 1835, included leading local colonizationists. The Cincinnati mob of July, 1836, included most of the city's
prominent colonizationists. The rioters who killed Elijah Lovejoy
at Alton, Illinois, in November, 1837, identified openly with African colonization. Almost automatically, as antislavery organizers
invaded one Northern community after another, zealous colonizationists became alarmed. They saw antislavery societies as men-
aces to their well-being, as threats to their holy cause, as killers of
their sacred dream. Time and again they aroused their townsmen
to violence and sought their enemy in battle.[17]

III

In adopting the position of the free Negro and in waging war
against the American Colonization Society, the abolitionists infuri-

---

[17] The last part of this paragraph is based on data from some 200 mobs.
It is impossible, of course, to gather information on the inner workings of
each mob. From the information that I have—which admittedly is uneven
—I would guess that local colonizationists played a significant role in at
least 50 per cent of the mobs, but not more than 75 per cent.

ated not only zealous colonizationists but Negrophobes as well. The antislavery alternative to African colonization—"immediate emancipation without expatriation"—accepted the proposition that some day the free Negro would be assimilated into American society. For most Northerners this proposition was anathema.

It was probably fear of racial assimilation that prompted the New York City mob of October, 1833, to discuss and to support mock resolutions favoring "immediate amalgamation." And it was certainly this fear that prompted men such as James Watson Webb, the key figure in the October mob and the North's most vehement anti-abolitionist spokesman, to support African colonization and to crusade against the abolitionists.

Webb supported African colonization, but he was never a "true believer." The thirty-one-year-old editor never believed that African colonization was God's plan for Christianizing Africa, aiding the free Negro, and eliminating Southern slavery. To Webb, an ardent Episcopalian, African colonization was not a holy cause; indeed, it was not even a practical one, for its cost would be twice that of the War of 1812. Nevertheless, he said it should be supported, for it was the "most effective barrier" against the abolitionists, and it served as a bulwark against the "heinous" and "pernicious" thought that some day the free Negro could become a vital and significant part of American society.[18]

Webb was basically a traditionalist. In general he reflected many of the crass, self-seeking, speculative aspects of the Jacksonian period, but essentially he was loyal to an older America. Due to this loyalty, the former army officer refused to alter his newspaper's traditional fare, to aim at a mass audience, to report prizefights or rape trials, to publish a Sunday edition, or to allow newsboys to hawk his paper on the streets; and eventually his newspaper folded when he clung to traditional ways in the face of the revolution in journalism. Fiercely proud of his lineage—which he could trace to early Puritan Massachusetts—Webb fancied him-

[18] New York *Courier and Enquirer,* May 12, June 13, September 20, October 3–12, December 17, 1833; January 1, May 12, June 13, July 8–22, August 9, 1834; March 26, June 6, 1835.

self as the staunch defender of country squires and gentlemen merchants, of ardent, brave, and magnanimous patricians, of superior breeding and of social deference. In particular he saw himself as the foremost protector of the interests and traditions of New York City's gentlemen merchants. Accordingly, he shunned impersonal relations in business, cuffed and caned "inferior" rivals on the street, fought one duel and caused another.[19]

For a man such as Webb, the question of future amalgamation was undoubtedly crucial. Webb's ideal America was not only traditional in its values, but was also of old American stock in its blood lines; the two, in his mind, stood or fell together. For this reason, he opposed vehemently any plan that promised the eventual assimilation of "inferior" breeds such as the Irish and the Latin-American into the mainstream of American society.[20] Above all, he denounced any proposal that even hinted that the Negro might someday become a part of his America. The proposals of Arthur Tappan and other "amalgamators," thundered Webb, amounted to treason; they threatened not only slavery and African colonization, but the "very fabric" of Northern society as well. To preserve their heritage, their institutions, and themselves, Webb thus called on gentlemen of the "highest character" to crush the "amalgamists" in the bud.[21]

This fear of assimilation, of being "mulattoized," of losing one's sense of identity, existed long before Webb and the New York mob expressed it. Indeed, it existed long before Northerners had ever heard of the *Liberator*. Everywhere in the North, as countless

[19] My understanding of Webb rests largely on his *Courier and Enquirer*, his *Reminiscences of Gen'l Samuel B. Webb, of the Revolutionary Army* (New York, 1882); the sketch of his life in James Parton *et al.*, *Sketches of Men in Progress* (New York, 1870), 349–404; James L. Crouthamel's "James Watson Webb and the *New York Courier and Enquirer*, 1827–1861" (Unpub. Ph.D. dissertation, University of Rochester, 1958); and Crouthamel's "James Watson Webb: Mercantile Editor," *New York History* 41 (October 1960), 400–22.

[20] Webb, a "high" churchman, was not anti-Catholic.

[21] New York *Courier and Enquirer*, July 4, 8, 18, 22, 1834; Abdy, *Journal*, Vol. I, p. 347; Crouthamel, "Webb," 319, 255–57, and *passim*. See also the citations in footnote 19.

travelers noted, Negrophobia and racism flourished, and Northern whites—either legally or illegally—made the lot of the Negro miserable in "a thousand ways." Indeed, it was largely because Northern Negrophobia was so vicious and so pervasive that colonizationists insisted that their cause was holy. Anything as unyielding and malicious as Northern fear and hatred of the free Negro, they argued, was obviously "an ordination of Providence, and no more to be changed than the laws of nature." Northern thought was so permeated with racism, argues Leon Litwack, that even the abolitionists accepted many of its most pernicious tenets. Even the *Liberator* talked about the Negro as "branded by the hand of nature with a perpetual mark of disgrace." [22]

Northern Negrophobia was not manifested merely in social and legal prescription, in barring Negroes from jury boxes and election polls, in excluding Negroes from white men's schools and railroad cars, in limiting Negroes to "Nigger work" and "Nigger pews." It hounded Northern Negroes from cradle to grave. Indicative was a potter's field in Cincinnati, where whites were buried east to west and blacks north to south.[23] Among the dead, Northerners insisted that white supremacy must prevail.

This antipathy frequently expressed itself in violence. Often whites suffered from black felons, who apparently abounded under these circumstances. And in September, 1824, about 150 Philadelphia Negroes attacked white officials as they were taking a runaway to jail.[24] But in nine instances out of ten, whites were the aggressors, and blacks the victims. Northern law and custom left Negroes unprotected, and they suffered continually at the hands of frustrated whites, practical jokers, and village sadists.

[22] George Wilson Pierson, *Tocqueville and Beaumont in America* (New York, 1938), 565; *An Address to the Public by the Colonization Society of Connecticut* (New Haven, 1828), 4–5; *Address to the American Society for Colonizing the Free People of Colour* . . . (Washington, D. C., 1818), 27–28; *African Repository*, I (1825), 68; Cyrus Edwards, *An Address at the State House in Vandalia, on the Subject of Forming a State Colonization Society* (Jacksonville, Illinois, 1831), 6; Leon Litwack, *North of Slavery* (Chicago, 1961), Chapter VII; *Liberator*, January 22, 1831.

[23] Abdy, *Journal*, Vol. III, p. 7.

[24] *Niles' Register* 27 (September 11, 1824), 32.

Occasionally whites tried to expel free Negroes forcibly from their communities. In Providence, where anti-Negro feeling was "very bitter," several attempts were made in the 1820's. On one occasion, respectable whites became alarmed about "Hardscrabble," a predominantly Negro slum which also harbored most of the city's drunkards, sailors, and prostitutes. The whites raised a mob which drove Negroes from their homes, tore down their houses, and carried off their furniture and sold it at auction in Pawtucket. Another time, a brawl between blacks and whites broke out on Olney Street, another disreputable neighborhood. After the death of a white sailor, lower-class whites invaded the Negro quarter and began razing Negro homes. To stop the destruction, the Governor of Rhode Island called out the militia and finally ordered them to fire. This resulted in further destruction, and by the time peace was restored, Olney Street was virtually uninhabitable.[25]

The most serious incident of this kind occurred in Cincinnati in August, 1829. For two decades the city fathers had ignored the provision of Ohio's infamous Black Laws that compelled free Negroes entering the state to post a $500 bond as guarantee of their good behavior and providence. But between 1826 and 1829, which were the years of greatest Negro migration to the state, Cincinnati's Negro population suddenly jumped from about 4 to 10 per cent of the total population. White citizens became alarmed. The Cincinnati Colonization Society, which had been formed in 1826 for the express purpose of "forwarding to Africa the free blacks of Cincinnati," received increasing support, and the number of local colonization societies in Ohio increased from one in late 1825 to forty-five by 1830. In 1828, the city council appointed a committee to consider a petition asking for measures to stop the inpouring of free blacks. In the spring of 1829, the Negrophobes scored heavily in a ward election that centered around the question of enforcing the Black Laws. And in July, the city fathers responded positively to this sentiment; in their role as Overseers of

[25] *Niles' Register* 27 (November 6, 1824), 160; *The Life of William J. Brown, of Providence, R. I.* (Providence, 1883), 86, 88–96.

the Poor, the Trustees of Cincinnati announced that after thirty days they would enforce the $500 bond requirement.[26]

Almost immediately, white bands began raiding Negro quarters. These assaults reached a climax on the weekend of August 22, when several hundred whites invaded "Bucktown," spreading terror and destruction. By the end of 1829, about half of the Negro population had left the city. Unfortunately, wrote the editor of the Cincinnati *Gazette*, the "sober, honest, industrious, and useful portion of the colored population" left, and thus the enforcement of the Black Laws, which he had supported, only served "to lessen much of the moral restraint, which the presence of respectable persons of their own color, imposed on the idle and indolent, as well as the profligate." But never again in the ante-bellum period did Cincinnati's Negro population exceed 5 per cent of the total, and for many whites this fact alone justified the excesses.[27]

It is clear, then, that violent antipathy toward the free Negro existed before the founding of the *Liberator* in January, 1831. It is

[26] E. Drake and E. D. Mansfield, *Cincinnati in 1826* (Cincinnati, 1827), 57–58, 37; *The Cincinnati Directory for the Year 1829* (Cincinnati, 1829), n. p.; Alice D. Adams, *The Neglected Period of Antislavery in America, 1808–1831* (Boston, 1908), 106; Staudenraus, *African Colonization Movement*, 137; Henry N. Sherwood, "The Movement in Ohio to Deport the Negro," *The Quarterly Publication of the Historical and Philosophical Society of Ohio*, VII (June 1912), 55ff.; *African Repository*, V (1829), 248; Richard C. Wade, "The Negro in Cincinnati, 1800–1830," *Journal of Negro History* 39 (January 1954), 48–57; Allan Peskin, ed., *North Into Freedom: The Autobiography of John Malvin, Free Negro, 1795–1880* (Cleveland, 1966), 38–40, 47–48; "Public Warning to Cincinnati Negroes and Commentary on Their Reaction," *Journal of Negro History* 8 (July 1923), 331–32.

[27] Cincinnati *Gazette*, September 17, 1829, quoted in Wade, "The Negro in Cincinnati," 56–57; Abdy, *Journal*, Vol. II, pp. 381–83; Charles Cist, *Cincinnati in 1851* (Cincinnati, 1851), 46.

Invariably historians maintain that the extreme racism that prevailed in Cincinnati was due to a large number of settlers from Virginia and Kentucky. The argument is false. Less than 15 per cent of the city's adult population was Southern-born. For every Southerner in Cincinnati, there were three or four settlers from the Northeast. See the tables of nativity for adult males in *The Cincinnati Directory for 1825*, 7, and *The Cincinnati Directory . . . for 1840*, 484.

also obvious that antislavery men did not cause Northern Negro-phobia, as some of their opponents later argued; they merely in-herited it. And it was this legacy of fear and hate—rather than any concern about the practicality or the impracticality of immediate emancipation—that caused many Northerners to side with the col-onizationists in their war with the abolitionists. It was not the doctrine of immediatism, as Gilbert Hobbes Barnes insists, but the heritage of racism that generated much of the controversy in the North.[28]

Anti-abolitionists, as Barnes and others maintain, invariably de-nounced immediatism as unsound doctrine. They always took ad-vantage of the abolitionists' confusion of terms, the abolitionists' inability to define what immediate abolition really entailed. On those rare occasions when antislavery men actually spelled out a program, their opponents picked at details. And on those numer-ous occasions when antislavery men refused to make their position clear, their enemies chided them for vagueness and impracticality. If the abolitionists proposed that state legislatures immediately free the slaves, then anti-abolitionists denounced them for wanting to flood the country with millions of black paupers and vagabonds. If the abolitionists suggested that "immediate abolition" did not necessarily circumscribe all forms of compulsory labor, such as vil-leinage, copyhold, or apprenticeship for years, then anti-abolition-ists reproached them for wishing the substitution of one kind of slavery for another.

But these attacks and denunciations were primarily parries and counterthrusts, rather than reflections of anxiety about immediatism.[29] Anti-abolitionists rarely showed any interest in finding practical solutions to the slavery question. And they cer-tainly did not offer any. With the notable exceptions of the New York *Herald* in the 1830's and the New York *Day Book* in the

[28] *The Antislavery Impulse.*

[29] Gerrit Smith, William Ellery Channing, and Catherine Beecher may have been deeply concerned about immediatism—as a legion of historians have pointed out. But the Smiths, the Channings, and the Beechers did not demand gag laws, write anti-abolition tracts, or form mobs. They often became aboli-tionists or fellow travelers.

1850's, both of which favored slavery, anti-abolition journals invariably supported ill-conceived plans for transporting millions of unwilling American Negroes to Africa, Brazil, or Central America. And mobs constantly thundered their approval of the same schemes. For most anti-abolitionists, it seems that a plan's practicality depended on whether it promised an all-white America.

It is also clear that before the New York philanthropists assumed control of the antislavery movement, a community's initial response to immediatism hinged largely on the race question. That is, it depended primarily on whether the doctrine was identified with Negro uplift or racial assimilation. Throughout New England, for example, there was almost no response—either positive or negative—to immediatism until the late summer of 1832, and then only a stirring until the summer of 1835.[30] Even in Boston, we may recall, civic officials did not learn of the *Liberator* or its editor until October, 1831, and then Mayor Otis dismissed the whole operation as trifling. Indeed, it was not until 1835 that he really became alarmed.[31] But there was a notable exception to this over-all tranquility, and that exception was Connecticut.

In Connecticut, the promotion of immediate abolition coincided with an attempt to establish a Negro college in New Haven. In June, 1831, Simeon S. Jocelyn, a white pastor of a New Haven Negro church, Arthur Tappan, and Garrison proposed such a college to a Negro national convention. The enterprise would "produce a band of educated men to take up the pen" for Negro rights. New Haven, they agreed, was an ideal site because of its location, its intellectual fame, and the "friendly, pious, generous, and humane" character of its inhabitants.[32]

The friendly inhabitants disagreed. Almost immediately they became alarmed, and after the Nat Turner insurrection broke out in Virginia in August, their apprehension increased. In September, a

[30] This generalization is based on reading New England newspapers from 1831 to 1835. In general, my reading was limited to newspapers that subsequently took a stand against immediate abolition.

[31] Morison, *Otis*, Vol. II, pp. 270–76; Boston *Atlas*, August 25, 1835.

[32] *Minutes and Proceedings of the First Annual Convention of the People of Colour* (Philadelphia, 1831), 5–7.

month before Boston officials had heard of the *Liberator,* the mayor and aldermen of New Haven called a town meeting. And by a vote of approximately 700 to 4, the citizens of New Haven denounced the proposal for a Negro college and denounced Garrison and the abolitionists for "unwarrantable and dangerous interference with the concerns of other states." Calling "the institution a *College,*" Jocelyn reported to Garrison, "touched the very *quick* of oppression," for "it carries the assurance of equality with it." [33]

Although Jocelyn, Garrison, and the other abolitionists accepted defeat and abandoned the project, local newspapers continued to berate them for sponsoring amalgamation and causing New Haven Negroes to become "impudent and insolent." Several newspapers demanded the suppression of vice in "New Liberia," the Negro ghetto. Finally, in October, 1831, one mob stoned Arthur Tappan's house on Temple Street, another tore down a Negro shanty on "Sodom Hill," and still another invaded "New Liberia" and attacked amalgamation where it actually existed, capturing four white women and fourteen white men.[34]

A year and one-half later, but still six months before the New York City mob of October, 1833, an almost identical reaction occurred in nearby Canterbury, Connecticut. This was the famous Prudence Crandall incident. In the spring of 1833, Miss Crandall, a young Quaker schoolmistress, who had just been publicly rebuked for admitting a Negro day student, decided to challenge the community's prejudice in a radical way. Securing the support of antislavery leaders, she opened her boarding school exclusively to black girls.

Immediately the townfolk, led by Andrew T. Judson, town selectman and later United States district judge, Democratic politician, and an officer of the local colonization society, called a town meeting and denounced the scheme. Ignoring this condemnation

[33] *Connecticut Journal,* July 20–September 13, 1831; Robert Austin Warner, *New Haven Negroes: A Social History* (New Haven, 1940), 53–56; *College for Colored Youth: An Account of the New Haven City Meeting and Resolutions* (New York, 1831); W. P. and F. J. Garrison, *Garrison,* Vol. I, p. 260n.

[34] *Connecticut Journal,* September 20–November 1, 1831; Tappan, *Tappan,* 258; Warner, *New Haven Negroes,* 57–59.

and pleas from angry citizens, Miss Crandall received between ten and twenty girls. To offset this devilish plot to make "New England . . . the Liberia of America," the town fathers called a second meeting, which condemned the school as a "rendezvous . . . designed by its projectors . . . to promulgate their disgusting doctrines of amalgamation and their pernicious sentiments of subverting the Union." The angry citizens drew up a petition to the General Assembly "deprecating the evil consequences of bringing from other states and towns, people of color for any purpose, and more especially for the purpose of disseminating the principles and doctrines opposed to the benevolent colonizing system." In May, the state legislature, responding to pressure, enacted a statute designed to outlaw Miss Crandall's boarding school.[35]

Miss Crandall defied the law, was twice tried, and finally was found guilty. Throughout her ordeal, the abolitionists, with healthy stipends from Arthur Tappan, effectively used the trials for propaganda purposes. By declining to furnish bail, for example, they threw on the prosecution the responsibility for lodging the young Quakeress in a cell that had been previously occupied by a notorious wife-murderer. Subsequent woodcuts, prints, and calico kerchiefs of the delicate young lady in a murderer's cell provided organized antislavery with more dynamite than thousands of pages of argument. Eventually, in late 1834, an appellate court quashed the case on a technicality.[36]

Meanwhile, the exasperated citizens of Canterbury resorted to violence. Townfolk harassed Miss Crandall continuously. Vandals

[35] Prudence Crandall to Simeon S. Jocelyn, February 26, April 9, April 17, 1833, in "Abolition Letters Collected by Captain Arthur B. Spingarn," *Journal of Negro History* 17 (1933), 80–84; Prudence Crandall to Garrison, March 19, 1833, Garrison Papers; *Liberator*, April 6, 1833; *A Statement of Facts, Respecting the School for Colored Females, in Canterbury, Ct.* (Brooklyn, Connecticut, 1833), Ralph Foster Weld, *Slavery in Connecticut* (New Haven, 1935), 20–21. Of the many accounts of this whole affair, perhaps the most useful is May, *Reminiscences*, 40ff.

[36] May, *Reminiscences*, 54ff.; Helen T. Catterall, ed., *Judicial Cases Concerning American Slavery and the Negro* (5 vols.; Washington, D. C., 1926–1937), Vol. IV, pp. 415–16, 430–33.

filled the school's well with manure, stoned the schoolhouse frequently, and even tried to burn it down. All these efforts, however,
failed to stop Miss Crandall. Finally, in September, 1834, a band
of men attacked her house at night and rendered it uninhabitable;
Miss Crandall at last gave way and departed for Illinois.[37]

Connecticut remained the most inhospitable of the New England states. From 1833 through 1837, antislavery journals reported
16 anti-abolition and anti-Negro mobs there. Of the New England
states, only Massachusetts, with 17 mobs, surpassed Connecticut.
But Massachusetts had not only a much larger population but also
much more antislavery activity. Between 1833 and 1837, antislavery men organized 243 auxiliaries in Massachusetts and only 46 in
Connecticut. If we regard the number of auxiliaries formed as a
reasonable indicator of antislavery activity, then the relative hostility of Connecticut and the other New England states becomes
clear. Connecticut, as the following table indicates, had a much
higher percentage of mobs for auxiliaries organized than any of
the other New England states: [38]

Connecticut	34.8%	(46 auxiliaries—16 mobs)
New Hampshire	16.4%	(79—13)
Rhode Island	15.4%	(26—4)
Maine	8.3%	(48—4)
Massachusetts	7.0%	(243—17)
Vermont	6.7%	(104—7)

Even in Cincinnati, which bordered a slave state and depended
heavily on the Southern trade, there was little reaction to immedia-

[37] May, *Reminiscences*, 50–51, 70–71; W. P. and F. J. Garrison, *Garrison*,
Vol. I, pp. 317n., 321; Abdy, *Journal*, Vol. I, pp. 199–203, Vol. III, pp. 208–
13, 303–7; George Benson to William Lloyd Garrison, March 5, 1833, Henry
E. Benson to Samuel J. May, March 31, 1833, Almira Crandall to Henry E.
Benson, April 30, 1833, Almira Crandall to George Benson, July 9, 1834—
all Garrison Papers.

[38] Information on mobs computed from data, *Liberator*, 1833–1837, *Emancipator*, 1833–1837, and *Philanthropist*, 1836–1837. I arrived at the number
of auxiliaries by taking the listing given in American Anti-Slavery Society,
Fifth Annual Report (New York, 1838), 128–52, and subtracting the number
formed before January 1833 as reported in the *First Annual Report . . . of
the New England Anti-Slavery Society* 43.

tism until it became associated with amalgamation and Negro uplift. The earliest penetration of antislavery sentiment into the Queen City came in early 1834, when Theodore Dwight Weld and his fellow students at Lane Theological Seminary formed an anti-slavery society. Contrary to historical belief, their call for the "immediate emancipation of the whole colored race" met little re-sistance either at the seminary or in the city of Cincinnati.[39] Only the *Cincinnati Journal* bothered to comment, and it found "noth-ing exceptionable" in the society's goal. Indeed, the editor of the *Journal* was happy that the antislavery movement was "falling into the hands of men, who express their views clearly and kindly." [40]

It was not until the Lane students opened schools in "Little Af-rica" or "Bucktown" and associated publicly with Negroes, particu-larly "sable belles," that the editor of the *Journal* and other Cincin-natians expressed alarm. Weld often visited Negro homes, and Augustus Wattles, the most zealous supporter of Negro education and uplift, boarded with a Negro family. One student, who had been seen leaving town with a black girl and returning with her a few hours later, caused a stir; few believed his claim that he was only giving directions. On another occasion, a carriage of Negro students visited Lane Seminary, and it soon became common gos-sip that the Lane students paid "marked attention" to the girls. And thus rumor followed rumor, and gossip became nastier and nastier.[41]

In May, less than two months after he had praised the Lane stu-dents, the editor of the *Journal* reprimanded them for lacking com-mon sense and being overzealous in their efforts. At the same time, the illustrious James Hall, editor and co-owner of the *Western*

[39] Weld's advocates have blown the Lane "debate" way out of proportion. There was little opposition, little conflict, and consequently little debate. The best presentation of the Lane Rebellion is Robert S. Fletcher's *History of Oberlin College* (2 vols.; Oberlin, 1943), Vol. I, pp. 150ff., and *passim*.

[40] March 28, 1834.

[41] Theodore Dwight Weld to Lewis Tappan, March 18, 1834, March 9, 1836, in Barnes and Dumond, *Weld-Grimké Letters*, Vol. I, 133–35, 273; *Proceedings of the Ohio Anti-Slavery Convention Held at Putnam* (Cin-cinnati, 1835), 34; *Fifth Annual Report of Lane Seminary, Nov. 1834* (Cin-cinnati, 1834), 38–41; *Cincinnati Journal*, October 17, 1834.

Monthly Magazine and an ardent supporter of African colonization, denounced the crusade for immediate emancipation, the activities of the students, and "the idea of inoculating . . . embryo
clergymen" with radical political and social ideas and "thus *pre-
paring* a trained band of missionaries to traverse the land and in-
oculate a particular creed." In August, the board of trustees of
Lane Seminary, responding to numerous complaints, outlawed the
antislavery society. In October, forty members of the society left
Lane, many of them bound for newly established Oberlin College.
Thus the first antislavery controversy in Cincinnati was short-
lived.[42]

But Cincinnati, which had anti-abolition and anti-Negro riots in
1836, 1841, and 1843, remained sensitive to questions of Negro
uplift and racial assimilation. Repeatedly cries of "Amalgamationists! Amalgamationists! Amalgamationists!" rang through the
Queen City. The "bugbear of 'amalgamation,'" reported one traveler, permeated southern Ohio. Even the notable Lyman Beecher
was "so far jaundiced" that he supported African colonization, because "he considered it a salutary preventive of that amalgamation, which would confound the two races and obliterate the
traces of their distinction."[43] And after the riot of September,
1841, which was the most violent and destructive of Cincinnati's
outbursts, zealous Negrophobes organized themselves into the
Anti-Abolition Society of Cincinnati. The society's primary goal
was to secure the expulsion of the Negro from Ohio, either by the

[42] *Cincinnati Journal,* May 16, 1834; "Slavery and Education," *Western
Monthly Magazine,* III (May 1834), 266–273; Theodore Dwight Weld to
James G. Birney, May 28, 1834, in Dumond, *Birney Letters,* Vol. I, p. 114.

[43] Abdy, *Journal,* Vol. II, pp. 399–400. Amalgamation, Abdy added, was
"neither to be dreaded nor deprecated, as it would destroy animosity by
destroying its causes."
Cincinnatians may have had reason to be extremely sensitive on questions
of race, sex, and marriage. According to Abdy, one justice of the peace performed four interracial marriages in the course of one winter. See Vol. III,
pp. 17–18. And, judging from innuendoes in the press, illicit relationships
between white men and Negro women apparently abounded. In the 1850
census, Cincinnati had fourteen mulattoes for every ten blacks; Connecticut,
three for ten; New York City, three for ten.

enactment of harsher anti-Negro legislation or by enforcement of the Black Laws of 1804 and 1807. Its only enemies, the society declared, were those "white traitors" who favored a "mixture of races." After the same riot, Dr. Gamaliel Bailey, the editor of the *Philanthropist*, issued a public disclaimer. It began: "We are not *amalgamationists*." [44]

Across the nation, abolitionists made the same disclaimer time and again, but to no avail. Throughout the ante-bellum period, anti-abolitionists repeated no charge with greater pertinacity than that of amalgamation, and none could more effectively stir up the rancor and the brutality of a mob. It was this charge—rather than any complaint about the technical difficulties of immediate emancipation or the future of the Southern trade—that generated the more savage anti-abolition mobs, such as those in New York City in July, 1834, and in Philadelphia in May, 1838.

IV

It is difficult to avoid the conclusion that this charge of amalgamation touched the heart of what Tocqueville called the "all-pervading disquietude" about the future of the two races in America.[45] Underlying anti-abolition pamphlets and harangues to mobs was the assumption that only miscegenation would solve the American race problem. Repeatedly, of course, anti-abolitionists denied the feasibility of miscegenation. They argued that the two races found one another physically repulsive—often in the face of overwhelming evidence to the contrary.[46] At the same time, however, they assumed that miscegenation was the only practical answer to America's racial dilemma.[47]

[44] *Daily Cincinnati Enquirer*, September 21, 25, 1841; *Cincinnati Post, and Anti-Abolitionist*, January 22, February 12, March 26, 1842; Bailey's disclaimer appeared in the *Cincinnati Daily Gazette*, September 17, 1841.

[45] Tocqueville, *Democracy in America*, Vol. I, p. 392.

[46] Judge Nathaniel C. Read, who as a young man participated in the Cincinnati mob of 1836, expressed such sentiments in *Edwill Thacker v. J. Hawk et al.*, 11 Ohio Reports 376. The case involved a mulatto trying to pass over!

[47] This paragraph and the ones that follow are based on my analysis of a

For many Northerners, the probable alternative to slavery and African colonization was *either* race war *or* miscegenation. For Northern anti-abolitionists, this alternative was as immutable as the law of gravity or the Ten Commandments: if slaves were freed, it followed that the two races must completely separate or wholly merge. To free millions of slaves and then leave them as a distinct race, to leave them in wretchedness and disgrace as the North had done with its few Negroes, was nothing less than to build a house with powder kegs. Destruction was certain.

The slave, as anti-abolitionists saw him, was contented and cowardly; he had been, as one ardent defender of the Lovejoy mob put it, "despoiled by Slavery." [48] But once the spirit of freedom and hope revived his dormant passions, he would be a new creature. He would never be satisfied with a few limited freedoms. He would want more and more. He would, in fact, never be content until he had access to women of both races, as white men had had for centuries, and particularly until he married the master's daughter. Onto the Negro the anti-abolitionists projected their own view of the American way. Marrying "well," they assumed, was the only real sign that an "inferior" had arrived. And since all "inferior" nationalities and classes measured their standing on the basis of their

wide assortment of anti-abolition literature and harangues to mobs. For a sample of what anti-abolitionists had to say, perhaps the place to start is with Oliver Bolokitten [pseud.], *A Sojourn in the City of Amalgamation in the Year of our Lord, 19—* (New York, 1835), which is a Rip Van Winkle story—anti-abolition style. See also James Trecothic Austin, *Remarks on Dr. Channing's Slavery* (Boston, 1835), *Review of the Rev. Dr. Channing's Letter to Jonathan Phillips, Esq.* . . . (Boston, 1839); Jesse Burden, *Remarks* . . . *in the Senate of Pennsylvania, on the Abolition Question* (Philadelphia, 1838); Simon Clough, *A Candid Appeal to the Citizens of the United States* (New York, 1834); Richard H. Colfax, *Evidence Against the Views of the Abolitionists* (New York, 1833); W. P. N. Fitzgerald, *A Scriptural View of Slavery and Abolition* (2nd ed.; New Haven, 1839); David M. Reese, *A Brief Review of the "First Annual Report of the American Anti-Slavery Society"* (New York, 1834), *Letters to the Honorable William Jay* (New York, 1835); William Willcocks Sleigh, *Abolitionism Exposed!* (Philadelphia, 1838); Thomas Russell Sullivan, *Letters Against the Immediate Abolitionists* . . . (Boston, 1835); Job Roberts Tyson, *A Discourse Before the Young Men's Colonization Society of Pennsylvania* (Philadelphia, 1834).

[48] Austin, *Review of Channing's Letters to Phillips*, 67.

access to a "superior's" women, it followed that the most "inferior" of all would do likewise.[49]

Once the slave became a new creature, he would also wield the sword with all the terror and the ferocity of deep revenge. The anti-abolitionist imagery of racial war, of slaughter, of carnage rested on the foreboding that the Negro had a score to settle with the white American. With dread anti-abolitionists looked forward to the day when the white man stood before the judgment seat of the black man. When that day came, as the expression went, "Quaker hats would be in quick demand."

The only alternative to that day and the only penance for their sins, anti-abolitionists feared, was the horror of horrors—amalgamation. For most white Americans, such thoughts were undoubtedly painful. But for the James Watson Webbs—for Americans who desperately dreaded being cut off from deep and permanent ties of family, clan, class, community, and position—amalgamation touched the heart of their passions: their dread of sinking below their forefathers' station and their nightmare of becoming cogs in a mass society.

For such men, African colonization offered the happy illusion of excluding the Negro not only from "society" but from the country as well. By attacking the American Colonization Society and by

[49] On the subject of race and sex, anti-abolition thinking differed somewhat from earlier and later apprehensions in at least two respects. First, anti-abolitionists, even in their crudest moments, rarely portrayed the male Negro as a sexual giant or a sexual athlete. I have encountered many startling comments concerning Negro sexuality, but very few even hint that the black man might be a stallion. This fact is worth noting, because the imagery of the black man as a stallion is not of recent origin; it was well established in the colonial period. (See, for example, Winthrop Jordan, *White Over Black: American Attitudes Toward the Negro, 1550–1812* [Chapel Hill, 1968], 158ff.) Second, anti-abolitionists frequently portrayed the black man as a potential rapist, but their rape complex lacked the vehemence of the horrifying rape complex that developed after the Civil War. Their complex, in fact, hardly compares with the later one. No anti-abolitionist, so far as I know, ever contended that the only way to protect white womanhood from the uncontrollable lusts of black men was through the liberal use of the lynching mob, the rope, and the faggot. This kind of thinking developed after the Jacksonian period.

closely identifying themselves with the free Negro, the abolitionists made it clear that they entertained a far different vision. They
proposed to lift the Negro not only out of bondage but out of the
gutter as well. They proposed to give the free Negro citizenship—
second-class citizenship to be sure, but citizenship nevertheless.
Many anti-abolitionists were thus alarmed, and some resorted to
violence. It took, however, the sudden appearance of a "powerful
combination" to heighten their fears into fury and to generate a
general outburst of violence.

3

Generation of Anti-Abolitionist Violence:
New York Phase

It is fitting that Governor Marcy of New York should have spent much of the Christmas season of 1835 wrestling with the "Williams question." For R. G. Williams, the publishing agent of the American Anti-Slavery Society, symbolized organized power, rather than vehement epithets and abuse. In demanding his extradition, the state of Alabama did not even pretend that Williams' words were as biting as Garrison's. And the grand jury of Tuscaloosa, which had returned a true bill against Williams on September 26, did not claim that Williams was even an important abolitionist. Indeed, it was largely because Williams was "an unimportant individual" that he was "selected from the mass of the Northern Abolitionists, as a fit subject for indictment." [1]

What Williams represented, primarily, was the "machinery" of

[1] Draft letter of William L. Marcy to John Gayle, Governor of Alabama, December 1835, Miscellaneous Collection—Alabama, New York Historical Society; Charles Zebina Eastman, *Messages from the Governors* . . . (11 vols.; Albany, 1909), Vol. III, pp. 594–604; *Alabama Senate Journal* (November 1835), 12–14; *New York Assembly Journal* (1836), 38–48; Thomas M. Owen, "An Alabama Protest Against Abolitionism in 1835," *Gulf States Historical Magazine* 2 (July 1903), 26–34.

organized antislavery—not bitter denunciation, or hopeless ideal-
ism, or reckless fanaticism—but "new measures," "increased energy," "enormous exertions," "systematic agitation," and "concerted
action." These words and their equivalents—which appear time
and again in anti-abolitionist literature—were associated with New
York City, rather than with Boston. It was Arthur Tappan and his
New York associates, rather than Garrison and his Boston radicals,
whom James Gordon Bennett and other Americans saw as frightening Americans "out of their senses." And it was principally "Arthur
Tappan and the infuriate demoniacs associated with him" whom
Governor Gayle of Alabama and public meetings throughout the
nation condemned for establishing "250 anti-slavery societies" and
"about thirty presses" and "overflowing this country . . . with licentious and incendiary publications." [2]

What frightened Governor Gayle and other Americans was the
apparent power and efficiency of Arthur Tappan and his New
York associates—their ability to establish numerous societies and
presses rapidly and to flood the country with their literature. Anti-
abolitionists, to be sure, always denounced their enemies as fanatics, hopeless idealists, reckless incendiaries, and incompetent non-
entities. Antislavery men, argued anti-abolitionists, were such
misfits that they were incapable of any argument other than vilifying the opposition; they were such reckless visionaries that they
were completely unaware of the consequences of their acts; they
were merely mice trying to destroy a mountain. In the next breath,
however, anti-abolitionists invariably pictured their enemies as
masterminding slave conspiracies from South Carolina to Mississippi, waging a relentless propaganda campaign throughout the
nation, infiltrating churches and missionary enterprises, subverting
the entire democratic process by a cleverly conceived petition
campaign, and molding large segments of the Northern population
—primarily women and children—into helpless puppets responding to every beck and call of a highly organized, central bureauc-
racy.

This vision of a highly efficient, well-organized propaganda ma-

2 New York *Herald*, September 1, 1835; *Alabama Senate Journal* (November 1835), 12–14.

chine terrified anti-abolitionists. As long as organized antislavery had been identified with a few fiery Boston radicals—with merely "licentious and incendiary" abuse—the abolition movement generated only teapot tempests. But once it became identified with New York—with the power, money, organization, and systematic agitation that Williams symbolized—then anti-abolitionist fears crystallized into violence.

II

After outmaneuvering John Neal and his fellow colonizationists in October 1833, the New York philanthropists, with a prod from Garrison, formed a national society at Philadelphia the following December. For the next five or six years, the antislavery movement operated out of New York. The decision-making power of the American Anti-Slavery Society rested largely in the hands of Elizur Wright, Jr., Joshua Leavitt, Lewis Tappan, and other New Yorkers. The symbolic leader was the New York silk merchant Arthur Tappan. The society's budget in the early years depended almost entirely on the largesse of Arthur Tappan, John Rankin, William Green, Jr., and other New York City merchants. Theodore Dwight Weld and the famous "Seventy" agents received their agencies, their orders, their reading material, and their paychecks from New York.[3] Even the New England Anti-Slavery Society, which had pioneered organized antislavery in America, recognized the shift in power; in February, 1835, it reluctantly adopted the lesser title of Massachusetts Anti-Slavery Society.[4]

[3] Cf. American Anti-Slavery Society, Agency Committee Minutes, 1833–1838, and Executive Committee Minutes, 1837–1838—both in Boston Public Library. See also, American Anti-Slavery Society, *Annual Reports, 1833–1839* (New York, 1833–1839).

[4] In mid-1834 the Executive Committee decided to bypass the regional primacy of the New England Society; the Garrisonians of course objected. Cf. Elizur Wright to A. A. Phelps, June 20, 1834, Amos Phelps Papers; B. C. Bacon to Elizur Wright, June 16, 1834, Letter Book of the New England Anti-Slavery Society, 1834–1835—both in Boston Public Library. Maine and New Hampshire became auxiliaries of the national society in the fall of 1834, and the New England Society capitulated. *Third Annual Report of the New England Anti-Slavery Society* (Boston, 1835), 4–5.

The great reaction to the activities of the New York associates
first came in the summer of 1835, one and one-half years after they
had formally organized. Why then? Why did so many Southern
communities put a price on Arthur Tappan's head in that year?
Why did prominent Northerners like Whig merchant Philip Hone
in New York City, Jacksonian Governor William Marcy in Albany,
former Federalist Harrison Gray Otis in Boston, "America's School-
master" Noah Webster in New Haven, Democratic journalist
Henry O'Reilly in Rochester, war hero and presidential hopeful
William Henry Harrison in Vincennes, General John Chandler in
Portland, state senate speaker Jesse Burden in Philadelphia, former Congressman Robert Lytle in Cincinnati—why did these men
and hundreds like them suddenly become alarmed and play conspicuous roles in anti-abolitionist rallies? And why did these rallies
draw record-breaking crowds in the summer, fall, and winter of
1835? [5]

Again, how do we account for the sudden outpouring of anti-abolition violence in the summer of 1835? Or for the sudden upturn
in our earlier graph?

Or how do we explain the sudden interest that politicians took
in the antislavery question? The absorbing and unusual attention
that antislavery received from the first session of the Twenty-
fourth Congress in the winter months of 1835–1836? [6] The consideration and concern that Northern governors and legislatures
gave to suggestions and measures designed to silence the

[5] Bayard Tuckerman, ed., *Diary of Philip Hone, 1828–1851* (2 vols.; New
York, 1899), Vol. I, pp. 156–57 [entries for August 26–27, 1835]; *Albany
Evening Journal*, September 5, 1835; Boston *Atlas*, August 25, 1835; New
Haven *Register*, September 5, 12, 1835; Rochester *Daily Democrat*, September
24, 26, 1835; excerpts from Harrison's Vincennes speech, quoted in *Emanci-
pator*, January 16, 30, 1840; *Kennebec Weekly Journal* (Augusta, Maine),
August 26, 1835; *Niles Register* 48 (August 29, September 19, 1835), 45,
188–89; *Hazard's Register of Pennsylvania* 16 (August 29, 1835), 138–39;
Robert T. Lytle's Scrapbook, entry for January 27, 1836, Lytle Papers,
Cincinnati Historical Society.

[6] At this session, debate over slavery and abolition consumed by far the
greatest amount of time. See *Register of Debates*, 24 Congress, 1 Session
(1835–1836), *passim*.

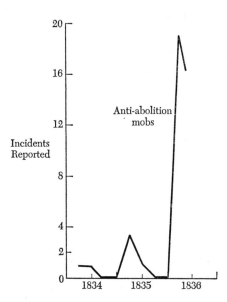

abolitionists? [7] President Andrew Jackson's denunciations of organized antislavery in his annual message in December, 1835? His call for "severe penalties" to suppress their "unconstitutional and wicked" activities? [8]

The answers to all these questions lie in what historians call the "pamphlet campaign" or the "postal campaign" of 1835. President Jackson and all others—either directly or indirectly—were react-

[7] *Resolves of the General Court . . . of Massachusetts, 1836* (Boston 1838), 296–98; *Resolves of the Sixteenth Legislature of Maine* (1836), 47–50; *Journal of the House of Representatives of . . . New Hampshire, June Session, 1836* (1836), 38–43; *Journal of the House of Representatives of . . . New Hampshire, November Session, 1836* (1837), 310–11, 326, 328, 330; Lincoln, *Messages from the Governor,* Vol. III, pp. 570–84, 594–604; *Laws of New York,* 59 Session (1836), 811–12; *Journal of the House of Representatives of . . . Ohio,* 34 General Assembly, 1 Session (1835–1836), 19–20, 927–28; *Journal of the Senate of . . . Ohio,* 34 General Assembly, 1 Session (1835–1836), 564–68, 990–91.

[8] James D. Richardson, ed., *Messages and Papers of the Presidents, 1789–1897* (Washington, 1896), Vol. III, p. 175.

ing to the American Anti-Slavery Society's attempt to flood the country with antislavery tracts, newspapers, kerchiefs, medals, emblems, and even blue chocolate wrappers. To overcome public apathy and to "beat up for a march," the abolitionists launched this campaign in the late spring of 1835. In the previous year, the national society had distributed only 122,000 pieces of literature; in 1835, it distributed 1,100,000. In July alone, the New York presses turned out 175,000 items, of which some 20,000 passed through the Post Office, bound for the South.[9] By late July, the tracts and newspapers reached Southern ports. And by mid-August, we may recall, the South was hysterical and New York City was a powder keg.

III

Historians have explained the great reaction to the pamphlet campaign in three distinct ways. All three have a certain substance; one is interesting; and none can be disproved.

A favorite explanation rests largely on the charge of Jackson and others that the "inflammatory appeals" of the abolitionists aimed at "the passions of the slaves" and intended "to stimulate them to insurrection, and to produce all the horrors of servile war." [10] Southern historians have argued that Jackson's fear was well grounded. They emphasize the simplicity of the texts and the vividness of the pictographs. They conclude that, whatever the abolitionists' intentions, such propaganda undoubtedly would have aroused the "colorful imaginations" of illiterate slaves.[11]

This view has some strong points. Even Northerners, as Tocque-

---

[9] American Anti-Slavery Society, *Second Annual Report* (New York, 1835), 48, and *Third Annual Report* (New York, 1836), 34; Lewis Tappan to Rev. John J. Shiperd, August 19, 1835, Lewis Tappan Papers, Library of Congress.

[10] Richardson, *Messages and Papers of the Presidents*, Vol. III, p. 175.

[11] Among recent proponents of this old argument are Charles M. Wiltse, *John C. Calhoun: Nullifier, 1829–1839* (Indianapolis, 1949), 268–71; and Henry H. Simms, *Emotion at High Tide: Abolition as a Controversial Factor 1830–1845* (Richmond, Virginia, 1960), 24ff. and *passim*.

ville pointed out, "perpetually" feared that the slaves would rebel in the near future. And in Maine alone, public meetings in Portland, Augusta, Bangor, Hallowell, Brunswick, Bath, Waterville, and "many other Towns too numerous to mention" passed resolutions denouncing antislavery "incendiaries" months before Jackson's annual message.[12] By the time of the message, in fact, such sentiments had become trite. Ironically, the triteness probably strengthens the position of Southern historians. For it is unlikely that such political virtuosos as Jackson, Governor Marcy of New York, Governor Isaac Hill of New Hampshire, and Governor Edward Everett of Massachusetts could have completely misread the public temper. Their use of such commonplaces in their annual messages almost assures us that many people responded to the ring of their argument.[13]

A second explanation often begins by dismissing Jackson's fear as contrived. Did Jackson and others, many historians have asked, really believe that the texts might stimulate the passions of *illiterate* slaves? Or did they fear that the tracts might produce intolerable "psychic tensions" among literate, but guilt-laden whites? Slavery, argue Charles Sellers and William Freehling, was a "travail" for Southern whites, and it was primarily to subdue this anguish about slaveholding that Southern radicals overreacted.[14]

This view is perhaps more satisfying. It has a ring of modernity. It does not assume that men fear what they say they fear. Nor

[12] Tocqueville, *Democracy in America*, Vol. I, pp. 391–92; *Resolves of Sixteenth Legislature of Maine*, 48; *Kennebec Weekly Journal*, August 26, 1835; Portland *Eastern Argus*, August 11, 1835.

[13] To be sure that his remarks would find public favor, Marcy sounded out such skillful politicians as Martin Van Buren and Silas Wright. See Marcy to Van Buren, November 22, December 3, 1835; Van Buren to Marcy, undated draft, Van Buren Papers, Library of Congress (microfilm); Wright to Marcy, December 18, 1835, Marcy Papers, Library of Congress.

[14] Cf. Nye, *Fettered Freedom*, 67–76; Charles G. Sellers, Jr., "Travail of Southern Slavery," in Sellers, ed., *The Southerner as American* (Chapel Hill, 1960); William Freehling, *Prelude to Civil War* (New York, 1966), Chapters 9 and 10. None of these interpretations, of course, is as flat and one-sided as the argument that I present here; I have merely abstracted from them what seems to me to be a central line of historical argument.

does it assume that skillful politicians harp on deep-seated public fears. And it finds strong confirmation in the statements of Duff Green and other Southern firebrands. In one respect, however, it rests on a false assumption. Usually its proponents assume that the abolitionists relied almost entirely on the written word. But what about the etchings, the woodcuts, the kerchiefs, and the chocolate wrappers? What about the full-page pictographs on the cover page of the *Anti-Slavery Record*, the pamphlet with by far the greatest distribution? [15] Abolitionists, said the antislavery *Herald of Freedom*, "know the influence of visual impressions. They know that such impressions are more powerful and permanent, than those which are derived from mere inscription." [16]

Still a third explanation centers upon obvious categories of self-interest. Southern planters, historians have relentlessly argued, primarily feared losing their human property. New York and Cincinnati merchants, responding to threats of Southern boycott, sold their souls for the profits of their Southern trade. Perceptive politicians such as James Buchanan and Franklin Pierce became "Northern men with Southern principles" to ensure their political futures. Prominent Northern Methodists such as Nathan Bangs and Wilbur Fisk denounced abolitionist dissenters to protect their positions in their church's national hierarchy. Northern workers opposed antislavery because they feared that abolition might flood the Northern labor market with cheap Negro labor. Such matters, the American Anti-Slavery Society noted in 1837, "are too common to excite surprise." [17]

[15] There were 385,000 copies distributed in 1835—or about 150,000 copies more than any other abolition publication. On the cover of the May issue was a white planter, holding a slave baby by the wrist and whipping the child's weeping mother with the other hand. For August, a Negro mother and her three children begging "A Generous Planter" with hard-earned coins for father's freedom. For September (second edition), a slave mother killing her twin infants, who apparently were to be sold away from her, with an ax. Advertisements of various kinds of lithographic prints, etc., appear in the *Emancipator*, August, September, December, 1835; February, May 5, 12, 19, 26, June 3, July 7, 1836; description of handkerchiefs, January 5, 1837. The *Slave's Friend*, which was sent to Charleston, was designed for children.

[16] *Herald of Freedom,* quoted in *Emancipator,* February 1836.

[17] American Anti-Slavery Society, *Fourth Annual Report* (New York, 1837), 57.

Despite its obvious merits, this view has limitations. There were too many Northern mobs in cities and towns such as Montpelier, Utica, Lockport, Troy, and Granville—in places that had little or no dependence on Southern patronage. Too many antislavery societies lived by the fat donations of a few wealthy merchants, most of whom engaged largely in the Southern trade. We might note here Henry G. Chapman, Francis Jackson, Samuel Philbrick, and Ellis Gray Loring of Boston; Christian and William Donaldson of Cincinnati; and particularly Arthur Tappan, John Rankin, and William Green, Jr. of New York. Above all, as the American Anti-Slavery Society lamented in 1837, much of the bitterest opposition came from men who cared not a whit for Southern patronage, Southern friendship, Southern hospitality, or Southern slavery.[18] What motivated men such as Isaiah Tiffany, a timid book dealer in Utica, and Holmes Hutchinson, a civil engineer on the Erie Canal, to join a mob? What induced Congregational clergymen to pass a gag law barring antislavery lecturers from Connecticut pulpits?

And what was it, precisely, about the pamphlet campaign that made men afraid? What did Southerners see in these tracts and newspapers that made them react so vehemently? Why did so many Northern gentlemen respond quickly and forcefully to Southern demands for suppression of organized antislavery?

The message that men received from antislavery journals in the summer of 1835 was often far different from what historians have described. The complaints and denunciations about "incendiary literature" and "inflammatory pictures" represented only the top of the iceberg. The antislavery argument that slavery was a "SIN," the South "a brothel," and the only remedy "IMMEDIATISM" may appear to be the primary message to twentieth-century readers. But contemporaries complained as much about the price of the papers as they did about the contents.

What, then, was the message? For insight let us turn to a speech that historians have often cited, John Tyler's tirade at Gloucester Courthouse, Virginia, on August 22, 1835.[19]

18 *Ibid.*, 59–60.

19 The speech, which the *African Repository* and many Northern newspapers reprinted in September and October 1835, appears also in Lyon

The future President, like most speakers that summer, began by assuring his fellow Virginians that he was no alarmist, that "until recently" he had never believed that abolition could make any headway in the United States. But the "unexpected evil is now upon us," he warned his audience; "it has invaded our firesides, and under our roofs is sharpening the dagger for midnight assassination. . . ." Thus Tyler propounded the standard argument that the "incendiary pamphlets" would arouse the slaves to rebellion and carnage.

But let us consider in some detail what followed, as it was later reported by the Richmond *Whig:*

> A society has sprung up whose avowed object it is to despoil us of our property at the hazard of all and every consequence. It had been Tyler's duty, occupying as he did a public station which devolved on him the obligations of a sentinel . . . to make himself acquainted as far as practicable with the rise and progress of that society, and with its means to do mischief; and his opinion was, that it was now powerful, and if not speedily checked in its mad career, was destined to attain much greater power. He had seen it in its origin, some two years ago, consisting of a mere handful of obscure persons, who were the subjects of ridicule from one end of the Union to the other. That small association, thus despised and thus contemned, had already established two hundred and fifty auxiliaries, and at a single meeting contributed $30,000 towards the furtherance of its scheme,—some half of which was paid down promptly. It has established numerous presses, four of which circulated from the city of New York, with copies of three of which they had been so *extremely kind* as to favor me through the mail. These papers were circulated gratuitously among us, and at mere nominal prices to actual subscribers. He had then in his possession one of those publications, and he would exhibit it for the inspection of those present. (He here drew from his pocket the *Anti-Slavery Record.*) Here, said he, is a picture upon the external covering, designed to represent each of you, gentlemen. A scourge is in your hand, and three victims bound and kneeling

Gardiner Tyler, *Letters and Times of the Tylers* (3 vols.; Richmond, Virginia, 1884–1894), Vol. I, pp. 573–81. Typically, Tyler's remarks were his "most intemperate . . . on the slavery question." Robert Seager II, *And Tyler Too: A Biography of John and Julia Gardiner Tyler* (New York, 1963), 104.

at your feet. You are represented as demons in the shape of men; and by way of contrast, here stands Arthur Tappan, Mr. Somebody Garrison, and Mr. Foreigner Thompson, patting the greasy little fellows on their cheeks and giving them most lovely kisses. *They* are the exclusive philanthropists—the only lovers of the human race—the only legitimate defenders of the religion of Christ. But I propose to show to you the cheap rate at which these papers are delivered out to actual subscribers. [He read from the external sheet: "*Human Rights*, twenty-five cents per annum; *Anti-Slavery Record*, one-dollar-and-a-half *per hundred*; *Emancipator* (a paper larger than the *Whig* or *Enquirer*), fifty cents per annum; *Slave's Friend*, a single number, one cent."] He had not seen the *Slave's Friend*; judging, however, from the other papers, he concluded it . . . should rather be called the *slave's enemy*, since its circulation among us . . . had produced a curtailment of privileges. . . . In addition to these, there was a numerous tribe of tracts, and he believed, prints designed to make impression on the minds of children. Here, then, Mr. Chairman, are evidences of a powerful combination. . . .

When he came to be informed that numbers of the reverend clergy in the North were lending themselves to this work, he could not doubt but that it would grow into greater magnitude. All felt and acknowledged their influence. Standing as pastors at the head of their flocks . . . these men . . . mean that their influence shall be felt.

Woman is to be made one of the instruments to accomplish their mischievous purposes. . . . Yes, woman is to be made the instrument of destroying our political paradise, the Union of these States; she is to be made the presiding genius over the councils of insurrection and discord; she is to be converted into a fiend, to rejoice over the conflagration of our dwellings and the murder of our people. . . . Under such counsels and such counselors she is already lending herself to these fanatical schemes. I state a fact, which my situation as chairman of the District of Columbia Committee of the Senate the last winter brought to my knowledge. A petition was presented to the Senate and referred to that Committee, praying the abolition of slavery in that District, signed by fifteen hundred women. . . .

Such, then, are the means which are now invoked by the abolitionists—such their growth, and such their resources. I am told that they are also addressing themselves to the growing generation through horn-books and primers—that the youthful

imagination is filled with horror against us and our children by
images and pictures exhibited in the nursery. How are they
to be met and overthrown? . . .

How were the John Tylers of Jacksonian America—how were
men without cheap presses, 250 auxiliaries, and other means of
widespread manipulation—to meet the onslaught of "a powerful
combination" of "vicious" advertisers and propagandists? How
were they to meet the challenge of an organization that not only
made women "instruments" of their purposes but also corrupted
young minds in the nursery? How were they to operate in a world
full of free newspapers, tracts at "one dollar-and-a-half *per hundred*," petitions "signed by fifteen hundred women," "horn-books
and primers," and children weaned on a steady diet of horrifying
"images and pictures"?

Outraged Northerners shared these fears. Consider, for example,
Boston's response. On the day before Tyler spoke in Virginia, an
overflowing crowd gathered in Faneuil Hall for an anti-abolition
meeting, which had been called by the Boston *Atlas*, the Webster
paper, and the *Morning Post*, the Jackson and Van Buren paper.
The high point of the meeting was a speech by Harrison Gray
Otis.[20] The old Federalist, who had never taken Garrison seriously, warned his fellow Bostonians that there was now cause for
alarm. It had become certain, said Otis, that a "dangerous association" had arisen in a "neighboring state." This organization is "a
revolutionary society—combined and affiliated with auxiliary and
ancilliary societies, in every state and community, large or small,
in the eastern and western states." Not only did this society invite
"all men" to join in their "holy crusade," but it also asked women
to "turn their sewing parties into abolition clubs." The society even
intended to teach "little children when they meet to eat sugar
plumbs or at the Sunday schools . . . that A B stands for abolition." "Sir," exclaimed Otis, "I do not exaggerate—there is the
book—[an antislavery pamphlet which lay on the table] . . . men,

[20] The speech, which appeared in the Boston *Atlas*, August 25, 1835, was
widely reprinted in September, 1835, appearing in metropolitan papers of the
North, as well as *Niles' Register*, which of course enjoyed national influence.

women and children are stimulated, flattered and frightened in order to swell their numbers."

What is even worse, continued Otis, is the society's obvious intention of becoming a "political association." Already it had "interrogated" one Congressional candidate. "And can you doubt, fellow citizens, that these associations will act together for political purposes? Is it in human nature for such combinations to forbear?" Who among us "can calculate the amount of trouble and calamity which will ensue, upon the perseverance of the antislavery society?" What will become of this nation? What will become of the union? "I pray . . . that my grave may close over me before the union descends into hers."

At the same time, the Boston *Courier* ran a serial entitled "Letters Against Immediate Abolition," by Thomas Russell Sullivan, a resident of New Hampshire.[21] Sullivan, who called for penal legislation against the abolitionists, had little quarrel with their goals. But their methods exasperated him. How could "our own New England men," Sullivan asked, engage in such activities? They "*ought* to know how we do business in the new world." Instead they "have pitched upon a system of operations as contrary as well could be to the practice of our citizens, under our republican forms." That is, they have begun "*the agitation of a legal, constitutional, or political reform . . . by measures adopted to inflame the passions of the multitude,*" including the women and children, the boarding-school misses and factory girls. . . ." In "a systematic, and, as far as practicable, simultaneous effort," they have tried to stir up the passions of every man, woman, and child "through organized societies, public meetings, authorized agents, foreign emissaries, regular publications, and the incessant circulation of cheap tracts, pamphlets, handbills, &c." Their avowed intention is to build up enormous Northern pressure groups to coerce the "man-owners at the South." How could well-bred men descend to such measures?

[21] These letters appeared later in pamphlet form, and the pamphlet went through at least three editions; I am quoting from the pamphlet, *Letters Against the Immediate Abolition of Slavery* (Boston, 1835).

In their proper place, argued Sullivan, women, children, and ill-bred men were harmless, useful, and desirable. But once their voice was brought to bear on important matters, then disaster followed. In her proper "sphere," for example, woman moves "regularly and calmly . . . as lovely as the evening star." But whenever she is "*dis-orbed*," not even "the disastrous shock of comets, striking our trembling globe, outmeasures the evil that might follow. . . ." And children? It was well to remember, said Sullivan, that once a child's mind was stirred, he "never forgot." How then, could any sensible man, any lover of "truth and reason," systematically appeal to women and children, organize them into "powerful combinations," and thus try to influence public opinion?

Sullivan's answer—and the answer of most anti-abolitionists to this question—was that even good causes seemed to be moving in this direction. The temperance movement, it was commonly argued, was a noble cause. It arose to meet a great emergency. But once temperance men stopped acting as individuals upon others, and began to operate as societies, then the nature of the movement changed. Individual persuasion gave way to corporate influence; reason gave way to inflammatory appeals; and appealing to the conscience of the individual gave way to overbearing him with the power of the multitude. The abolitionists, then, were not unique. They were simply the cutting edge of a far-reaching change that anti-abolitionists saw enveloping American society. The abolitionists, in anti-abolitionist thinking, simply carried organized agitation and the techniques of "popular excitement" to an extreme.[22]

Despite these sentiments, only a few anti-abolitionists were desperate defenders of individual action. Most, in fact, assumed that the day of individual action was long past, and that forming associations was the normal means for solving problems. But

---

[22] This paragraph and the ones that follow are drawn from a wide assortment of anti-abolitionist literature and harangues to mobs. For a sample of what troubled anti-abolitionists, compare Sullivan, *Letters Against Immediate Abolitionists*, 13ff.; Calvin Colton, *Thoughts on the Religious State of the Country* (London, 1837), 68ff. and *passim*; Colton, *Abolition, a Sedition* (Philadelphia, 1839), 18off. and *passim*; David Meredith Reese, *Humbugs of New York* (New York, 1838), 161ff.

nearly all held that such associations should be restrictive—or, to use their term, "elective." Organizers should follow the example of the colonizationists and seek out only prudent, judicious "gentlemen of property and standing" as members. Or, at the very least, they should seek only certain elements of the community as members. They should never indiscriminately gather into their societies a mixed and impetuous multitude of young and old, men and women, enlightened and unenlightened. They should never try to stir up the passions of *all* men, women, and children by heartrending stories and horrifying pictures. Nearly all organizations, anti-abolitionists admitted, violated one or more of these hallowed injunctions. But antislavery men violated all of them. They preached their doctrine even to Negroes. Worst of all, they gathered these "despicable outcasts" into their societies. Among abolitionists, it seemed as if no distinctions were sacred.

Not only social distinctions but also social control seemed to be at stake. Anti-abolitionists invariably envisioned the New York associates and their agents as metropolitan monsters invading rural paradises and imposing abnormal standards on the local citizens. Otis' image of the New York philanthropists indoctrinating children with a revised primer was commonplace. Indeed, many speakers and pamphlet writers described the New Yorkers as not only teaching that "A B stands for abolition" but also as instilling the desirability of amalgamation into children's minds. Underlying such notions was the fear that social control was shifting from local elites to organizations and metropolitan centers.

The very nature of antislavery operations enhanced this fear. By forming a network of centrally organized societies, for example, the New York associates created an obvious tension between central and local control. If local antislavery societies were simply the "instruments" of Arthur Tappan and his central bureau, as men generally believed, then it followed that this metropolitan agency might try to impose uniform patterns of behavior on the local community. By flooding the country with free literature in the summer of 1835, the New York abolitionists multiplied this apprehension at least tenfold. Throughout the North, men quickly became convinced that Tappan and his associates intended to impose uniformity.[23]

Thus anti-abolitionists saw their opponents as the vanguard of a challenge to basic prerogatives. Antislavery men, they feared, defied the right of settlers and residents to impose their own patterns of behavior. Their direct appeals to women and children threatened the authority of fathers and husbands. Above all, their methods and appeals bypassed the authority of city fathers. They challenged the dominion of local elites. How were men who were reared to expect social deference, raised for traditional leadership, trained in older ways of manipulation—how were these men to face the emergence of a strange and hostile world of pressure groups and mass media? This question haunted the outpourings of the Tylers, the Otises, and the Sullivans of Jacksonian America. Their kind might not only lose property and profits, but might also become a leadership group without a following, an elite without a function.

IV

These anti-abolitionist fears were intensified by the national uproar —particularly in the Northeast—against "foreign emissaries" and "foreign agents" in the summer of 1835.

It was understandable that some Northerners might see the American Anti-Slavery Society as part of a foreign and an alien movement. In 1833, Tappan and his associates purposely identified their society with the successful campaign in England. They timed

[23] In New York State, for example, this rise in apprehension can be followed in July through October issues of the New York *Courier and Enquirer*, New York *Evening Star*, New York *Commercial Advertiser*, Albany *Advertiser* (all of which not only sympathized with mobs but also favored penal legislation against abolitionists), and the Albany *Argus* and the Utica *Observer* (both of which sympathized with the Utica mob and favored some "legislative action"). It is perhaps noteworthy that James Gordon Bennett, who also began employing mass media techniques in 1835, responded somewhat ambivalently to the hysteria of 1835; frequently—but not consistently—he dismissed and ridiculed the anti-abolitionist uproar as unfounded nonsense. See New York *Herald*, September–October 1835.

its organization, for example, to coincide with the arrival of news from England that slaves in the British West Indies finally had been freed. Such timing, they reasoned, would give their movement momentum and the appearance of universality. Openly and self-consciously, they patterned the American Anti-Slavery Society on the British model.[24] More important, in 1834 and 1835, the society had the services of Charles Stuart and George Thompson, two of the British movement's leading agitators.

Northern anti-abolitionists centered their fire on George Thompson. Thompson, who had been the English society's chief organizer, came to America in the fall of 1834 at Garrison's invitation. Quickly he became the American society's most notorious agent. Not only Tyler but also other Americans associated "Arthur Tappan, Mr. Somebody Garrison, and Mr. Foreigner Thompson" in the same breath. Thompson was even referred to indirectly in Jackson's annual message in December, 1835. In his discussion of the slavery question, the President applauded the "strong and impressive" response of Northerners "against . . . emissaries from foreign parts who have dared to interfere in this matter." [25]

And what was this "strong and impressive" response? Thirty-six hours after Thompson's arrival at New York in September, 1834, his fellow lodgers followed the promptings of James Watson Webb's *Courier and Enquirer* and forced the manager to evict Thompson, his wife, and his children. A mob at Augusta, Maine,

[24] American abolitionists *said* they used the British movement as a model. Whether they merely copied British ideas, tactics, and organization has become a subject of historical debate. For a sample of this debate, see Frank Thistlethwaite, *America and the Atlantic Community* (Harper Torchbook edition, New York, 1963), Chapter 4; Thomas F. Harwood, "British Evangelical Abolitionism and American Churches in the 1830's," *Journal of Southern History* 28 (August 1962), 287–306; and David Brion Davis, "The Emergence of Immediatism in British and American Anti-Slavery Thought," *Mississippi Valley Historical Review* 49 (September 1962), 209–30.

[25] Richardson, *Messages and Papers of the Presidents*, Vol. III, p. 175. Given the common expressions that men used in 1835, Jackson's comment applied only to Thompson—and perhaps Stuart. Stuart's visit was not too unusual. Since the mid-1820's, he had flitted between the British Isles, Canada, and western New York. Men objected to his antislavery activities, but never as fervently as they objected to Thompson's.

attacked the home of Thompson's host, frightening Thompson's wife and children. Another mob at Concord, New Hampshire, threw stones and eggs at a ladies' meeting at which Thompson was speaking. Still another mob at Lynn, Massachusetts, pelted Thompson's audience with rotten eggs and stones and forced Thompson to accept the escort of three hundred ladies to get out of the place. Still another mistook the poet John Greenleaf Whittier for Thompson and plastered him with eggs, mud, and stones. And the famous Boston mob of October, 1835, sought Thompson, found Garrison, and dragged the latter through the streets at the end of a rope. Finally, in November, 1835, after some two hundred lectures and perhaps as many as twenty mobs, Thompson fled the country by rowing a boat out to a New Brunswick-bound brig. Like Jackson, he knew the strength and impressiveness of Northern anti-abolition.[26]

The North's reception of Thompson owed its intensity to several sources. At the time of his arrival, even antislavery sympathizers were dubious about the propriety of using the talents of a foreigner, particularly an Englishman, to stir up American society at its most sensitive point. American Anglophobes immediately raised an outcry against this "intermeddling." Later, news began circulating that Thompson was a former thief, that he had been convicted of having stolen about £160, or about $750, from his employers— "and that, after having been forgiven for a previous offense of the same character." [27] Still later, the rumor developed that Thompson

[26] Elizur Wright, Jr., to his father, September 24, 1834, Wright Papers, Library of Congress; *Emancipator*, November 4, 1834; *Liberator*, November 1, 29, December 6, 13, 1834, August 15, September 12, 1835; *Niles' Register* 47 (1834), 51, 134, 48 (1835), 439; *Boston Daily Evening Transcript*, August 8, October 29, 1835; New York *Herald*, September 10, 1835; Samuel T. Pickard, *Life and Letters of John Greenleaf Whittier* (2 vols., Boston, 1894), Vol. I, pp. 149–53; *Letters and Addresses by George Thompson, During His Mission in the United States, from Oct. 1st, 1834, to Nov. 27, 1835* (Boston, 1837), *passim*.

[27] *Boston Daily Evening Transcript*, October 16, November 16, 1835; New York *Journal of Commerce*, November 14, 1835.

Although anti-abolitionists exaggerated the extent of Thompson's criminality, their charge was essentially correct. Thompson had been an embezzler.

said that "every slaveholder ought to have his throat cut." In September, 1835, the New York *Commercial Advertiser* printed a statement to this effect from a student at Andover Theological Seminary, where Thompson allegedly had advocated throat-cutting "distinctly" and "repeatedly." Thompson immediately denied the charge in a public letter. But the *Commercial Advertiser* responded with a testimonial from three of the student's most eminent professors, who swore that the young man's "veracity" was "unimpeachable." And thus the public had the choice of believing either a former thief or an honest seminarian.[28]

But to Northern anti-abolitionists, Thompson was more than a "cutthroat." He became the symbol of a well-planned British plot to destroy the American way of life. He became only the most visible sign of a satanic foreign conspiracy to scatter firebrands in the South and sow seeds of war, rape, and carnage throughout the United States. Why, asked anti-abolitionists time and again, has the United States been singled out from the rest of the world as a target for the great guns of British philanthropy? Why has the English press failed to call on the monarchs of France, Spain, or Portugal to give immediate freedom to the slaves of their colonies? Why did the British government suddenly abolish slavery in its colonies? From a newborn zeal of humanity? Hardly! English philanthropists still turned only deaf ears to the cries of the paupers in London and particularly in Ireland. The British simply wanted to appear humane so that they might send missionaries among Americans to preach sedition, to advocate the cutting of throats, and to sow the seeds of disunion.[29]

His employers displayed an unusual amount of Christian charity, and thus he never was committed to prison. For a full account of Thompson's life, see Raymond English, "George Thompson and the Triumph of Philanthropic Radicalism" (Unpub. Ph.D. dissertation, Trinity College, Cambridge, England, 1948). See also C. Duncan Rice, "The Anti-Slavery Mission of George Thompson to the United States, 1834–1835," *Journal of American Studies* 2 (April 1968), 25–26.

[28] New York *Commercial Advertiser,* quoted in Boston *Atlas,* September 30, October 17, 1835. See also *Boston Daily Evening Transcript,* October 17, 1835, and *Letters by Thompson,* 58–59, 93–98, 121.

[29] Anti-abolitionists, particularly after the summer of 1835, could hardly

Not every Englishman, conceded anti-abolitionists, wanted to destroy the United States. But it could hardly have escaped the notice of Americans that the most devoted adherents of aristocracy were the loudest supporters of Negro emancipation. Even **Tsar** Nicholas himself, the most despotic of Europe's monarchs, favored immediate emancipation of Negro slaves in the American South. The second loudest supporters of Negro freedom, argued anti-abolitionists, were the lords of European manufacturing and trade. How was it, anti-abolitionists often asked rhetorically, that European abolitionists invariably turned out to be the enemies of liberty in Europe? As long as the United States remained the lighthouse of liberty to the degraded masses of the Old World, it obviously threatened European despotism. An America that made rapid advances in population, wealth, manufacturing, and commerce threatened the money barons of Europe.

Thus Northern anti-abolitionists concluded that British aristocrats, with the aid of English merchants and manufacturers, had launched a conspiracy against the American republic. By abolishing slavery in the West Indies and raising a clamor against Southern slavery, these conspirators hoped to placate their own downtrodden masses with a false issue. Then, as years passed, they hoped to destroy American vigor either by fomenting war and carnage or by debilitating American manhood through widespread miscegenation.

This paranoia developed out of the American Colonization Society's debacle in 1833. Many colonizationists blamed Garrison for their society's troubles, but others blamed English abolitionists,

open their mouths or write a pamphlet without alluding to this "conspiracy." For a sample of their paranoia, which outlived even the Civil War, see James Kirke Paulding, *Slavery in the United States* (New York, 1836), 109ff.; *Mr. Tyson's Letter to the Abolitionists of Philadelphia* (Philadelphia, 1840); George Junkin, *The Integrity of our National Union* (Cincinnati, 1843); John H. Van Evrie, *Negroes and Negro Slavery; the First, an Inferior Race—the Latter, Its Normal Condition* (New York, 1853), 12ff.; Nehemiah Adams, *A South-Side View of Slavery* (Boston, 1854), 180ff.; George Lunt, *The Origin of the Late War* (Boston, 1867), 71–103; R. G. Horton, *A Youth's History of the Great Civil War* (Seventy-five-thousandth edition; New York, 1868), iii–v, 15–64. As a rule, later works filled in details, but the basic "plot" remained.

and some soon discovered "evidence" of a British plot. In late 1834, the Philadelphia Colonization Society published a pamphlet warning "against the insidious attempts of foreign stratagem." Englishmen, said the pamphlet, denounced African colonization as absurd, and now they have two agents in the Northeast fomenting disunion—"can we doubt of the existence of a well-defined object, a settled and systematic design?" It seems clear that "Anti-Slavery Societies, from their principles, connexions and acts, are of foreign parentage—that their formation was *dictated* by English party politicians," who hoped "to compass their objects at home" by directly assaulting the American union. A few months later, at their third annual meeting, New York City colonizationists made a similar claim. They insisted that the denunciation of African colonization by British philanthropists and the newborn zeal and recklessness of American abolitionists were telltale signs of the antislavery movement's "foreign origin" or of "its subservience at least to foreign interests and views." [30]

Within a few years, this conspiracy theory settled into a cut-and-dried response; but in 1834 and 1835, it was hazy and uneven. Men appeared to be searching for explanations rather than parroting hackneyed phrases. Nearly all anti-abolitionists agreed that Thompson was a foreign agent. But whom did he represent? Some suggested that he was the hireling of a "bevy of old maids at Glasgow," and thus Americans had little to fear.[31] Then, sometimes in almost the next breath, they insisted that he represented Daniel O'Connell, Frances Wright, and other British radicals. Or they maintained that he was the agent of English tories or of the crown itself. Not until the pamphlet campaign did the conspiracy theme begin to crystallize, and even then its details remained somewhat hazy.

The chief difficulty with the "tory plot" was Daniel O'Connell,

[30] Job Roberts Tyson, *A Discourse Before the Young Men's Colonization Society . . . 1834* (Philadelphia, 1834), 39ff.; *Proceedings of the Colonization Society of the City of New York, at their Third Annual Meeting . . . May, 1835* (New York, 1835), 12f.

[31] Expressions such as "old maids of Glasgow," "pussy cats of Glasgow," etc., which were frequently coined by James Watson Webb's *Courier and Enquirer,* became household phrases in 1835.

the champion of Ireland. American newspapers rang with the Irish
liberator's derisions of American slaveholders as "two-legged
wolves," men with "hearts of tigers," "monsters in human shape."
Why should O'Connell help his archenemies, the nobles and bish-
ops and money barons of England, in their attempt to destroy the
American republic? "There must be something extraordinary, some
cement eminently adhesive," wrote James Kirke Paulding in November, 1835, "to have produced this miraculous conjunction of op-
posing bodies." Yet it had happened. "Let it no more be said that
oil and vinegar will not mix together, when we see Sir Robert Peel
and Mr. O'Connell uniting in denouncing the Colonization
Society . . . at a meeting of abolitionists in the city of London."
So deceitful and so cunning was the enemy that it duped even the
champion of Ireland! [32]

This frenzied and fanciful rhetoric gained strength not only
from the uproar over Thompson's mission but also from several
other sources. Undoubtedly it was nourished by the well-known
tendency among Jacksonian Americans to overreact to British crit-
icism, to "twist the lion's tail," and to picture their enemies in gargantuan and conspiratorial terms.[33] Much of its imagery, in fact,
was a compound of traditional stereotypes about designing aristocrats and scheming Jesuits, papal plots and crown conspiracies.

This feverish language acquired strength from concrete ethnic
rivalries and face-to-face conflicts within American society. Irish
immigrants in the 1840's and 1850's almost immediately identified
with the anti-abolitionists. One reason was that they dismissed abolition as a British import.[34] Perhaps another was that English

[32] Slavery in the United States (New York, 1836), 115.

[33] For suggestive, but conflicting approaches to this period's conspiratorial
outlook, see John Higham, "Another Look at Nativism," Catholic Historical
Review (Washington) 44 (July 1958), 147–58; and David Brion Davis,
"Some Themes of Counter-Subversion: An Analysis of Anti-Masonic, Anti-
Catholic, and Anti-Mormon Literature," Mississippi Valley Historical Review
47 (September 1960), 205–24. For American Anglophobia, see Max Berger,
The British Traveler in America, 1836–1860 (New York, 1943), and Thomas
A. Bailey, Diplomatic History of the American People (New York, 1958),
Chapters 14 and 15.

[34] Cf. Madeleine Hook Rice, American Catholic Opinion in the Slavery

and Welsh immigrants invariably identified with the abolitionists. In Utica, New York, which was one of the hotbeds of the antislavery movement, about one-third of the active abolitionists came from Wales or England. And in Cincinnati the antislavery movement depended on the largesse of English immigrants.[35] Anti-abolitionist mobs, moveover, tended to save some of their roughest treatment for English immigrants. As we will see in some detail later, one of the chief targets of the New York City mob of July, 1834, was the English stage manager of the Bowery Theatre, and the special target of the Cincinnati mobs of 1841 and 1843 was an English confectioner.

The image of antislavery as subversive served to legitimize anti-abolition behavior. Anti-abolition mobs saw themselves defending the established order against the encroachments of internal subversives and foreign agents. Self-consciously and self-righteously, the mobs identified with the Sons of Liberty, the Minute Men, and similar groups. The Philadelphia mob of August, 1835, even tailored its behavior to resemble the Boston Tea Party. The mob seized some antislavery pamphlets, hauled the material out into the middle of the Delaware River, ripped the papers into thousands of pieces, and dumped the debris overboard. Before the Cincinnati mob of July, 1836, was formed, a town meeting passed a resolution praising "the noble and fearless example set us" by the Boston patriots who acted "*without* the sanction of law, but in the plentitude of the justness of their cause." And after the Alton mob killed Lovejoy in November, 1837, the Attorney General of Massachusetts, James Trecothic Austin, told a large audience at Faneuil Hall in Boston that the mob acted in the hallowed tradition of Samuel Adams, James Otis, Charles Warren, and the other heroes of 1773.[36]

The view of antislavery men as subversive tories allowed anti-

---

Controversy (New York, 1944), 84, 103–5; Bernard Mandel, *Labor: Free and Slave* (New York, 1955), 69.

[35] Notably Christian and William Donaldson, and Rees Price.

[36] *Hazard's Register of Pennsylvania* 16 (August 29, 1835), 138–39; *Narrative of the Late Riotous Proceedings Against the Liberty of the Press, in*

abolitionists not only to visualize themselves as guardians of the
past, defenders of orthodoxy, and protectors of the Union, but also
to proclaim their faith in freedom, democracy, and equal rights.
They could defend the Founding Fathers' compromise with slavery and argue relentlessly that this compromise was the cornerstone of national unity. Yet they could also subdue their own "psychic tensions" and their own guilt feelings about slavery. They
could see themselves as champions of equality and American democracy, the hope of mankind and the wave of the future, fighting
off the challenge of antislavery reactionaries and effete monarchism. By concentrating on the imaginary threat of a tory conspiracy, then, anti-abolitionists could fight aggressively for the established order, yet style themselves progressives.

Finally, the imagery of the British plot reflected changes that
anti-abolitionists saw taking place in American society. We can
only wonder if anti-abolitionists projected their own cunning and
deceit, their own desires for fixed social distinctions and for an established order onto imaginary British conspirators. There is no
need, however, to be equally cautious about their fantasies of unscrupulous tories using "foreign" means and "foreign" stratagems
to destroy the Union and to subvert local authority. For anti-abolitionists insisted time and again that the American Anti-Slavery Society's "system of operations" was un-American, that both its goals
and its "machinery" were of "foreign parentage," and that the
pamphlet campaign and the organizational drive of 1835 had been
stimulated by "an impulse derived from abroad." [37] Anti-abolitionists, moreover, always ascribed to their imagined enemies all the
evil characteristics that they saw permeating American society.
George Thompson and other "conspirators," in the eyes of many
anti-abolitionists, were simply parts of a machinelike organization

---

Cincinnati (Cincinnati, 1836), 25; Henry Wilson, History of the Rise and Fall
of the Slave Power in America (3 vols.; Boston, 1872), Vol. I, 384ff.;
Henry Tanner, The Martyrdom of Lovejoy (Chicago, 1881), 174–75.

[37] Sullivan, Letters Against Immediate Abolitionists, 4 and passim; Tyson,
Discourse Before the Young Men's Colonization Society, 39ff. Paulding,
Slavery, 134ff.

that was directed by a central agency in England. The central agency, through cheap pamphlets and emissaries like Thompson, blinded and corrupted thousands of women and children—and sometimes even good and able men—by subtle and devious propaganda. Once the agency had these dupes in its meshes, it directed them like puppets in the battle against free society and local authority.[38] Thus the ultimate symbol of concerted action, systematic agitation, and centrally imposed conformity was the British plot. Like amalgamation, it went to the heart of anti-abolitionist nightmares and dramatized their dread of becoming indistinguishable parts in a mass society.

V

But how could the American Anti-Slavery Society—a small organization that employed only thirteen agents and collected only $25,000 in 1835—generate such fears? James Kirke Paulding insisted in the fall of 1835 that American abolitionists had the backing of foreign funds. How else could they "obtain the means of gratuitously distributing so many papers, pamphlets, and pictures, or of supporting such a number of brawling incendiaries"? And even such an experienced and cautious observer as Hezekiah Niles reported in September, 1835, that abolitionists had "lately subscribed more than $100,000 to forward *their* work!"[39] Why were estimates of the New York associates' power so grandiose?

The answers to these questions lie partly in the identification of the American society with the British antislavery movement, but largely in a revolution in printing that occurred in the 1830's. Labeling any technological change as "revolutionary" is suspect, but if any change merits this label, it was the rapid transformation of printing in Jacksonian America. Consider, for example, what hap-

[38] The same fears were also central to anti-Mormon, anti-Catholic, and anti-Masonic literature. See Davis, "Some Themes of Counter-Subversion," 208, and *passim*.

[39] Paulding, *Slavery*, 135; *Niles' Register* 49 (September 12, 1835), 20.

pened in the pace-setting city of New York within only two years.
In 1833, James Watson Webb's *Courier and Enquirer,* with 4,500
readers, had the largest daily circulation in the city; it cost slightly
more than six cents a copy. In 1835, after the famous New York
fire, the *Sun* published a morning edition of 23,000 and an extra of
30,000 at only one penny a copy. Two years before, neither the
Sun nor any other newspaper could have published 53,000 copies
in a single day. The *Sun's* press then had a capacity of only 200
impressions per hour, which was normal for the time. In 1834, the
Sun installed a machine press with a capacity of 1,000 copies per
hour; and in 1835, a steam press with a capacity of 5,500 per hour.
From sixpenny papers to one penny, from presses with a daily out-
put of 2,000 prints to ones of 55,000—the transformation was indeed "revolutionary." [40]

The printing revolution—which was the result of the fusion of
the recent development of the steam press, the paper-cutting machine, the Transportation Revolution, the technique of converting
colored rags into usable paper, and the idea of the penny press—
undoubtedly had enormous impact on society; but few historians
have explored its cultural and social ramifications. Certainly Gu-
tenberg's introduction of movable types in 1453 opened a new age
in the history of culture. Yet I suspect that the mechanization of
printing and the mass production of print in the 1830's had even
more far-reaching effects. Not only did the printing revolution create a mass audience, but it also shifted the centers of opinion-mak-
ing from county seats and capital cities such as Albany, Richmond,
and Washington to metropolitan centers. [41]

On a national scale the printing revolution was first apparent in

[40] James L. Crouthamel, "The Newspaper Revolution in New York, 1830–
1860," *New York History* 45 (April 1964), 91–113; Frank Luther Mott,
American Journalism (Third edition; New York, 1962), 200–7, 215ff.; Charles
H. Levermore, "Rise of Metropolitan Journalism," *American Historical Re-
view* 6 (April 1901), 446–65; Robert Hoe, *Short History of the Printing Press*
(New York, 1902), 15ff.; Dard Hunter, *Papermaking* (Second edition; New
York, 1947), 340ff.; Louis Tillotson Stevenson, *The Background and Eco-
nomics of American Papermaking* (New York, 1940), 11ff.

[41] Suggestive on the impact of the printing revolution are Harold Innis,

the pamphlet campaign of 1835.[42] Both the campaign itself and its hysterical reception owed their existence to the transformation of printing technology. In 1834, the New York associates' printing costs averaged nearly three cents per publication. In 1835, their costs dropped to slightly more than one and one-half cents per publication.[43] Thus they were able, as the Executive Committee later reported, to distribute *"nine* times" as many publications "at only about *five* times the expense." [44]

Reduced costs and accessibility to steam presses enabled the Tappan group to take advantage of the cheap postal rates that newspapers had long enjoyed, and to flood the mail with tracts and papers. It also encouraged them to distribute free pamphlets to people unaccustomed to buying newspapers. Accordingly, the *Anti-Slavery Record,* the paper that John Tyler showed to his Virginia audience, aimed at the "millions," while the *Slave's Friend* aimed at children. And finally, the printing revolution made the American Anti-Slavery Society appear stronger and wealthier than it actually was. Until men became fully adjusted to the reduced costs in New York printing, they invariably overestimated the strength and affluence of the abolitionists. Thus the transformation in printing indirectly contributed to the anti-abolitionist notion of a monstrous Anti-Slavery Society stimulated both by foreign influence and by foreign funds.

VI

The postal campaign itself was easily blocked. Shortly after the hysteria about "incendiary literature" began, Charleston Postmas-

---

The Bias of Communication (Toronto, 1951), 156ff.; Louis Dudek, *Literature and the Press* (Toronto, 1960), and Richard D. Birdsall, *Berkshire County: A Cultural History* (New Haven, 1959), Chapter 7.

[42] Many of the complaints against antislavery pamphlets were raised later against the metropolitan newspapers. Cf. the reports of the Postmaster General (1836 and after), in the *Congressional Globe.*

[43] The cost included books.

[44] American Anti-Slavery Society, *Third Annual Report* (New York, 1836), 35.

ter Alfred Huger wrote Samuel L. Gouverneur, Postmaster of New York City, requesting aid. The mail of July 29, 1835, Huger informed Gouverneur, had "literally filled" the Charleston Post Office with copies of the *Emancipator, Anti-Slavery Record, Slave's Friend,* and *Human Rights.* Other Southern postmasters also called on Gouverneur for assistance in suppressing the New York papers.[45]

Gouverneur, in turn, wrote an express letter to Amos Kendall, President Jackson's Postmaster General, requesting instructions for dealing with the crisis. Meanwhile he adopted the policy of forwarding "none of the offensive papers" by mail. After a short delay, Kendall advised Gouverneur that this policy was undoubtedly illegal, but it had the administration's blessing. "As a measure of great public necessity," explained Kendall, "you and the other postmasters who have assumed the responsibility of stopping these inflammatory papers, will, I have no doubt, stand justified in that step before your country and all mankind." The Postmaster General also informed Gouverneur "that the President, the Secretary of State, the Secretary of War and the Secretary of the Navy entirely concur with me in my general views of this subject and approve the attitude which has been assumed." With this support, Gouverneur continued his policy of excluding antislavery papers from the mail. Thus he stymied the postal campaign at its point of origin.[46]

Nevertheless the specter of the pamphlet campaign continued to haunt the South, while the vision of a well-organized, centrally di-

[45] Huger to Gouverneur, August 1, 1835, Samuel L. Gouverneur Papers, New York Public Library. The entire controversy can be followed in Gouverneur's correspondence, since he preserved both the letters he received and copies of the letters that he sent out. See the letters from August 1 through September 20, 1835.

[46] Gouverneur to Kendall, August 7, 10, 18, 1835; Gouverneur to Alfred Huger, August 8, 1935; Kendall to Gouverneur, August 16, 22, 1835—all in Gouverneur Papers. Much of this correspondence—particularly Kendall's advice to Gouverneur—became public knowledge as it was turned over to the press. For Jackson's view of this matter, see Kendall to Jackson, August 7, 1835, and Jackson to Kendall, August 9, 1835—both in Andrew Jackson Papers, Library of Congress (microfilm).

rected propaganda machine obsessed Northern anti-abolitionists. In almost every Northern community where abolitionists attempted to establish a stronghold, they encountered violent resistance. Its intensity varied from state to state, county to county, town to town, but over all its pattern remained constant. The pattern, in fact, changed so little that we might regard it as almost automatic.

Consider, for example, the patterns of violence that emerge from data collected for New Hampshire, New York, Pennsylvania, and Illinois. In each of these states, the frequency of anti-abolitionist mobs rose and fell as the abolitionists' organizational efforts increased and decreased. In New Hampshire antislavery men made their strongest attempt to organize in 1835–1836. Anti-abolitionist mobs reached their peak in the Granite State simultaneously. The following graph shows the number of *new* organizations formed per year and the number of mobs per year: [47]

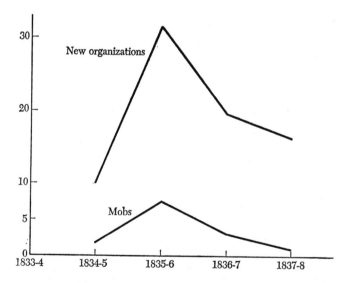

[47] We are *not* dealing with growth and decay; the *total* number of organizations always increased from year to year. By May 1835, the American Anti-Slavery Society had 225 auxiliaries; by 1836, 527; by 1837, 1,006; by 1838,

In both New York and Pennsylvania the high points of concentrated organizing and violence came the following year—in 1836–1837. Here are the relationships for each state: [48]

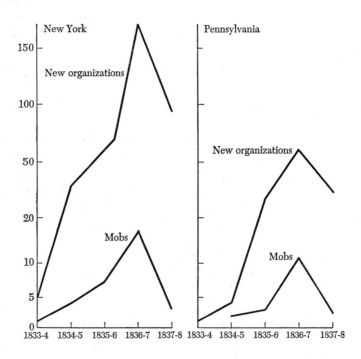

Relatively speaking, Illinois experienced few mobs and little organizational activity. Yet Illinois followed the same pattern as

1,346; by 1839, 1,650. Data on mobs came from *Liberator* (1833–1838), *Emancipator* (1833–1838), and *Philanthropist* (1836–1838); data on organizations from New England Anti-Slavery Society, *First* and *Second Annual Reports* (Boston, 1833–1834) and American Anti-Slavery Society, *Second* through *Fifth Annual Reports* (New York, 1835–1838). The New England Society's year went from January to January; the national society's year from May to May. Thus "1833–4" represents January 1833 to January 1834, but "1834–5" represents January 1834 to May 1835. All others ("1835–6," "1836–7," and "1837–8") are from May to May.

[48] Sources: same as footnote 47.

New York and Pennsylvania. The only difference is that the high points of organizing and violence came in 1837–1838, rather than in 1836–1837: [49]

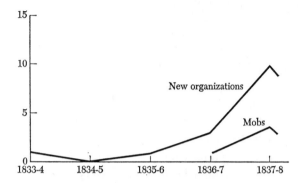

An endless number of illustrations showing the simultaneity of the rates of organization and of violence could be presented. But was there a real connection between organization and violence? Or were they only simultaneous? We may recall here that the three leading antislavery papers—the *Liberator*, the *Emancipator*, and the *Philanthropist*—recorded 165 mobs between 1833 and 1838.[50] Of these, nearly 60 per cent definitely were attempts to disrupt the formation of local societies. (If I had more complete data on the other mobs, the percentage probably would be considerably higher.[51]) Of the mobs that the antislavery papers reported,

[49] Sources: same as footnote 47.

[50] Again, I might add that the abolitionists reported more "mobs" than I have listed. They often used the word "mob" to describe any strong objection to their activities. I use the word only for incidents characterized either by violence or by turbulence.

[51] The problem here is twofold. First, the newspaper accounts often do not include sufficient data. Second, the abolitionists slanted their reporting to capitalize on the issue of free speech. Thus, while antislavery papers might indicate that an agent was mobbed for merely denouncing the "SIN of slavery," I often found that the agent was actually mobbed for trying to establish local auxiliaries. Contrary to abolitionist rhetoric, I found very few instances where an agent was attacked for just lecturing—and nothing more.

moreover, nearly 75 per cent were in counties that experienced intensive organization.[52]

It is possible, however, that the mobs may have occurred in the "right" places, but at the "wrong" time. Consider, for example, what might have happened if abolitionists organized a state in two distinct phases. That is, let us suppose that they organized counties A to L in 1835–1836, and counties M to Z in 1836–1837. And let us say that the high point of violence came in the latter year. If the violence happened primarily in counties M to Z, then our argument gains additional strength, for these were the counties that were intensively organized. But what if the mobs formed primarily in counties A to L? What if the violence ensued in counties that had been rapidly organized the year before? Then we could say that counties with a high level of antislavery activity had more mobs than counties with a low level; and perhaps we could safely add that the high-level counties experienced mobs only for a season, or until the local inhabitants recovered from the initial shock of being an abolitionist center.

A close inspection of the data, however, shows that the mobs generally occurred in the "right" counties at the "right" time. Ohio, which had more anti-abolitionist mobs than any other state, illustrates the pattern. Only about one-third of Ohio's counties experienced intensive organizing. In twelve of these counties, abolitionist efforts reached their peaks in 1835–1836; and in the remaining eleven counties, in 1836–1837. The following graphs, which set

---

[52] Neither the newspaper accounts nor the American Anti-Slavery Society's yearly reports recorded the counties consistently. Sometimes they recorded only town and state. To match the right town with the right county, I used two means. One was the township and county locator in the manuscript census division of the national archives. The other was a collection of old atlases. The former simplified matters considerably; the latter has no particular merit.

Fortunately, there were only a few instances of two townships in the same state having the same name. These were eliminated from the sample. Determining "intensive organization" presented few difficulties because there were relatively few borderline cases. I took care of borderline cases by applying the tag "intensive" only to counties in which three or more new organizations were formed within any twelve-month period.

forth data for the first twelve counties on the left and the second eleven on the right, show how the number of mobs increased and decreased along with organizational efforts: [53]

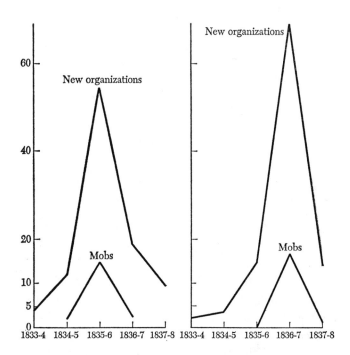

New York, which had the most anti-abolition mobs after Ohio, follows the Ohio pattern. In three counties, the high points of organizing and of mob violence were in 1835–1836; in fifteen counties, in 1836–1837.[54]

[53] Sources: same as footnote 47. The counties represented by the graph on the left are Ashtabula, Columbiana, Cuyahoga, Geauga, Huron, Knox, Licking, Lorain, Medina, Muskingum, Portage, and Stark; on the right—Adams, Brown, Clermont, Delaware, Hamilton, Highland, Jefferson, Logan, Richland, Trumbull, and Wayne.

[54] Sources: same as footnote 47. The counties represented by the graph on the left are Genesee, Oneida, and Washington; on the right—Allegany, Cattaraugus, Chautauqua, Clinton, Delaware, Erie, Herkimer, Madison, Monroe, New York, Niagara, Onondaga, Ontario, Oswego, Otsego.

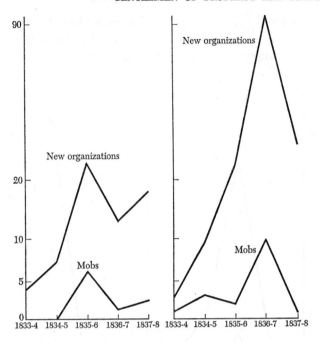

Although mob activity and the establishment of new organizations culminated in the same places at the same times, they did not develop at the same rate. I do not find a county with proportionate increases of, say, five new societies and two mobs the first year, ten new societies and four mobs the second year, and twenty new societies and eight mobs the third year. The proportion of mobs generally decreased after antislavery organizers established a beachhead. The graphs, unfortunately, fail to show this vividly, since they had to be cramped into limited space. And only a few counties experienced sustained organizing over several years. In each of these counties, mob activity tapered off. Nationally, the percentage of mobs for new societies organized also diminished.[55]

1835–1836	18.6%	(301 new societies/56 mobs)
1836–1837	14.6%	(479/70)
1837–1838	4.7%	(344/16)

[55] Sources: same as footnote 47.

The amount of violence in any given area, then, depended not only on the number of societies being organized but also on the number of societies already organized. It was far more dangerous, in other words, for antislavery organizers to establish six societies in an area that only had one than it was for them to form ten societies in an area that already had ten. Violent resistance decreased as an antislavery beachhead became an antislavery stronghold.

Thus the Northern anti-abolitionist mobs can be viewed as almost automatic responses to the New York associates' attempt to establish a network of auxiliaries. In saying this, I do not mean to imply that every Northern community reacted similarly. There were, as we will see in the next chapter, a great many local variations that it would be foolish to overlook. But it would be equally foolish to overlook the general pattern. And perhaps it would be even graver folly to ignore the context of fear in which this pattern developed.

For the over-all pattern and the anguished cries about "powerful combinations," "foreign agents," "concerted action," "systematization," and "amalgamation" indicate that anti-abolitionism was a reaction not only against "disunionists" and "fire-brands," but also against the direction in which Northern society was moving. The future looked grim. Through their centralized organizations, reform associations gave too much power to the men who ran them, while "their immense, combined, and variously ramified machinery" reduced local leaders to the level of mere onlookers or groveling subordinates.[56] Similarly, centralization enhanced the power and prestige of metropolitan centers at the expense of state capitals and county seats. Eventually even such isolated, self-contained communities as Berkshire and Ashtabula would be diminished to provincial outposts or—at best—dependent subcenters. Thus anti-abolitionists dreaded the prospect of becoming indistinguishable "instruments" in a centrally organized and centrally directed mass society.

[56] Colton, *Abolition a Sedition*, 181.

4

Types of Mobs

What were the Northern anti-abolition mobs like? How did they behave? These questions, I have learned, invariably evoke certain images. Some people automatically picture a spontaneous outburst by a rabble of ragged, desperate workingmen with ropes and torches in their hands. Others see a howling and undirected mob of "white trash" storming an antislavery meeting. Whatever the picture, most people assume that all mobs are primitive, emotional, and spontaneous responses of the poor and desperate.

The scholarly source for this point of view is Gustave Le Bon, whose book *La Foule* appeared in English in 1896 as *The Crowd*. Although Le Bon wrote in the relatively tranquil late nineteenth century, he managed to sound like an aristocrat dashing off a passionate indictment of the French Revolution several hours before it became his turn to meet the guillotine. Thus, in Le Bon's judgment, all mobs were "fickle," "credulous," "intolerant," and "brutish." Many of the individual members, he noted, might be inoffensive and timid citizens under ordinary circumstances, but once they were transformed into a crowd, they showed the violence and ferocity of "primitive beings." [1]

[1] Le Bon had a rather odd definition of "primitive beings," which included

Since Le Bon's heated descriptions of mob behavior, there have been many less colorful and less extravagant analyses. All the early giants of social psychology—Gabriel Tarde in 1903, William McDougall in 1920, Sigmund Freud in 1922, and Floyd H. Allport in 1924—contributed to the study of mob behavior. These scholars shrewdly detected flaws in Le Bon's reasoning, but they accepted his over-all impressions about the character of mobs. Indeed, it often seems as if their only sources were Le Bon's fiery descriptions of the crowds of the French Revolution and the Third Republic.[2] From their day until just recently, the study of mobs received little attention from social psychologists. Many contemporary textbooks, in fact, never mention the subject. Others are being hastily revised to include a section on "collective behavior" or "collective dynamics." Judging from the recent works that I have seen, the conventional stereotype of a howling and undirected rabble remains dominant.[3]

This conventional stereotype has only limited application to the Northern anti-abolition mobs. How, for example can one call "spontaneous" mobs that assembled at church meetings with bags full of rotten eggs? Or with a band? Some anti-abolition mobs, to be sure, displayed little organization. Many were disorderly. And many howled and screamed. Nevertheless, the typical mob congregated intentionally and planned and organized its action.[4]

women, children, savages, and the lower classes. These "inferior" forms of humanity, Le Bon insisted, regularly displayed the emotionality and irrationality to which civilized men gave way when they were in a crowd.

[2] Tarde, *The Laws of Imitation* (New York, 1903); McDougall, *The Group Mind* (Cambridge, England, 1920); Freud, *Group Psychology and the Analysis of the Ego* (London, 1922); Allport, *Social Psychology* (Cambridge, 1924).

[3] Today, of course, scholars rarely use such value-loaded words as "rabble," "howling," "fickle," "primitive," or "brutish." Thus the old stereotype is often couched in language that is disarmingly sterile.

[4] To some extent, the anti-abolition mobs were what some social psychologists now call "Bourbon" or "vigilante" mobs. In 1930 there were twenty-one lynchings in the United States. As each one became known, the Southern Commission on the Study of Lynchings sent an investigator to the scene. The resultant data showed that there were two kinds of lynching mobs. One, which corresponded roughly to Le Bon's descriptions, was called "proletariat."

While conditions varied significantly from mob to mob, two types may be broadly discerned. The first includes mobs that involved a substantial amount of prior coordination and design. Generally these mobs were smaller and less likely to get out of hand. Usually they had specific goals or targets. Their membership included many leading citizens whose primary goal was to preserve the status quo and their own supremacy. Often they had either the blessing or the acquiescence not only of the community at large but also of law-enforcement officials. This approval probably played a decisive role in many instances, where the leading citizens who took part in these mobs suffered from uneasy and divided consciences. Once the dominant forces in the community —the newspapers and the civic officials—endorsed a mob, these qualms of conscience apparently were quickly dispelled.[5]

The second category includes mobs that developed without prior coordination and design—or, to be more exact, mobs that at least appear to have formed without previous planning and organization.[6] Usually these mobs were larger and more likely to get out of hand. Frequently their members seem to have had no enduring identification with one another. Yet in these mobs there was always a division of labor. Some men gave directions. Others lit fires. Still others threatened firemen and constables. And many

The other, which was orderly and planned, was called "Bourbon" or "vigilante." Generally, social psychologists have treated organized mobs as exceptions, and screaming and disorderly mobs as the rule. See Arthur Raper, *The Tragedy of Lynching* (Chapel Hill, 1933); Hadley Cantril, *The Psychology of Social Movements* (New York, 1941); R. W. Brown, "Mass Phenomena," in Gardiner Lindzey, ed., *Handbook of Social Psychology* (2 vols.; Cambridge, 1954), Vol. II, 852f.; Roger Brown, *Social Psychology* (New York, 1965), Chapter 14.

5 In "Good People and Dirty Work," *Social Problems* 10 (Summer 1962), 3–11, Everett Hughes argues that frightful brutalities, such as those of the Nazi SS, depend on the acquiescence of the immediate community. See also, William A. Westley, "The Escalation of Violence through Legitimation," *Annals of the American Academy of Political and Social Science* 364 (March 1966), 120–26.

6 I make this reservation simply because of my own research experience. On too many occasions I found that apparently spontaneous outbursts involved coordination and design.

simply stood by and cheered.[7] Generally these mobs included more lower-class citizens than the planned mob. This fact, according to contemporaries, accounted for their tendency to engage in mass terrorization and destruction. The toiling masses, so middle-class Americans liked to believe, were inherently more violent than their "betters." Perhaps! But it was just as likely that the increased violence was simply the result of larger numbers. And occasionally it was the result only of stiffer resistance. These mobs generally encountered more resistance than the others, and unless this resistance was overwhelming, it only escalated the violence. Finally, the increased violence was the result of having Negroes as primary targets. Invariably such mobs were more anti-Negro than anti-abolition, and as we have already seen, ante-bellum Northerners had very few inhibitions against tormenting and terrorizing Negroes.

II

In most respects the Utica mob of October 21, 1835, typified the conventional Northern anti-abolition mob. Its membership included many of the town's leading citizens. Bankers and lawyers, merchants and tradesmen, state and local politicians assembled intentionally, formed a meeting, passed resolutions, and dispatched some of their membership to do the dirty work. The mob had limited objectives. And nearly everyone in the community knew in advance what would probably happen.

Almost two years before, the city of Utica, which had a population of about ten thousand, had experienced some difficulties over the antislavery question. In December, 1833, the Reverend Joshua

[7] There is a tendency to dismiss these enthusiasts and to consider only the "active nucleus" as the mob. This is a mistake. In a study of the Chicago race riots of 1919, the Chicago Commission on Race Relations noted: "Without the spectators, mob violence would probably have stopped short of murder in many cases. An example of the behavior of the active nucleus, when out of sight of the spectators, bears this out. George Carr . . . outstripped all but the vanguard of the mob. . . . The young men who had followed Carr left him without striking a blow, upon his mere request for clemency." *The Negro in Chicago* (Chicago, 1922), 23.

Dansforth, the American Colonization Society's most zealous agent, and Beriah Green, the president of Oneida Institute, engaged in a heated debate over the advisability of African colonization. Was colonization a Christian and practical endeavor? Yes, screamed Dansforth. No, thundered Green. After more than a week of tongue lashings and denunciations by both sides, a crowd marched through the streets of Utica, shouting that the abolitionists were traitors. One group burned an effigy of Green and of Alvan Stewart, another nascent antislavery man. Later, the City Council not only denounced antislavery as "little short of treason toward the government of our country," but also came one vote shy of indicting Green for treason.[8]

Tempers subsided until the late summer of 1835, when Uticans became alarmed about the activities of the New York City philanthropists. On September 3, a public meeting at the courthouse adopted resolutions denouncing the "incendiaries." And on September 17, the grand jury of Oneida County declared that those who were "getting up" antislavery societies "for the purpose of printing pictures and inflammatory publications" were guilty of sedition and ought to be punished. Moreover, said the grand jury, it was the "duty of all our citizens" who were "friendly to the Constitution" and the "future quiet and happiness of this people" to destroy these publications "*whenever and wherever* found." [9]

It was in this atmosphere that the Utica Anti-Slavery Society issued a call for a state convention to be held in the city on October 21, for the purpose of forming a state society. Actually the impetus for the convention came from the central bureau in New York City. But "we thought," Elizur Wright confided to Amos Phelps, that the call "would have a much better effect, coming from Utica than if published here." Both the Utica abolitionists and their New York associates made strenuous efforts to bring to this gathering the chief protagonists of emancipation in the state. Others, such as

8 Thomas F. Gordon, *Gazetteer of the State of New York* (New York, 1836), 576; Daniel E. Wager, *Our County and Its People: A Descriptive Work on Oneida County,* New York (Boston, 1896), 312f.; *Emancipator,* January 21 and 28, 1834.

9 Utica *Observer,* September, 1835; Albany *Argus,* September, 1835; Wager, *Our County,* 313f.; *American Anti-Slavery Almanac,* 1837, 22.

the land baron Gerrit Smith, were invited to be present in the hope that they might be converted to the cause. It was no longer a case of when or how black men should be freed, Smith was told; rather it had become the "awful moment" when all good men should step forward "to the rescue and deliverance of the rights of the press, freedom of speech and conscience." If Smith had differed with abolitionists on "minor and subordinate points," here was "new ground . . . on which a Hampden, a Sidney, a Warren and a Montgomery might lay down their lives." By mid-October, it became clear that Smith and perhaps seven hundred others would travel to Utica for the state convention.[10]

Meanwhile, anti-abolitionists of both political parties raised the alarm. Almost daily, James Watson Webb's *Courier and Enquirer*, a Whig paper, demanded that the convention be "put down" either by the laws of New York, or by "the law of Judge Lynch." In upstate New York, the Utica *Whig* called for the suppression of the proposed convention. For once the Albany *Argus* and the Utica *Observer*, both Van Buren papers, agreed with their political enemies. If sectional tensions persisted, advised the *Observer*, Van Buren might lose in his bid for the presidency. At a county convention on October 15, Oneida County Democrats resolved that "the citizens of Utica owe it to themselves, to the state, and to the union that the contemplated Convention of incendiary individuals is not permitted to assemble within its corporate bounds." All the churches, the court, the academy, and the schoolrooms should "be closed against these wicked and deluded men." Thus for many Jacksonian Democrats, the editor of the Utica *Standard and Democrat* later lamented, "the enforcement of '*prudential restrictions*' against the abolitionists" became "a party measure." [11]

In Utica, where certain "prominent and respectable gentlemen"

[10] Wright to Phelps, September 4 and 16, 1835, Elizur Wright Papers, Library of Congress; Amos Phelps to Smith, October 2, 1835, and Alvan Stewart to Smith, October 2, 1835, Gerrit Smith Papers, Syracuse University Library (microfilm); New York *Herald*, October 19, 1835.

[11] New York *Courier and Enquirer*, September–October 1835; Utica *Whig*, October 1835; Albany *Argus*, October 1835; Utica *Observer*, October 1835; [William Thomas], *The Enemies of the Constitution Discovered* (New York, 1836), 62.

daily warned street-corner audiences of the coming "calamity and disgrace," the excitement soon became intense. On October 8, an anti-abolition meeting at Miller's Hall, with Mayor Joseph Kirkland presiding, protested against the convention's assembling in Utica. Over all, the meeting was calm. The resolutions, which denounced the abolitionists whether their motives were "charitable or wicked," were relatively mild. Attorney William Tracy, who later took part in the mob, chastised the abolitionists but still argued for the right of free discussion. "It is that," said he, "for which our fathers bled." Judge Chester Hayden, who later led the mob, then gave a metaphysical disquisition on slavery. But then came the highlight of the evening—a rousing speech by Congressman Samuel Beardsley.[12]

"No man," said the staunch Jacksonian, ". . . can doubt that every movement of this kind, instead of elevating the condition of the slaves, renders their condition more degraded, debased, and oppressive than before." Why then, asked Beardsley, are the abolitionists holding a convention here to promote such nonsense? "It is intended to insult us . . . to degrade the character of the city in the esteem of the world . . . to treat us with the utmost contempt —insult us to our faces, where they cannot raise a corporal's guard." At this point the audience had become excited, and cheers followed nearly every sentence. ". . . The laws of propriety," continued Beardsley, "forbid that they should come here. We are to be picked out as the head-quarters of Abolitionism in the state of New York. Rather than have this, I would almost as soon see it (the city) swept from the face of the earth, or sunk as low as Sodom and Gomorrah!" These words brought deafening cheers! "Nothing," said Beardsley as the roar subsided, "is due to these men if they come here. They are resolved to press forward with their designs, and thus endanger the south and our own institutions.—So a man may contend he has a right to smoke a cigar in my powder house!" Again the crowd cheered. ". . . The question is, whether the peace of this Union shall be disturbed or not? and

12 Utica *Observer*, October 12, 1835. Or see the *Emancipator*, November 1835, and [Thomas], *Enemies of the Constitution*, 58–62.

whether we are to be thus disturbed and disgraced?" "No, No, No," shouted the crowd. And with this final ring of approval in his ears, Samuel Beardsley—the subsequent chieftain of the mob, the next Attorney General of New York, and the future Chief Justice of the state Supreme Court—took his seat.

On October 16, the Common Council of Utica voted by 7 to 4 to let the convention be held in the courtroom. Bedlam followed, and on the next day anti-abolitionists posted handbills in "flaming" colors, calling a meeting at the courtroom that evening. Hundreds of Utica's leading citizens attended. Midway through the proceedings, Mayor Kirkland entered. Refusing the chair "from feelings of delicacy" toward the Common Council, over which he presided, the Mayor nevertheless expressed his "decided opposition" to the decision of the Council. Shortly thereafter, the meeting resolved that the Common Council acted in "flagrant usurpation of power," and that the meeting "will not submit to the indignity of an abolition assemblage being held in a public building of this city." As expected, Congressman Beardsley spoke in favor of the resolution. "I would rather," said he, "this building should be razed from its foundation, or be destroyed with fire from heaven, than be thus contaminated." [13]

Strong sentiments! But on this occasion Beardsley was outdone by Ephraim Hart, one of the meeting's vice-presidents. Hart, a sixty-two-year-old merchant from Connecticut, was a poor speaker. Nevertheless, his audience responded enthusiastically, interrupting him on several occasions with thunderous applause. "Those niggers at the south," said Hart, live "much happier than our free negroes." Southerners treat their slaves "as kindly as any one would his favorite race horse." Slaves, in fact, "fare better than our FARMERS do." Why, then, is there so much recent talk about slavery? Why do abolitionists insist on coming here? "There seems to be something behind the curtain. Old women looking at the picture of a slave with the blood running down his back, and four or five beating him, and then [the women] crying." If the abolition-

[13] Utica *Observer*, October 19, 1835. Or see *Emancipator*, November 1835, and [Thomas], *Enemies of the Constitution*, 63ff.

ists continue such agitation, soon "the niggers will be excited to rise and murder their masters, and the white popula- tion. . . . There is something abroad at work here. Why is this emissary sent from Europe? They are afraid of this govern- ment. The spirit of liberty reigns here." Their people are dissatis- fied "with the iron rod of despotism," and thus they want us to be ruled by a "king or bashaw," too. We do not want a "gag-law," concluded Hart, "but we don't like these hypocrites going about . . . setting our houses on fire, and debating in which cor- ner they shall put the firebrand." After the cheering subsided, someone objected that "we allow free discussion." He was hissed down.

Once the resolutions were passed, the meeting turned to the question of violence. Attorney William Curtis Noyes, who later supported the mob, indicated that he would leave the abolitionists alone, but that "the public" would not permit "their public build- ing to be desecrated." An unidentified speaker demanded that the abolitionists be left alone. He, too, was hissed down. Then Samuel Beardsley explained that "we do not intend to hunt them about the streets"; we only "wish to repel from this house this moral pes- tilence." As usual, Beardsley received a rousing ovation. As for me, said editor Augustine G. Dauby of the *Observer*, "I will be here on that morning, and do my duty manfully to prevent the meeting, *peacefully if I can, forcibly if I must.*" Bedlam followed. Finally, after much discussion, the meeting agreed to meet at the court- house one hour before the abolitionists assembled there. Remem- ber, said Beardsley as the crowd began to straggle out, "the first law is self-defense."

In response to the anti-abolition meeting, the Common Council reversed its decision, forcing the abolitionists to shift the site of their convention to the Presbyterian Church on Bleecker Street. On the eve of the convention, the "respectable mechanics" of Utica held a meeting in favor of free discussion and the suprem- acy of the laws. But anti-abolitionists, led by editor Dauby, state senatorial candidate David Wager, and district clerk Rutger B.

Miller, took over the meeting and shouted down all attempts to speak on the side of law and order.[14]

At 9 A.M. the next morning, anti-abolitionists assembled at the courtroom. After passing several resolutions, the chairman appointed a Committee of Twenty-Five to "wait" upon the abolitionists, who began their convention at 10 A.M. The Committee of Twenty-Five, led by Judge Hayden and Congressman Beardsley, then marched to the Bleecker Street church, where a large crowd had already gathered. The committee burst through the church doors, rushed down the aisle, and headed for the pulpit. About half-a-dozen men ripped the clothing off one abolitionist's back. Others threw hymnals or tore up antislavery documents and papers. Rutger B. Miller, later a United States Congressman, threatened to cane an aged minister. By and large, however, the mob stopped short of provoking a brawl. Outnumbered by at least 4 to 1, the Committee of Twenty-Five and its supporters largely contented themselves with shouting down the meeting. They performed well, for the abolitionists quickly decided that it was useless to continue. After the convention dissolved, many of the abolitionists reconvened at Clarke's Temperance House, where Gerrit Smith invited them to his estate, twenty-seven miles away. The mob meanwhile, returned to the courtroom, where they reported that the antislavery convention had "yielded to the pressure of public opinion." The anti-abolition meeting then passed several more resolutions and adjourned.[15]

That night, despite heavy rain, the mob attacked the office of the *Oneida Standard and Democrat*, a Van Buren paper that had supported the convention. After throwing types, cases, and other

[14] [William Thomas], *Enemies of the Constitution Discovered*, 68–70.

[15] Utica *Whig*, October 21, 1835; Utica *Observer*, October 21, 1835; Albany *Evening Journal*, October 22, 1835; Albany *Argus*, October 23, 27, 1835; *Oneida Standard and Democrat*, October 30, 1835, as quoted in [Thomas], *Enemies of the Constitution*, 82ff.; New York Anti-Slavery Society, *First Annual Report* (New York, 1835), 8–9. Some of the abolitionists were again mobbed near Vernon, about seventeen miles from Utica; a few were injured, and many had their carriages damaged.

printing materials into the streets, some of the rioters wanted to go home. Others raised a cry against Spencer Kellogg and Alvan Stewart, two leading abolitionists whose expensive brick houses stood only several blocks away. But only a few of the mob made their appearance at either of these places, for it was well known that both houses were prepared to give them a warm reception. Thus the attack was easily crushed.[16]

Such was the Utica mob of October 21, 1835. The gentlemen who engaged in this mob were censured in some quarters, but in general they were barely condemned. Many newspapers and politicians, in fact, assured them that they had done their duty. In the United States Senate, for example, Senator Silas Wright of New York cited the sacking of the *Oneida Standard's* office and the disruption of the antislavery convention as "evidences of the correct state of public opinion." David Wager, noted Wright, won a seat in the state senate two weeks after he had participated in the mob. And several months later, Samuel Beardsley became Attorney General of New York, receiving "a strong and almost unanimous vote" from the state legislature. "Could there," said Wright, "be anything equivocal in expressions like these?" [17]

III

The Utica pattern, involving a well-organized nucleus of respectable citizens who planned their actions in advance, might be regarded as the basic model for the Cincinnati mob of July, 1836, and the Alton mob of November, 1837. Some differences, however, must be noted. Neither the Cincinnati mob nor the Alton mob followed Robert's Rules of Order to the extent that the Utica mob did. And neither faced large numbers of abolitionists. In Cincinnati, where anti-abolitionists outnumbered their opponents by a

[16] *Oneida Standard and Democrat,* October 30, 1835, as quoted in [Thomas], *Enemies of the Constitution,* 86.

[17] *Register of Debates in Congress,* 24 Congress, 1 Session (1835–1836), 201–8. See also John A. Garraty, *Silas Wright* (New York, 1949), 165–66.

considerable margin, the mob encountered almost no resistance. But in Alton, where the mob and its opposition were more equal in strength, resistance was fierce, and the ensuing battle resulted in several casualties and two fatalities.[18]

Cincinnati, a city of about forty thousand people, witnessed the usual uproar against Arthur Tappan and his "murderous tracts" in the late summer of 1835. At least two of the city's newspapers even recommended that if any of Tappan's agents should be found in the city, the populace should lynch them.[19] Thus in the fall of that year, only a few citizens welcomed the news that James Gillespie Birney, an ex-slaveholder who had become an abolitionist editor, planned to establish an antislavery press in Cincinnati. In November, after distribution of an antislavery handbill, the "Declaration of Sentiment of the Cincinnati Anti-Slavery Society," Birney received a warning from Mayor Samuel Davies, the city marshal, and a leading editor that he might be mobbed that very night. The mob failed to materialize, but Birney stocked his house with about forty muskets and double-barreled shotguns. Later, he decided to establish his press at New Richmond, twenty miles from Cincinnati, and to travel back and forth either on horseback or by stage. This, reasoned Birney, would reduce the chance of violence.[20]

On January 1, 1836, the first number of Birney's *Philanthropist* came out. Its moderate tone made little difference, for leading Cincinnatians, goaded continually by the *Whig* and the *Republican*, already agreed that it was a malignant attempt to browbeat the

[18] In sociological terms, the Cincinnati mob was a terrorist action, because only one side fought, and the Alton mob was a riot, because both sides fought.

[19] Cf. the *Cincinnati Whig* and Cincinnati *Daily Evening Post*, August–September 1835. Less aggressive, but still strongly anti-abolitionist, was the *Cincinnati Advertiser and Ohio Phoenix*. See, for example, the issue for November 14, 1835.

[20] Birney to Gerrit Smith, November 11 and 25, 1835, Birney to Charles Hammond, November 14, 1835, in Dumond, *Birney Letters*, Vol. I, 257–74; William Birney, *James G. Birney and His Times* (New York, 1890), 207f.; Betty Fladeland, *James Gillespie Birney* (Ithaca, 1955), 126f.

public and turn Cincinnati into a citadel for antislavery fire-brands. [21] On January 22, some of the city's richest and most respected citizens—including Mayor Davies, postmaster and Methodist minister William Burke, former United States Senator Jacob Burnet, land office receiver Morgan Neville, and bank president Robert Buchanan—presided over a meeting of some five hundred anti-abolitionists. The announced purpose of the meeting was to bring the "full weight" of public opinion against the pamphlet campaign, the forming of abolition societies, and the establishment of Birney's press at New Richmond. Rumor had it, however, that in a store on Front Street the instigators of the public meeting had already formed a nucleus for a mob. Trouble thus was expected.[22]

The mob, however, never appeared, and the meeting turned out to be surprisingly calm. Birney attended and even spoke for forty-five minutes before being jeered down. The meeting resolved to recommend "prompt and efficient legislation" if the national antislavery society continued its "designs." It also agreed not to "suffer the inflammatory publications" of antislavery societies "to be introduced into our houses, counting-rooms, or workshops." And it promised to "exert every lawful effort to suppress the publication of any abolition paper in this city or *neighborhood*." [23]

Time and again speakers stressed two themes. One involved commerce. Cincinnati, said nearly everyone, could scarcely afford to become a "theatre" for antislavery "operations." Obviously it would jeopardize the city's Southern trade, and certainly it would undermine all plans for a railroad to Charleston. The other matter involved the Negro, and as usual the discussion centered around

[21] Cf. *Cincinnati Whig* and *Cincinnati Republican*, December 21, 1835–January 22, 1836. See also *Philanthropist*, January 8–22, 1836.

[22] Birney, *Birney*, 212ff.; Fladeland, *Birney*, 130–31.

[23] All the major Cincinnati papers reported the meeting, January 22–25, 1836. The most violent accounts appeared in the *Whig* and the *Republican*. A moderate account appeared in the Cincinnati *Gazette*. And Birney's account appeared in the *Philanthropist*, January 29, 1836. See also Robert T. Lytle's scrapbook, entry for January 25, 1836, Lytle Papers, Cincinnati Historical Society.

amalgamation. Birney, said Colonel Charles Hale, a prominent Whig from Pennsylvania, favored amalgamation. Hale said that when he visited Birney's house, he found him entertaining one of the "biggest and most blackest niggers" whom he had ever seen. Negroes, said Colonel Robert T. Lytle, a former Jacksonian Congressman and a native of Massachusetts, "must become divested of their bestiality before they can be improved." And the only way to elevate them, explained Lytle, is "to mingle with their blood foreign currents. You must cross the breeds, to make anything of them; or else, you must castrate the men and —— the women." [24]

No further outbursts occurred until April, when the *Philanthropist* moved to Cincinnati. During that month, rioters burned down a Negro tenement, while a large crowd watched and enjoyed the spectacle. The place, explained the *Republican*, was "notorious as a . . . resort for rogues, thieves, and prostitutes—black and white." [25] After the April riot, Cincinnati experienced a long lull. The storm came in July.

On the night of July 12, without warning of any kind, a band of about twenty men, equipped with a ladder and a plank, gathered in front of the office of Birney's printer, Achilles Pugh. The leaders were Joseph Graham, a native of Pennsylvania and the owner of a large paper mill; Archibald Gordon, a New Yorker and steamboat builder; Joseph S. Bates, a native of Massachusetts and the owner of a hat and cap store; Julien Neville, a Pennsylvanian and the son of one of the city fathers; and John A. D. Burrows, a native of New Jersey, a wholesale grocer, and the son of a prominent civic leader and trustee of Lane Seminary. These men, leaving their confederates as sentries, entered the building through a window on the roof, tore up the coming issue of the *Philanthropist*, took the press apart, and carried its smaller parts away. The city watch

---

[24] In deference to "delicacy," none of the papers that I examined reported Lytle's exact words. So we can only guess what he had in mind for the women. The word "castrate," I might add, does not appear in all the accounts; Lytle may actually have used a much cruder expression.

[25] April 13, 1836.

observed the affair, which took about two hours, but made no effort to arrest the vandals.[26]

The next day, Joseph Graham and a fellow Pennsylvanian, John Wood, the editor of the *People's Echo*, prepared a handbill. That night placards bearing the following suggestions appeared on the street corners: [27]

> ABOLITIONISTS BEWARE
>
> The Citizens of Cincinnati, embracing every class, interested in the prosperity of the City, satisfied that the business of the place is receiving a vital stab from the wicked and misguided operations of the abolitionists, are resolved to arrest their course. The destruction of their Press on the night of the 12th instant, may be taken as a warning. As there are some worthy citizens engaged in the unholy cause of annoying our southern neighbors, they are appealed to, to pause before they bring things to a crisis. If an attempt is made to re-establish their press, it will be viewed as an act of defiance to an already outraged community, and on their own heads be the results which follow.
>
> Every kind of expostulation and remonstrance has been resorted to in vain—longer patience would be criminal. The plan is matured to eradicate an evil which every citizen feels is undermining his business and property.

The handbill, however, failed to intimidate the Cincinnati Anti-Slavery Society. They resolved to continue publication. Pugh received a guarantee of $2,000 from the abolitionists, quickly repaired his press, which suffered only $150 damages, and thus resumed printing after only a slight delay. And on July 15, three days after the wreckage, the *Philanthropist* again hit the streets.

The persistence of the abolitionists led some anti-abolitionists to call for more drastic measures. On Sunday, July 17, a handbill appeared on street corners. Signed "OLD KENTUCKY," it offered $100 for James G. Birney, "a fugitive from justice," who in "all his

[26] Birney claimed that some of the vandals were from Kentucky, and that the wreckers acted on orders from Southerners. *Philanthropist*, July 15, 1836. I have found no evidence to support this assertion. The wreckers were later tried. See *Philanthropist*, June 19 and 26, 1838.

[27] Handbill reproduced in *Historical and Philosophical Society of Ohio Bulletin* 9 (October 1951), 258.

associations and feelings is *black*." On Tuesday, the *Whig* carried a letter by "PUBLIC SENTIMENT," who insisted that all Americans except Cincinnatians had done their duty. Bostonians were not "slaves of the law." They dragged Garrison, "the Missionary of Britain, and probably the hired stipendiary of the Autocrat himself," through the streets of "the cradle of Liberty." Like their forebears who dumped the tea in Boston harbor, they knew when to stop talking about "subserviency to the established institutions of the land" and how to deal with tories. Was Cincinnati not similarly threatened? And is there not reason to believe that many of the city's abolitionists are "in the pay, and doing the work of the Autocrats and lordlings of Europe"? On Thursday, the *Whig* printed another letter with the same message. Will Cincinnatians, asked the writer, "permit a band of fanatics, led on by an English emissary, to make this city the theatre of their operations, from whence they may throw fire-brands in the slave states"? On the same day, the *Republican* gave a pointed "*word of advice*" to Rees Price and Christian and William Donaldson, wealthy antislavery merchants from England: "If any of you are foreigners we would advise you, most especially to be silent on the subject of slavery. A large majority of our citizens, have taken the foolish notion into their heads that they understand their own institutions and their own interest quite as well as certain foreign dictators." [28]

It was in this context that the call went out for a public meeting at the Lower Market House on Saturday evening, July 23, to decide whether Cincinnatians "will permit the publication or distribution of Abolition papers in this city." About one thousand citizens attended. With the exception of Mayor Davies, who was conspicuously missing, the leaders were the same men who had presided over the January meeting. The resolutions, however, were stronger than those adopted in January. They warned that "nothing short of the absolute discontinuance" of the *Philanthropist* could "prevent a resort to violence." Chairman William Burke then

[28] *Narrative of the Late Riotous Proceedings Against the Liberty of the Press, in Cincinnati* (Cincinnati, 1836), 16ff.; *Cincinnati Whig*, July 19 and 21, 1836; *Cincinnati Republican*, July 21, 1836.

appointed a committee to inform the abolitionists of the "tone of public feeling in the city" and to warn them that if they persisted in the publication of their paper, the citizens at the meeting could not hold themselves responsible for the consequences. We hold "the most profound respect," the meeting agreed before closing, for the patriots of Boston, who "*without* the sanction of law . . . took the responsibility of *re-shipping* the *tea* cargo." The message, as even the most naïve acknowledged, was clear.[29]

After a week of negotiating, the Market House Committee made public on Saturday, July 30, the results of its endeavors. The committee had failed; the abolitionists refused to yield. That afternoon, with the aid of the *Whig* and the *Republican*, the news spread quickly through the city. That evening, at six o'clock, the mob organized. The leaders included the same men who had wrecked Pugh's press earlier in the month. Joseph Graham presided over the meeting, and John A. D. Burrows acted as secretary. In addition there were two new leaders: John O. Clark, a tailor originally from Connecticut, and Joseph Talbot, a carpenter from Virginia. These men, along with others, were assigned various tasks. A committee was formed to locate the residences of prominent abolitionists. Then, after adopting "Santa Anna" as their watchword, and agreeing to "proceed *peaceably, orderly* and *quietly* to destroy the press," the mob adjourned to the meeting of the Texas Aid Committee at the courthouse. There the mob heard resounding denunciations of the abolitionists for their stand against the Texas revolutionaries.[30]

Later that night, the mob assembled on the corner of Seventh and Main where Pugh's press was located. After a short consultation, the mob broke into Pugh's shop, scattered the type into the streets, tore down the presses, and dismantled the office. From there the rioters proceeded to Pugh's home, where they searched

[29] The official report of the meeting (i.e., the one signed by the officers) appeared in the *Cincinnati Advertiser and Ohio Phoenix*, July 27, 1836.

[30] Cf. the account in the Cincinnati *Gazette*, August 2–3, 1836, with reports of the subsequent trial in the *Philanthropist*, February 27, 1838, April 30, 1839. The court records, unfortunately, burned with the courthouse in the 1890's.

for additional supplies of ink and paper. Finding nothing there, the mob moved on to Christian Donaldson's home, where only ladies were present, and then to Birney's home, where the mob found only his young son. The rioters, young Birney recalled years later, displayed "no indication of popular excitement." They approached "without outcry, and quietly as if under control of leaders." Leaving Birney's, the mob proceeded to the office of Dr. Isaac Colby, another prominent abolitionist. There the rioters systematically piled the contents of the doctor's office in the street. Some insisted that the pile be burned, but Joseph Graham mounted the pile and talked against the idea. Nearby homes, argued Graham, might catch fire. Accepting Graham's reasoning, the rioters returned to Pugh's office and dragged the presses down the street and into the river. Thus ended the first phase of violence.[31]

The second phase began after the mob paused for refreshments at the Exchange Hotel. It differed from the first phase in two respects: leadership was more diffuse, and the primary targets were Negroes and amalgamationists, rather than abolitionists. The first target was "Church Alley," a place where "black and white men and women, of infamous characters, . . . huddled promiscuously together in five or six small buildings." After being initially repulsed by gunfire, the rioters attacked again, found the houses empty, and demolished the interracial brothels. Shortly thereafter, as the mob paraded down Main Street, the Mayor intervened. Mayor Davies, who had watched the destruction of the printing office earlier in the evening, advised the rioters that they were now "in danger of punishing the innocent with the guilty," and they were robbing themselves and others of rest. "We have done enough for one night," said the Mayor. ". . . I advise you all to go home." Taking the Mayor's advice, some of the rioters went home and caught up on their sleep.[32]

[31] Birney, *Birney*, 246–47. All major Cincinnati papers reported the details of the riot, August 2–9, 1836. Most sympathetic with the mob were the *Cincinnati Whig* and the *Cincinnati Republican*. Most critical was the Cincinnati *Gazette*.

[32] *Cincinnati Whig*, August 2, 1836; *Narrative of Late Riotous Proceedings*, 40.

Others gathered together an hour later in a part of Cincinnati commonly called the "Swamp." There they attacked six or seven Negro "houses of bad character." [33] In the course of the attack, a young silversmith from New Jersey, Edward Kinsey, received a severe hip wound from pigeon shot. But the mob easily overran the resisters, demolished their furniture, and shattered all their windows. Finally tiring at 3 A.M., Sunday morning, the mob went home.

The next two nights saw the people of Cincinnati again disturbed and excited. A newly formed mob searched for Birney and made several unsuccessful raids on the Negro section. On Monday night, volunteer organizations protecting the city kept the rioters under control. On August 2, the *Gazette* carried a notice, signed by forty men, calling for a meeting of the friends of law and order. The signers included many prominent merchants and lawyers; by and large, however, they had more lowly jobs than either the Market House Committee or the mob.[34] When these saddlers, bricklayers, hatters, and booksellers came to the Court House at the appointed time, they found to their astonishment that the "law and order" meeting was well under way. William Burke presided, and Joseph Graham acted as secretary! Thus the meeting, with the rioters and their supporters safely in control, blamed the abolitionists for causing the disorder. And, with the proper touch of gall, the meeting disapproved of mobs and offered its support in maintaining the peace! On this ironic note, the Cincinnati mob of July, 1836, disintegrated.

In its broad outline, then, the Cincinnati mob was merely a variant of the Utica pattern. So was the Alton riot of November 7, 1837. It, too, involved a well-organized nucleus of prominent citizens who coordinated their actions and selected their targets in advance. The Alton rioters, like their counterparts in Utica and Cincinnati, received stimulus and succor from town meetings, in-

---

[33] *Cincinnati Whig*, August 2, 1836.

[34] This generalization is the result of comparing the occupations of the men in the three groups. Their occupations can be found in the *Cincinnati Directory*, 1836–1837.

fluential editors, civic leaders, and state officials. But the Alton abolitionists, more than antislavery men in Utica and Cincinnati, also
had the forceful backing of many leading citizens. Indeed, had
they lacked this backing, mob violence at Alton probably would
have stopped short of the murder of Elijah Lovejoy.

Lovejoy had lived previously in St. Louis, where he had fallen
into disrepute because of his stand on the McIntosh case. McIntosh, a Negro, had been roasted alive over a slow fire of green
wood for killing a deputy. His tormentors, who were generally described as "well-dressed," never stood trial. Judge Luke Lawless,
in fact, instructed the grand jury that if they found the dreadful
act to be the result of an "electric phrenzy," then the case was "be-
yond the reach of human law." Lovejoy's *Observer*, a religious
paper which was then only mildly antislavery and vehemently
anti-Catholic, denounced the people of St. Louis and lashed Judge
Lawless as a papist whose legal doctrine came from a Jesuit school
in southern Ireland. The tumult that followed led Lovejoy to seek
a more peaceful setting upriver in Illinois. He decided on Alton, a
law-abiding and thriving frontier town of some three thousand
souls, which urged him to come. He arrived in July 1836.[35]

On Monday, July 25, the citizens of Alton were shocked to dis-
cover that Lovejoy's press, which had arrived at the dock on the
Sabbath, had been destroyed. Disorderly actions, everyone agreed,
might occur in other places, but Alton had a standard to maintain.
It was a progressive town. Its charter even provided that black
children should be admitted to the public schools on the same
basis as white children. Its leaders tried to attract settlers of the
better type by building fine schools and churches and by provid-
ing cultural enrichment through weekly meetings of the Lyceum.
The perpetrators of this outrage, said the city fathers, must have
come from St. Louis. There people mistook Lovejoy, obviously a

[35] Of Lovejoy's recent biographers, I am dependent largely on John Gill,
Tide Without Turning (Boston, 1959), and Merton L. Dillon, *Elijah P. Lovejoy, Abolitionist Editor* (Urbana, Illinois, 1961). For Lovejoy's anti-Catholicism, see "Elijah P. Lovejoy as an Anti-Catholic," *Records of the American
Catholic Historical Society of Philadelphia* 62 (September 1951), 172–80.

pious religious editor, for an abolitionist incendiary; but Altonians knew better. Nevertheless, concluded civic leaders, Altonians should raise the funds to replace the destroyed press and to restore the town's good name. Thus Alton welcomed the *Observer* and its editor.

Trouble came the following summer. In March 1837, the land boom failed, and the price of lead bought and stored by Alton entrepreneurs fell drastically. In this time of general collapse, Lovejoy began his attack on slavery, and by late June the *Observer* was taking an open, clear-cut, unqualified stand for organized antislavery.[36] It gave full support to the American Anti-Slavery Society's plan of circulating petitions for abolishing slavery in the District of Columbia. It called for the formation of local antislavery societies. And it even proposed the formation of a state society.[37] Thus the men of Alton, who were already suffering economic woes and had less confidence in the future than before, faced the terrifying prospect that their community might become a center for organized antislavery.

The reaction was immediate. Two days after the *Observer* proposed the formation of a state society, anonymous handbills, tacked along the streets of Alton, invited all citizens to a protest meeting. On July 11 and 18, "Friends of the *Observer* dissatisfied with its course" assembled at the Market House and censured Lovejoy for disseminating "the highly odious doctrines of modern Abolitionism" and for violating his "solemn pledge" to publish only a religious journal. A young lawyer, Junius Hall, insisted that organized antislavery would reduce American culture to the level of the Hottentot. The abolitionists, said he, favored intermarriage

[36] As late as January 1837, Lovejoy defended the Illinois Synod, which condemned immediate abolitionists. See *Philanthropist*, January 20, 1837. But once Lovejoy began to move toward organized antislavery, he moved rapidly. Cf. Alton *Observer*, March 16–July 6, 1837.

[37] Lovejoy did not issue the call for a state society on his own initiative. The New York philanthropists had applied pressure on Illinois abolitionists to organize. Cf. Alton *Observer*, July 6, 1837, with Elizur Wright, Jr., to James Gillespie Birney, August 14, 1837, and James Buchanan to Birney, August 18, 1837—both in Dumond, *Birney Letters*, Vol. I, 414, 416.

and slave revolt. Their schemes would bring carnage, inter-
breeding, mongrelization—and eventually, just as had happened
in Rome, decay and destruction. But Hall's harangue was the
exception. As a whole, the men who composed the meeting spoke
respectably and acted with restraint. They appointed a committee
to meet with Lovejoy and find out if he intended to persist in his
new and exasperating ways. Further action, they agreed, would
depend on Lovejoy's reply.[38]

Lovejoy made no effort to soothe public opinion. He proceeded,
in fact, as though the Market House meeting had never been held.
The *Observer* continued to carry vivid denunciations of slavery
and plans for a state antislavery convention. And on August 5, less
than a month after the public meeting had condemned the forming of antislavery societies, Lovejoy and other local abolitionists
formed the Madison County Anti-Slavery Society at Upper Alton.
The new society immediately endorsed the plan for a state anti-
slavery society and insisted that abolitionists had the God-given
and constitutional right to influence public opinion.[39]

Hostilities therefore increased, and by mid-August prominent
men of Alton began to suggest the possibility of mob violence.
Charles Howard, Whig candidate for mayor, maintained that putting down abolitionist sentiment would not destroy freedom of the
press; it would only destroy licentiousness. Young Dr. Benjamin
Hart from New York, a potential Democratic candidate for mayor,
expressed doubt about whether the community owed protection to
the *Observer*. Had it not forfeited all claims to such protection by
ignoring the wishes of the majority in Alton? Such sentiments, men
realized, undermined all restraints for law and order. Violence
thus was expected.

To avoid extreme violence, twelve of Alton's "most intelligent
and influential" citizens organized themselves into a secret society.

[38] Joseph C. and Owen Lovejoy, *Memoir of the Rev. Elijah P. Lovejoy*
(New York, 1838), 216ff.; Alton *Telegraph*, July 19, 1837; Alton *Spectator*,
July 13 and 20, 1837.

[39] Alton *Observer*, July 20 and August 17, 1837; *Emancipator*, September
7, 1837.

Among this group were three practicing physicians: Dr. Horace Beal, a young Marylander; Dr. James Jennings, a young Virginian; and Dr. William Emerson, a thirty-six-year-old native of Maine, a Harvard man, and formerly one of the town's trustees.[40] Closely associated with these men was another Virginian, Dr. Thomas Hope, a staunch Catholic, an ardent Democrat, and a future mayor of Alton. According to their attorney, these men were looking for a way to avoid "shedding . . . Lovejoy's blood." They finally agreed that their "only alternative" was to tar and feather Lovejoy, place him in a skiff, admonish him to stay out of Alton, and set the skiff adrift.[41]

The opportunity to carry out this plan came on August 21 at about nine o'clock in the evening. The doctors and their confederates met Lovejoy accidentally on the Huntersville Road, a short distance outside Alton. Before they recognized Lovejoy, he was in their midst. At length a number of them began shouting, "Damn him!" "Rail him!" "Tar and feather him!" Completely surrounded, Lovejoy asked only that they deliver some medicine to his wife without alarming her. This they promised to do, and one of their members took the medicine to her. Lovejoy then said, "I am now at your disposal." At this, the mob had qualms of conscience, and after a brief consultation the men released Lovejoy unharmed.[42]

They returned to Alton, however, to destroy Lovejoy's press. Between ten and eleven o'clock they began bombarding Lovejoy's office with stones and shouting threats and insults at the workers inside. Soon a large crowd of well-dressed citizens gathered to

[40] George T. M. Davis, the lawyer for two members of the group, described the principals, but omitted their names. See his *Autobiography* (New York, 1891), 58ff. Thus there has been some dispute among secondary accounts over the identity of the third doctor. Was he Emerson or Benjamin Hart? Earlier in his account (p. 49), Davis associated Hart with New York. Later (p. 60), he insisted that the third doctor came from New England. Emerson was the only doctor in Alton from New England. Hart, as Davis apparently realized, was a New Yorker. See *History of Madison County, Illinois* (Edwardsville, Illinois, 1882), 295; and W. T. Norton, compiler, *Centennial History of Madison County* . . . (Chicago, 1912), 471, 777–79.

[41] Davis, *Autobiography*, 58ff.

[42] Cf. Lovejoy, *Memoir*, 232–34, with Davis, *Autobiography*, 59–62. (The assailants awoke Davis later that same night for legal advice.)

watch. Only one man tried to dissuade the assailants from their plans. He suggested that they wait until morning, "peacefully" pack up the press and its editor, and send both south on the next boat. Ignoring his advice, the mob continued its assault, and finally the workers inside gave up all thought of defending the press and fled to safety. The mob then entered the deserted building and destroyed the press, the type, and other printing materials.

The destruction of the *Observer* caused Lovejoy's supporters to rally around the editor and quickly to raise money for another press. No sooner had this been accomplished, however, than some of his staunchest supporters began to have second thoughts. Was it really worth the effort to re-establish the *Observer* against such determined opposition? Should Lovejoy remain as the paper's editor? Division of opinion on such matters, Lovejoy's friends knew, could easily prove disastrous. If the friends of the *Observer* were seen to waver in its support, then its enemies would be only more determined to silence it permanently. Only the solid support of the *Observer's* backers, along with pressure from law-abiding citizens, could intimidate the mob. But the press arrived before such unity developed.

On September 21, near sundown, some of Lovejoy's friends received the new press from a steamboat and took it to a warehouse on Second Street. The Mayor posted a constable to guard it until eleven o'clock, when presumably everyone would be in bed, and all danger past. As soon as the constable left ten or twelve men broke into the warehouse, rolled the press across the street, and began taking it apart. While this work was going on, Mayor John Krum arrived. He ordered the mob to disperse. The mob replied that they would as soon as they were finished. And with the Mayor watching, the men completed their task, and by midnight the parts of Lovejoy's new press lay at the bottom of the river. The next day, estimated Lovejoy, four-fifths of the townspeople rejoiced that his press had been destroyed. It was, Mayor Krum allegedly reported, an unusually "quiet and gentlemanly mob." [43]

[43] *Alton Telegraph,* September 27, 1837; *Philanthropist,* October 8 and 22, 1837; Lovejoy to Joshua Leavitt, October 3, 1837, in Lovejoy, *Memoir,* 258–259. See also, Lovejoy, *Memoir,* 250ff.

The ineffectiveness of the Mayor and the hostility of public opinion led Lovejoy and his defenders to make a fateful decision: next time they would rely on pistols and muskets rather than on moral force.[44] Yet one last effort was made to unite all men in the defense of civil rights and to promote good feeling in Alton. Against their better judgment, Alton abolitionists agreed with Edward Beecher, president of Illinois College, that the state antislavery convention should be open to all "friends of free inquiry," rather than just to antislavery men. Thus, on October 26, when the convention convened in the Presbyterian church at Upper Alton, abolitionsts found to their dismay that some of the *Observer's* harshest opponents had arrived and taken their seats. Among those present were Colonel Alexander Botkin, proprietor of the State Street Mansion House and leader of the July Market House meetings; Dr. Benjamin Hart; the Reverend John Hogan, a former Methodist circuit rider, a wholesale merchant, a banker, a Democratic politician, and a vice-president of the recently revived Alton Colonization Society; William Carr, one of the most violent members of the mob; and their leader, Usher F. Linder, a young Kentuckian who had recently become Attorney General of Illinois.

Linder and his associates had little difficulty in controlling the meeting. By simply agreeing that slavery was a sin, they easily blocked an abolitionist attempt to exclude them. They failed to elect Dr. Thomas Hope permanent chairman; but by the time the third officer, a secretary, was chosen, they had enough votes to elect William Carr and to turn the convention into a farce. Linder submitted a "minority" set of resolutions, which the convention adopted and then adjourned *sine die*. Completely outmaneuvered in the public convention, seventy-five of the more determined abolitionists then met privately in a spacious stone house in Upper Alton. But Linder countered by organizing a mob to beat against the doors and disrupt the meeting. Not until the mayor and forty special constables cleared the streets could the abolitionists form a state society.

Before adjourning, the newly formed state society decided to

[44] Lovejoy to Leavitt, October 3, 1837, in Lovejoy, *Memoir,* 258–60.

reestablish the *Observer* in Alton and "to take such measures as shall secure its re-establishment and safety." [45] Several days later, when Beecher preached on slavery in Upper Alton, antislavery men maintained the peace with loaded muskets. Soon both sides were well armed, and moderates in both camps became increasingly frightened. Thus Beecher and the Reverend John Hogan agreed to call another public meeting to allay the explosive atmosphere. And on November 2, prominent merchants and professional men, together with some clergymen, gathered in Hogan's store. It was no longer a question of abolitionism, Beecher told them; rather it was now a matter of free speech and the authority of the law. If for no other reason, argued Beecher, men of wealth and property should maintain civil authority for their own material interests. This proposal, countered Linder and his followers, was nothing more than total surrender to the abolitionists. And it was too much to expect, added Linder, that men in that very room who "had promoted, or at least connived at what had been done" should now admit that they were entirely in the wrong. [46]

The next day, when the meeting reconvened, Linder was in full control. He excluded Beecher by guiding through a resolution that limited the meeting to citizens of Madison County. The basic issue, Linder argued later in the meeting, was whether "the interests and feelings of the citizens of Alton should be consulted," or whether they were to be "dictated to by foreigners" who cared only for self-gratification and establishing "certain abstract principles, which no one, as a general thing, ever thought of questioning." The prominent men of Alton not only rejected Beecher's argument that Lovejoy had a constitutional right to publish the *Observer*, but also approved Linder's resolution that under no circumstances should the *Observer* be reestablished. Thus the majority, even though they formally disapproved of "all unlawful violence," utterly refused to protect Lovejoy and his press. [47]

[45] *Proceedings of the Illinois Anti-Slavery Convention . . .* (Alton, 1838), 11.

[46] Edward Beecher, *Narrative of Riots at Alton* (Alton, 1838), 60.

[47] Alton *Telegraph*, November 8, 1837; Lovejoy, *Memoir*, 268ff.

But a sizable minority of the town's prominent men, along with some abolitionists, approached Mayor Krum and asked for authorization to form a military company. Krum refused to command such a company himself, but he readily admitted the need for an organized militia. Soon afterward the minority organized themselves into an informal company with William Harned, an innkeeper from Kentucky, as captain. Meanwhile, the abolitionists made careful plans to protect the new press once it arrived. They agreed to keep the press temporarily in Winthrop Gilman's stone warehouse directly beside the Mississippi River. The press could be unloaded at his wharf sometime between midnight and daybreak, rushed across the street into the warehouse, and remain safely there behind massive stone walls. In case of trouble, guns were stored in the warehouse.

On November 7, at three in the morning, the press arrived, and under the watchful eyes of Harned's volunteers and Mayor Krum, it was carried to the third floor of the warehouse. There, all agreed, the press would be safe. The warehouse was virtually a fort: only the gabled ends had windows and doors; the sides were solid masonry. A handful of men, it seemed, could easily defend the building. Thus the thirty men in Harned's company agreed to divide into five groups, each to stand watch on successive nights.

That day, however, disturbing news spread through the city. William Carr, Dr. Beal, Dr. Jennings, and others had learned of the press's whereabouts and were making plans to storm the warehouse. Snatches of conversation were overheard, and nearly everyone expected violence. That evening, forty-two men reported to Gilman's warehouse and volunteered their services. Only a few were abolitionists; the rest were primarily merchants and tradesmen who saw themselves as guardians of law and order. They expected some trouble, but they also expected "to have some crackers and cheese and hear some good stories." [48] None thought the situation was desperate, and so at eight o'clock over half the men went home. About an hour later, the fourteen remaining men

[48] Joseph Greeley's testimony, William S. Lincoln, *Alton Trials* (New York, 1838), 23.

learned to their dismay that they had underestimated the mob, which planned either to burn the building or to blow it up.

While the defenders of the press desperately sought further help, the doctors and their associates organized at Tontine's saloon. At ten o'clock the vanguard of the mob formed a column and marched toward the warehouse. As soon as the column reached the building, the rioters began stoning the windows and doors. Suddenly Gilman appeared above them, standing in an upper doorway, and asked what they wanted. "The press!" shouted William Carr. "We bear no ill feelings toward any of you, but we intend to get the press at the sacrifice of *our* lives!" [49] Gilman then withdrew. Shortly thereafter someone fired, and soon gunshot filled the air. Suddenly a scream went up from the mob; a young carpenter from western New York, Lyman Bishop, had been mortally wounded.

Stunned, the mob fell back temporarily, but then surged forward with even greater determination. Barefoot and in shirtsleeves, Solomon Morgan, a fifty-year-old farmer, ran about frantically—like "a dog in high rye." Mayor Krum stopped him, but Morgan, the father of six, tore himself away and shouted, "How would you like a damned nigger going home with your daughter?" When Justice Robbins ordered a young merchant, Levi Palmer, to go home, Palmer seized him by the shoulders and told him to "go away," for "the press would be had at all events." Dr. Beal, moving through the crowd, mumbled something about wanting "to kill every damned abolitionist in town." [50]

Mayor Krum, standing on a box, appealed to the mob, but they refused to leave at his command. Finally, Krum agreed to be an envoy for the rioters and carry an ultimatum to the men inside: unless Lovejoy surrendered the press, the warehouse would be burned. But Lovejoy and the other defenders refused to surrender,

[49] Cf. Krum's testimony, Gilman's testimony, and Samuel L. Miller's testimony, *Alton Trials*, 99, 103, and 110.

[50] Dillon, *Lovejoy*, 167; Webb Quigley's testimony, *Alton Trials*, 115; Usher F. Linder's summation, *ibid.*, 142; Sherman Robbins' testimony, *ibid.*, 108; Samuel Avis' testimony, *ibid.*, 113.

and when Krum returned with this news, the mob hastened preparations to set fire to the roof. Having already placed an extension ladder against the northeast corner of the warehouse, out of range of the snipers inside, the mob sent a boy up the ladder with a torch. But five defenders darted out of the warehouse with guns blazing, and the incendiary and his supporters had to scramble for cover. Then James Rock, a riverfront tough, agreed to carry the torch. With men covering him from behind a pile of lumber, Rock climbed the ladder and ignited the roof. This time, Royal Weller and Elijah Lovejoy dashed out of the warehouse and aimed their pistols at Rock. The men behind the lumber pile fired and hit both Lovejoy and Weller. Weller suffered only a minor wound. Lovejoy, hit by five bullets, dragged himself upstairs to his compatriots and fell dead at their feet.

With Lovejoy dead and the roof blazing, the defenders saw no point in prolonging the battle. They fled to the river while the mob harassed them with buckshot. A dozen men then entered the building and dropped the press out of a window on the third floor to the street below. They disturbed nothing else in the building except a few guns. Dr. Beal had warned them that "he did not want any property injured, nor anything taken away." Outside, the rioters were equally orderly. Dr. Hope helped put out the fire, while other men dragged the press to the steamboat landing and began smashing it with hammers. "It was done in a quiet sort of way," one witness said. "They seemed to be happy while engaged in breaking it in pieces." [51]

By midnight, peace finally came to Alton as the rioters and spectators went home. Yet for years to come, Alton was to bear the stigma of being an unusually bloodthirsty and riotous city. In the East the general revulsion became so great that the New York associates held an emergency session to consider how to take advantage of the situation; and thus Lovejoy was scarcely dead before antislavery papers, banners, stationery, sermons, and a commissioned memoir honored "the first MARTYR to American LIB-

[51] Samuel L. Miller's testimony, *Alton Trials*, 111; Joseph Greeley's testimony, *ibid.*, 23; Henry H. West's testimony, *ibid.*, 95–96.

ERTY." Soon the city of Alton, once known for its churches and its orderly and industrious citizens, became a symbol for Western lawlessness and brutality.

Yet it would be a mistake for us to reach the same conclusion. The "respectable" character of the mob, the purposeful and limited nature of its goals, and even its consideration for human life differed only slightly from conventional anti-abolitionist mobs. What distinguished most Eastern mobs from their Alton counterpart was not the inherent moderation of their respectable, middle-class participants; rather it was the almost total lack of resistance to mobs by other respectable people in the community. Had *all* of Alton's citizens followed the example of many of their harshest Eastern critics—had *all* of them simply watched while the Linders, the Beals, and the Carrs raised a mob and attacked Lovejoy —Alton's reputation probably would have been only slightly soiled. But some resisted, and this resistance intensified the mob's grievances and escalated the violence.[52]

IV

The other broad category of anti-abolitionist mobs comprises only about one-fourth of the total. These mobs apparently formed without prior coordination and design and had much in common with the stereotypical mobs of revolutionary France or pre-Victorian England. To many contemporaries, in fact, they often seemed as irrational, fickle, and primitive as the abstractions described by Gustave Le Bon and most social psychologists.

But the *real* European mobs of the late eighteenth or early nine-

[52] The systematic comparison of data in almost any sociological or historical narrative indicates that the number of deaths depends largely on the amount of opposition. For a good discussion of this point in another context, see Gordon Wood, "Note on Mobs in the American Revolution," *William and Mary Quarterly* 23 (October 1966), 635–42. It has been recently argued by a psychologist that violent opposition intensified the commitment of anti-slavery men. See Silvan S. Tomkins, "The Psychology of Commitment . . ." in Martin Duberman, ed., *The Antislavery Vanguard* (Princeton, 1965), 270–98. The same argument holds for the Lovejoy mob.

teenth century had little in common with the capricious, unreasonable, murderous rabble that Jacksonian Americans usually envisioned. On the contrary, argues George Rudé, the typical English and French mobs "rioted for precise objects and rarely engaged in indiscriminate attacks on either properties or persons." The Gordon rioters of 1780, for example, "carefully earmarked their victims" and took "meticulous care" to avoid damaging neighboring property. Even those mobs that appeared "most spontaneous," says Rudé, displayed "remarkable single-mindedness and discriminating purposefulness." With "unfailing regularity" European mobs destroyed property, but they rarely murdered or maimed. Of the 285 persons who died during the Gordon Riots, not one was killed by the mobs. Throughout the period between 1730 and 1848, concludes Rudé, it was generally "authority rather than the crowd that was conspicuous for its violence to life and limb." [53]

In most respects, anti-abolitionist mobs of the second category resembled these lower class European mobs. They, too, directed their energies against specific targets. The mob that burned down Pennsylvania Hall in May, 1838, not only took pains to avoid setting fire to neighboring property, but also took up a collection to pay for accidental damages to a nearby dwelling. And like their European counterparts, these mobs were destructive, but rarely bloodthirsty. Unlike some of the mobs that Rudé describes, however, these mobs never faced vigorous or overzealous magistrates. They never encountered constables or troops who gleefully charged with fixed bayonets or fired into their midst. Invariably American magistrates were both unwilling and unable to crush an anti-abolitionist disturbance with bullets and bayonets. On the one hand, many city magistrates sympathized with the mobs—either entirely or partially—as long as the rioters confined their activities to destroying the property of abolitionists and Negroes. Thus they were only halfhearted in carrying out their duties. On the other hand, all city officials faced the awesome task of mobilizing sufficient force to put down a riot. Everywhere the constabulary was

[53] *The Crowd in History, 1730–1848* (New York, 1964), 253–57.

inadequate, and the procedure for calling out the national guard or the city militia was so cumbersome that it was virtually impossible to act with speed and efficiency.[54] Thus neither the authorities nor the mobs were conspicuous for their violence to life and limb.

Typical of this class of anti-abolitionist mob were the New York City riot of July, 1834, and the Cincinnati riot of September, 1841. Both had strong lower-class support; both apparently developed without benefit of a committee of planners; both were very destructive; and both directed their greatest ferocity not at white friends of the Negro, but at Negroes themselves.

In New York City history, 1834 is known as "the year of the riots." Within a period of ten months, Manhattan had five disturbances, and for the first time in the city's history civil authorities had to call on the military for aid in policing the city. Both the anti-abolitionist mob of October, 1833 (which we noted earlier), and a similar anti-abolitionist outburst of May, 1834, caused little alarm. But the election riot in April, the anti-abolition riot in July, and the stonecutters' riot in August—all necessitated calling out the National Guard. Of these three disturbances, by far the most formidable was the July riot. The 27th National Guard, which readily routed both the election rioters and the stonecutters, had difficulty handling the July rioters. Indeed, at the high point of rioting, the mobs were so uncontrollable in the more respectable neighborhoods of Manhattan that troops were not even sent to the "Five Points" slum, where rioting was worse. For three days anti-abolitionist rioters held the city at bay, destroyed at least sixty dwellings, demolished six churches, and seriously damaged other homes and meeting houses.[55]

[54] For a recent analysis of this period's police problems, see Roger Lane, *Policing the City: Boston, 1822–1885* (Cambridge, Massachusetts, 1967).

[55] There are many secondary accounts of this riot. For a sampling of viewpoints, see Gustave de Beaumont, *Marie, or Slavery in the United States* (Barbara Chapman translation; Stanford, 1958), Appendix L; Henry Fowler, *The American Pulpit* (New York, 1856), 367–77; J. T. Headley, *Pen and Pencil Sketches of the Great Riots of New York City* (New York, 1882), 81ff.; William L. Stone, *History of New York City* (New York, 1872), Chapter VII; Lewis Tappan, *The Life of Arthur Tappan* (New York, 1871), Chapter XII;

Why the disorder? New Yorkers asked themselves this question dozens of times, and they offered a wide variety of explanations. A few noted the brief recession in the local economy. Some called attention to labor troubles, particularly in the building trades; contractors had begun to purchase marble at Sing Sing and to employ prisoners to cut and hew the material before bringing it to the city; stonecutters and masons were incensed.[56] Other New Yorkers called attention to frightening rumors and news reports that cholera, which had ravaged the city in 1832, was once again heading toward New York. Still others blamed rabble-rousing politicians and virulent newsmen. Abolitionists always insisted that they had to thank William Leete Stone, secretary of the New York Colonization Society and editor of the *Commercial Advertiser,* and James Watson Webb, editor of the *Courier and Enquirer,* for the attacks on their homes and businesses. These two editors, abolitionists argued, never missed an opportunity to stir up the fury of the populace. Stone, Webb, and many other New Yorkers, in turn, blamed the abolitionists for ignoring public sentiment, for printing inflammatory placards, for threatening the future of the Union, and for sponsoring the most radical of social doctrines—amalgamation.

However New Yorkers arranged their lists of causes, they invariably assumed that the primary issue was amalgamation. Throughout June and early July, ugly and fantastic rumors spread through the city. One was that abolitionists asked their daughters to marry Negroes. Another was that a prominent New York abolitionist had adopted black children. Still another was that Arthur Tappan had divorced his wife and married a Negro. Still another was that abolitionist ministers regularly conducted interracial mar-

Asher Taylor, *Recollections of the Early Days of the National Guard, Comprising the Prominent Events in the History of the Famous Seventh Regiment* (New York, 1868), 147ff. I generally found more recent accounts to be of little use; one exception is Linda K. Kerber, "Abolitionists and Amalgamators: The New York City Race Riots of 1834," *New York History* 48 (January 1967), 28–39.

[56] News that New York University was to be built with Sing Sing marble and prison labor touched off the stonecutters' riot in August.

riages. And still another was that abolitionists encouraged Negroes to assume "airs," to parade up and down Broadway on horseback and with canes and "dandy" dress, seeking white wives. From "morning to night," reported one English traveler, even the "nicest people" talked about "sexual passion, with a vehemence of manner, and in a tone of earnestness, utterly abhorrent from the generally received notions of propriety." Even "young women" could not see "the indelicacy of discussing the subject of 'amalgamation.'" Even William Leggett of the *Evening Post,* whom antislavery men regarded as their staunchest defender during the riot, assumed that the Tappan brothers and their associates advocated "promiscuous intermarriage of the two races." Throughout the city, men and women believed that the abolitionists "had entered into a conspiracy against the human species, by promoting marriage between the blacks and whites." [57]

But what about the traditional historical explanation? What about the old argument that the July riot was the result of increasing competition between white and black labor? If there was such a problem in 1834, few New Yorkers were aware of it. Linda Kerber's recent reassessment of the riot adheres to the traditional explanation. But she rests her argument on one quote from Duff Green's *United States Telegraph,* a Washington, D. C., newspaper. On the basis of this quote, she implies that the rhetoric of amalgamation was only a cover for the tension between white and black labor.[58] I disagree: the behavior of the rioters indicates that the rhetoric of amalgamation reflected their deepest fears.

The riot began—as did most riots of this type—after a series of precipitating incidents. The first occurred during the abolitionists' Fourth of July celebration at Chatham Street Chapel. Weeks before the meeting, Stone's *Commercial Advertiser,* the city's leading colonization paper, began raising a hue and cry against the pro-

[57] Abdy, *Journal,* III, 123–28; New York *Evening Post,* July 8, 1834. Samples of the rumors appear in all major New York City papers, July 1–15, 1834. On August 19 the *Emancipator* printed a list of some of the rumors.

[58] "Abolitionists and Amalgamators," 34. Later, when hordes of unskilled Irish laborers flocked to New York City, black and white labor collided frequently. In 1834, however, the draft riots were a long way off.

posed assemblage of traitors and instigators of slave insurrections. On the morning of the meeting, this notice appeared throughout the city:

> The friends of the UNION and of the SOUTH are requested to attend the ANTI-SLAVERY MEETING at Chatham Street Chapel, at 11 o'clock this morning. Remember, freemen, what this Society aims at—THE DISUNION of the STATES.
> MANY FRIENDS OF THE COUNTRY.

At eleven o'clock a mob led by George Bull, an official reader of the Board of Aldermen, arrived at the meeting. They found the two races "obnoxiously mixed." But they waited until the principal speaker rose to speak, and then with shouts of "Treason! Treason! Hurrah for the Union!" they broke up the meeting. Afterward, some of the most vociferous went to a nearby park and started a brawl with some blacks. Eventually the police interfered, and six of the mob were arrested.[59]

The second incident occurred on July 5. In a hotel near the Bowery Theatre, a butcher overheard an English actor and stage manager, William Farren, say "damn the Yankees, they are a damn set of jack-asses, and fit to be gulled. . . ." The butcher objected, and Farren smashed him in the face. Most people who heard of the incident did not associate it with the abolitionists. But others did. They identified the Farren incident with British attacks on American slavery, with British opposition to African colonization, and with British aid to the American Anti-Slavery Society.[60]

The third incident occurred on July 7 at Chatham Street Chapel. The New York Sacred Music Society had leased the chapel for every Monday and Thursday evening. But since the society was not planning to use the chapel on Monday the seventh, it sublet the hall to Negroes who wanted to celebrate their freedom and to hear speeches on American independence.[61] Unfortunately, not all

[59] New York *Commercial Advertiser,* June 9, July 7, 1834; *Emancipator,* July 8 and 15, 1834; New York *Sun,* July 7, 1834.

[60] New York *Sun,* July 8, 1834; Headley, *Great Riots,* 85.

[61] Negroes had planned to celebrate on the evening of July 4, but they postponed their meeting due to that day's disturbance.

the directors of the Sacred Music Society were aware of the ar-
rangement, and thus one of the officers, discovering the black
meeting in progress, became incensed and ordered the audience to
disperse. The audience refused, but the officer of the Sacred Music
Society gathered a band of about fifteen men and tried to drag the
Negro speaker and his friends from the stage. A fight ensued,
loaded canes were used freely, lamps and chairs were broken, and
some persons were seriously injured. The Negroes succeeded in
pitching some intruders out of doors and windows, but then the
police came and cleared the building. Outside, a large white
crowd soon gathered and forced the blacks to flee.

This incident, of course, created great excitement in the city.
Some newspapers, which had been bellowing for days against the
integrated antislavery meeting of July 4, fanned this excitement
into fury. They blamed the incident on the "amalgamators" and
their incendiary placards.[62] The *Commercial Advertiser* reported
that "gangs of black fellows" gathered at street corners through the
night, "some of them threatening to burn the city, and declaring
that the next time they would be in sufficient force to overcome
the whites." Webb's *Courier and Enquirer,* under the heading of
"Negro Riot," maintained that these "disgraceful negro outrages"
would continue "until Arthur Tappan and his troop of incendiaries
shall be put down by the strong arm of the law." Last night's riot,
said Webb, was strictly a Negro riot. The whites were entirely innocent. Still "they were beaten—yes, beaten, fellow-citizens, by the
bludgeons of an infuriated and an *encouraged* negro mob! How
much longer are we to submit? In the name of the country, in the
name of heaven, how much more are we to bear from Arthur Tappan's mad impertinence?"[63]

After this incident, the frequency of violence quickly increased.
On July 8 there were two episodes. First, a fire mysteriously broke

[62] The abolitionists had posted a placard headed "LOOK OUT FOR
KIDNAPPING!!" Underneath was a cut of a mounted slave-driver with a
double-thonged whip, driving before him a Negro, whose wife and children
were clinging to him to prevent the unnatural separation.

[63] New York *Commercial Advertiser,* July 8, 1834; New York *Courier and
Enquirer,* July 8, 1834.

out in a building where a notorious abolitionist, John Rankin, had his store. Later a large group of enraged whites, having discovered that the Moral Lyceum was holding an integrated antislavery meeting at Clinton Hall, burst into the meeting and forced the Negroes to withdraw. In reporting this occurrence, Webb warned "that if the blacks continue to allow themselves to be made the tools of a few blind zealots, the consequences to them will be most serious." [64] On July 9 there were frequent rumors of impending attacks during the day, and there were three serious disorders during the night. About dusk a large crowd gathered outside Chatham Street Chapel to break up another integrated antislavery meeting. When the antislavery meeting failed to materialize, the crowd broke into the chapel, listened to William Wilder describe the miseries that sudden abolition brought to Santo Domingo, shouted colonizationist vows, and agreed to adjourn until the next meeting of the antislavery society. Then a part of the audience took off for the Bowery Theatre and succeeded in ruining a benefit night for "damn the Yankees" Farren. After the authorities had managed to clear the theater, the mob proceeded to the home of Lewis Tappan on Rose Street. There they broke doors and windows, overcame city watchmen, and burned about $500 worth of furniture in the street. On July 10 and 11, violence increased a hundredfold. Rioters roamed the city almost at will. First they concentrated on the homes, businesses, and churches of white abolitionists and "amalgamators"; then they attacked the churches of prominent black abolitionists; and finally they razed and ransacked the Negro quarters.

Contrary to Le Bon's abstractions, the New York mobs became more methodical and better organized as the rioting intensified. From the beginning, potential rioters knew where to meet, when to assemble, and whom to attack. Such information made the rounds at the marketplace. Occasionally it appeared in a handbill, but usually it spread verbally. Tappan's house, for example, was earmarked as a prime target hours beforehand. News of the impending attack, in fact, became so widespread that Tappan's

[64] New York *Courier and Enquirer,* July 9, 1834.

friends advised him to evacuate his family. Accordingly, he took
his family out of town about the time the potential rioters were
gathering at Chatham Street Chapel.[65] The Tappan mob, then,
was hardly spontaneous.

Nevertheless, the Tappan mob lacked the precision and disci-
pline of subsequent mobs. On July 10 and 11, the rioters not only
chose their primary targets carefully in advance, but also made
battle plans for the evening's work. The ringleaders, according to
one informer, agreed under oath to form small and detached units
at nightfall and to proceed to general rendezvous. There they would
destroy their first target. Then they would organize themselves
into a square with the weaker men in the middle and the stronger
men on the outside; the weaker men would be armed with stones
and other missiles, and the stronger men would carry loaded clubs.
In this fashion they would ward off attacks by the military, who allegedly had been forbidden to fire on the mob, and would proceed
to their subsequent targets.[66]

Even when such well-laid plans went awry in the course of battle, the rioters rallied with startling speed and coordination. Before
attacking a Presybterian church on Spring Street, for example, the
rioters deliberately fortified their position. They chained carts and
wagons across the streets to prevent the authorities from interfer-
ing. Then they smashed the doors and windows, stormed the
church, and demolished the organ, the pulpit, and the pews. They
were in the process of tearing down the galleries when a regiment
of national guard arrived. After two city aldermen failed to secure
favorable terms from the mob, the military broke through the bar-
ricade, split the rioters into four fragments, and finally sent them
fleeing pell-mell in several different directions. Yet while the regiment congratulated itself on restoring peace and quiet to that sec-

[65] Lewis Tappan to Theodore Dwight Weld, July 10, 1834, *Weld-Grimké
Letters*, Vol. I, 153.

[66] "One who by concealing his own sentiments, has become acquainted
with the designs of others" to Mayor C. W. Lawrence, n.d.; Miscellaneous
Riots—1834, New York Historical Society. The Mayor received notes from
several informers. This particular one predicted the evening's events with
such accuracy that he must have been an insider as he claimed.

tion of the city, the rioters were reassembling before the home of the Reverend Henry G. Ludlow, the pastor of the Spring Street church, and began another attack. Such was the preparation of the mob of July 11.

Even more methodical, and certainly more destructive and more devilish, were the mobs that roamed "Five Points" on July 11. They had messengers to keep one another informed, and they developed a simple, but ingenious scheme to distinguish black dwellings from white. Taking their cue from the Book of Exodus, the rioters spread the news that white families should keep their candles lit and stand before their windows so that they might be identified and their homes passed over; the mob would attack only homes with darkened windows or with dark faces at the windows. This procedure enabled the rioters to sack and demolish Negro homes with efficiency and dispatch. It proved so effective, in fact, that Philadelphians adopted the same tactics during the famous Passover Riot of August, 1834.

During the two nights of intense rioting, then, the New York rioters behaved neither spontaneously nor capriciously. They displayed as much rhyme and reason, as much purposefulness and singlemindedness, as the rioters whom Rudé describes. Their choice of primary targets, therefore, strikes me as one way to gain insight into some of their central concerns. If one carefully analyzes all of the newspaper reports and all of the eye-witness accounts, it becomes readily apparent that the mobs attacked at least four places with unusual determination and vehemence. One was a house on Leonard Street, which was attacked by a band of sailors who had personal grievances against the Negro owner.[67] The other three were churches and parsonages.

All three of the churches had pastors who were popularly identified not only as abolitionists but also as "amalgamators." Dr. Samuel Cox, whose Presbyterian church was attacked on both nights,

[67] These particular rioters were arrested and tried by the Special Court of Sessions. Information on their motives and summations of their trial appeared in the New York *Journal of Commerce*, July 16, 23, and 26, 1834, and the New York *Sun*, July 14, 22, and 23, 1834.

had gained notoriety before the rioting by denouncing "Nigger pews" and favoring integration within the church. In one sermon he argued that Christ was of a dark Syrian color, probably darker than many Negroes, and that He undoubtedly would be turned out of the church. This comment of course generated an enormous uproar. James Watson Webb, among others, fiercely denounced Cox for saying that "the Saviour of mankind was a negro." And with clenched fist, one merchant expressed very aptly the city's prevailing mixture of religion, profanity, patriotism, and racism: "He's against slavery, and the South, and the Union! And would you believe it? he called *my Saviour* a nigger! God damn him!" The second pastor was the Reverend Henry Ludlow, whose misfortunes we have already noted. Allegedly he had promoted miscegenation and had given practical proof of his faith in amalgamation by marrying a white to a black. He later published a denial of these charges. The third man was the Reverend Peter Williams, the first Negro priest in the Episcopal Church and the pastor of the St. Phillip's African Episcopal Church. Following a rumor that he had officiated at an interracial marriage, a large mob spent about two hours demolishing both his home and his church. He later denied the rumor and severed all ties with the American Anti-Slavery Society.[68]

The American Anti-Slavery Society also published a "DISCLAIMER." On Saturday, July 12, the Society posted a handbill in different parts of Manhattan. It began: "We entirely disclaim any desire to promote or encourage intermarriages between white and colored persons." On the following Monday, James Watson Webb, who had been repeatedly cheered by the mobs, took pride in his contribution "in producing this desirable state of public feeling." He trusted that "the immediate abolitionists and amalgamators" now realized that New Yorkers "have determined to prevent the

[68] Fowler, *The American Pulpit*, 374–75; H. G. Ludlow to the editors of the *Journal of Commerce*, July 24, 1834, in the *Journal of Commerce*, July 26, 1834; *Emancipator*, July 29, 1834; New York *Mercantile Advertiser*, July 12, 1834; Beaumont, *Marie*, 248–49; Carter G. Woodson, ed., *The Mind of the Negro as Reflected in Letters Written during the Crisis, 1800–1860* (Washington, D. C., 1926), 629–34.

propagation among them of their wicked and absurd doctrines, much less to permit the practice of them." William Leete Stone of the *Commercial Advertiser* disavowed the mobs, but he blamed the abolitionists for raising "the whirlwind," for vilifying the American Colonization Society, and especially for kindling the fury of the rioters by seeking to "*mulattoize* our posterity" and degrade "a nation of white men . . . to the condition of mongrels." [69] Thus in the wake of violence both the abolitionists and their staunchest opponents presumed that the dread of amalgamation had been the rioters' primary motivation.

Seven years later, a similar riot occurred in Cincinnati. There, as we have already noted, the issue of amalgamation had been central for years. The fear of racial mixing, in fact, probably had deeper roots in Cincinnati than in New York. For Cincinnati's mulatto population outnumbered its black population.[70] Thus visible data discredited the old myth that white men found Negro women physically repulsive. The same evidence, moreover, probably undermined the standard antislavery argument that once slavery ended, the two races would never mix. At any rate, local abolitionists never convinced their fellow Cincinnatians that the fear of widespread miscegenation was nothing more than a bugaboo. After the riot of September, 1841, Cincinnati abolitionists once again issued a disclaimer; it began, "We are not *amalgamationists*." [71]

Despite the disclaimer, neither the abolitionists nor their enemies assumed that the dread of amalgamation was the primary

[69] New York *Courier and Enquirer*, July 14, 1834; New York *Commercial Advertiser*, July 10–14, 1834.

[70] I have been unable to find exact figures for the ratio of mulattoes to blacks in 1841. But in 1850, Cincinnati had fourteen mulattoes for every ten blacks, while New York City had three for ten. See J. D. B. De Bow, *Statistical View of the United States* (Washington, D. C., 1854), 68, and Manuscript Census Returns—1850, Hamilton County, National Archives. Cincinnatians, like most Northerners, were sensitive to the presence of mulattoes in their midst. Generally they blamed Southern slaveholders for spawning the city's halfbreeds. But the Manuscript Census Returns hardly supports their contentions: it appears that most of the city's mulattoes were born in Ohio.

[71] Cincinnati *Gazette*, September 17, 1841.

cause of the September riot Both sides agreed that it was an underlying cause, but not a precipitating one as it had been in New York. Cincinnati's most virulent anti-abolitionist paper, John and Charles Brough's *Enquirer*, frequently portrayed Oberlin College as a hotbed of interracial sex, but in the spring and summer of 1841, the *Enquirer* was primarily concerned with other "malign influences" of abolitionism. One was the concessions made to the abolitionists by "Federalist" politicians, particularly their support of a petition from 105 Negroes and their vote to incorporate an interracial school in Brown County. Such concessions, argued the Jacksonian *Enquirer*, encouraged Negroes to come to Cincinnati and gave them "pretensions and privileges that they neither deserved nor could appreciate." Another evil of abolitionism, said the Brough brothers, was that it fed on the carelessness and apathy of most Cincinnatians, particularly those citizens who regarded the Black Laws of 1807 as a dead letter. Thus hordes of black vagabonds, receiving aid and encouragement from the "white fanatics," had come and squatted in Cincinnati without posting a $500 bond. These "impudent wretches" crowded out white labor "when they worked at all," but "more frequently" they lived by stealing from the white workingmen.[72]

By far the worst of the antislavery influences, said the Broughs and other anti-abolitionists, was the rapid increase in "negro stealing." The abolition influence had become so prevalent, insisted the *Enquirer*, that a slaveholder could not come to Cincinnati to trade, to spend the summer, or even to pass the night "without having his negro servants decoyed or stolen away." Southerners even found that they could not safely employ slave labor on steamboats that touched Cincinnati landings. Soon Southerners became indignant, and more and more began to go elsewhere and turn over the profits of their trade and travel to Chicago and other communities. Thus Cincinnati suffered because of "a miserable clique of fanatics, white and black, among us." The city's boat-building,

[72] Cincinnati *Enquirer*, September 9–11, 1841; see also June–September, *passim*. Until the *Cincinnati Post, and Anti-Abolitionist* was established in the fall of 1841, the *Enquirer* was the city's leading anti-abolitionist paper.

its foundries, its machine shops, its manufacturing generally—
"they all have a direct interest in preserving friendly relations
with, and preserving the trade and travel of, the South." But the
"pestilent incendiaries" have "sported with" all these interests and
injured them "materially and vitally." [73]

The Southern trade and "negro stealing" became concomitant issues after the so-called Mahan Affair of 1838. John B. Mahan, a
clergyman of Brown County, Ohio, won notoriety for assisting fifteen slaves on their way to Canada. Kentuckians raised a hue and
cry, and the Ohio legislature responded by passing a stiff fugitive
slave law. Nevertheless the activities of the Underground Railroad
increased measurably in 1839 and 1840. Then in June, 1841, the
Supreme Court of Ohio held that every slave brought voluntarily
by his master into Ohio was free. After this decision the excitement about "negro stealing" became intense. Cornelius Burnett, an
Englishman very active in the Cincinnati Anti-Slavery Society,
openly sheltered a fugitive slave. On June 25, Burnett, his three
sons, and three other abolitionists refused to turn the black man
over to the authorities. A brawl ensued. Burnett and his men were
arrested, charged with assaulting a constable, and sent to jail. A
mob then attacked Burnett's home, but the rioters were dispersed
before much damage had been done. Shortly thereafter, Cincinnatians became excited about a letter allegedly written by a fugitive
slave. It directed runaways to Burnett or to any other abolitionist
whom Negro hands on steamboats pointed out. The letter proved,
said the *Enquirer*, that the "nefarious conspiracy . . . against
Southern rights, and our own business interests, was reduced to a
perfect system." [74]

Tension increased with the summer heat. One slave after another reportedly took refuge in Cincinnati's Negro community.
Chicago boasted about the huge amount of trade and tourism
that it had won from Cincinnati. Negroes reportedly took

[73] Cincinnati *Enquirer*, September 9–11, 1841; see also June–September,
passim.
[74] Cincinnati *Gazette*, June 26, 1841; *Philanthropist*, July 7, 1841; Cincinnati *Enquirer*, June 26, September 9, 1841.

the inside of the pavement on all occasions, swaggered and swelled, and entered places where they had been formerly excluded. Several blacks, who were caught robbing blackberries, killed the German owner with bowie knives. The number of disparaging remarks about Negroes and "negro stealers," "English fanatics," and "foreign abolitionism" soared with the temperature.

Then came the precipitating incidents. On Tuesday, August 31, a quarrel between some blacks and whites ended in a brawl. On Wednesday, about midnight, a band of whites, armed with clubs, attacked a Negro boardinghouse and demanded the surrender of a fugitive. The ensuing battle resulted in several injuries, and some reported that the Negroes had fired at the assailants. On Thursday evening, a few white boys threw gravel upon some blacks who were passing by. A fight followed. One white boy received four knife wounds, and another was so badly cut that "his bowels fell out." News of this incident enraged the white community, and on the following day, September 3, the riot began.[75]

From about eight o'clock on Friday evening until three o'clock on Sunday morning, Cincinnati was almost entirely at the mercy of a mob. According to newspaper reports printed during the riot, the various crowds ranged from 200 to 1,400 people, dozens of whites and blacks were killed, and scores were injured. Such reports increased the tension considerably, but they proved to be wild exaggerations. As far as I can tell, the crowds were about half as large as reported; only J. Nicholson of Newport, Kentucky, was killed; and about thirty men were seriously wounded. Nevertheless the number of serious injuries was far greater than in the New York riot of 1834. Again, the reason for this disparity can be

[75] All the Cincinnati dailies reported the riot, September 1–11, 1841. The *Gazette*, the *Chronicle*, and especially the *Republican* sympathized with the Negroes and the abolitionists. All were Whig papers. The *Enquirer* blamed the riot on the Negroes and the abolitionists.

The *Gazette*, which had tendencies toward anti-Catholicism and nativism, implied that the white rioters were predominantly Irishmen. The *Enquirer* published several denials. Among the wounded, only a few names were Irish.

For the antislavery version of the riot, see *Philanthropist*, September 8, 1841, and *Emancipator*, September 23, 1841.

attributed to the difference in resistance. In New York City the Negroes offered little resistance, and the authorities eventually put down the riot through the use of troops, but not bullets. In Cincinnati the authorities were ineffective, but the Negroes were well armed and more than willing to defend their homes with bullets. The result was more physical violence, but less destruction.

There was one other major difference between the New York and Cincinnati riots. In New York the rioters concentrated their initial attacks on the white abolitionists; then they shifted the focus of their attacks to the Negroes. The Cincinnati rioters reversed this order. During the first night they concentrated their attention on razing and ransacking the Negro quarters; then during the second night they expanded their operations to include the shops and homes of white abolitionists, particularly Englishmen.

Otherwise, there were few differences between the two riots. Like the New York riot, the Cincinnati riot was hardly spontaneous. On Friday, September 30, potential rioters learned at the marketplace about the impending attacks upon Negro residences in McAlister, Sixth, and New streets. The news spread so widely that it came to the attention of the police and the Negroes. The police did virtually nothing, but the blacks armed themselves and prepared for the night's assault. News of their arming increased the excitement. That the city's Negroes had access to guns and ammunition was indeed frightening! Where did they get their firearms? Had they made previous plans to slaughter the whites? Such questions buzzed through the white community.

Shortly before eight o'clock in the evening, a mob, which included some Kentuckians, openly assembled in the Fifth Street Market.[76] Neither the police nor private citizens interfered. The mob, armed with clubs and stones, then marched deliberately toward Broadway and Sixth Street. There they attacked a Negro

---

[76] Some of the newspapers later blamed the mob on Kentuckians. Although there was a grain of truth to this charge, the charge was obviously an attempt by prominent Cincinnatians to shift the responsibility to outsiders. Being known as an antislavery center may have been bad for business, but being known as "mob town" was worse.

confectionery and demolished the doors and windows. About this time Mayor Samuel Davies came up and exhorted the rioters to obey the law. They shouted him down and moved onward. The blacks opened fire. The mob scattered, but rallied quickly. The Negroes fired again, and again the mob took cover. This same pattern was repeated again and again and again. Finally, about one o'clock, the rioters got a cannon from near the river, loaded it with boiler punchings, and against the frantic pleas of the Mayor pointed it down Sixth Street. With the firing of the cannon and the firing of guns on both sides, the riot resumed, and the whites began to gain ground as many blacks fled to the hills. About two o'clock, some of the military, upon the call of Mayor Davies, arrived and succeeded in keeping the rioters at bay.

The following day, Saturday, was extraordinary. Martial law was established, but only in the Negro quarter. Throughout the city, blacks were seized and herded into the riot area. A meeting of citizens at the courthouse, over which the Mayor presided, agreed to uphold the law, but also agreed to the demands of the rioters. The meeting called for the arrest of the Negroes who had knifed the two white boys, the rigid enforcement of the Black Laws of 1807 until the city was delivered from the evil effect of "modern abolitionism," the prompt return of all fugitive slaves, the disavowal of abolitionism and abolitionists by "every good citizen," and the immediate disarmament of Cincinnati's black population. Prominent Negroes met at a church and agreed to comply with these demands. At three o'clock the authorities proceeded to the riot area and disarmed the Negroes. Enough arms, complained the *Enquirer*, were found to outfit "an Algerine pirate vessel. . . . How was it that almost every black among us, carried concealed about him, *deadly weapons*, prepared, at any moment, to steep his hands in human blood?" It was terrifying! Undoubtedly, concluded the *Enquirer*, the abolitionists were at fault.[77] While being disarmed, some Negroes posted bond and received permission to leave the riot area with their sureties. But the mob would have none of it;

[77] Cincinnati *Enquirer*, September 9, 1841.

they refused to allow any blacks to leave the quarter. Thus at five o'clock the authorities decided to appease the mob and prevent disorder by putting the male Negroes in jail!

That night the mob was more efficiently organized than it had been the evening before. The rioters gathered early in the evening, divided their force, made attacks at different points almost simultaneously, and thus distracted the combined attention of the police, the military, and the *posse comitatus*. At best the law enforcement agencies were only half-hearted in carrying out their duties. They shot at no one, and they even failed to post guards at such obvious targets as the office of the *Philanthropist* and the confectionery of Cornelius Burnett. Thus the rioters encountered few difficulties. They broke up the office of the *Philanthropist* and threw the presses into the river. They leveled Burnett's shop. They ransacked the Negro quarters, destroyed a Negro church, and drove Negro women and children from their houses. Some rioters "even went so far as to ravish the person of a young black girl!" [78] The rioters failed in their attempt to destroy the hardware store of Christian Donaldson, an Englishman, and they were driven off by the police when they attacked the book store of two abolitionists, William Truman and Winthrop Smith. Otherwise their evening was successful.

On Sunday, Governor Thomas Corwin arrived in Cincinnati, issued a decree, and took steps to put down further violence. Had it not been for his timely arrival, said the *Philanthropist*, there would have been further violence.[79] Once the violence ended, abolitionists rallied around the *Philanthropist*, paid their long-overdue subscriptions, and determined that the paper must remain in Cincinnati. Thus the *Philanthropist*, which had been languishing before the riot, gained new vigor and prospered.[80] But the blacks suffered. On Tuesday, September 7, three-fourths of the Negro men

[78] *Cincinnati Republican*, September 7, 1841.

[79] *Philanthropist*, September 8, 1841.

[80] Joel Goldfarb, "The Life of Gamaliel Bailey Prior to the Founding of the *National Era* . . ." (Unpub. Ph.D. dissertation, U.C.L.A., 1958), Chapter XVI.

were released from jail. Most executed bonds or produced certificates of nativity; the rest either agreed to leave Cincinnati or were discharged by the court. In short, the Black Laws were enforced for the first time in years. On September 23 the Cincinnati anti-abolitionists organized themselves into a society, declared "war against Abolitionists—*white men*—who, disregarding the misery of the whites, make a parade of their kindly feelings toward the blacks," and damned the abolitionists "for assisting the blacks in mobbing and shooting the whites on the 3d." The society failed in its campaign against the abolitionists, but it succeeded in achieving stiffer controls of the city's Negroes.[81] In balance, then, the Cincinnati mob of 1841 achieved its purpose.

V

We have seen in this chapter that the conventional picture of mobs painted by Le Bon and inherited by later social psychologists has little application to Northern anti-abolitionist mobs. Words such as "spontaneous," "unorganized," "fickle," "indiscriminate," and "purposeless" do not describe even the most impulsive anti-abolition mobs. "Murderous" has more meaning, but only when applied to mobs that encountered violent resistance. More useful are the terms favored by George Rudé: nearly all anti-abolition mobs were "destructive," "discriminating," and "purposeful." In most respects, moreover, the lower-class anti-abolition mobs, such as the New York mob of 1834 and the Cincinnati mob of 1841, resembled the European mobs that Rudé describes.

Yet the conventional anti-abolition mobs, such as the Utica mob of 1835 and the Cincinnati mob of 1836, differed markedly from the mobs that interest Rudé. They were neither revolutionary nor lower-class. They involved a well-organized nucleus of respectable, middle-class citizens who wished to preserve the status quo rather than to change it. They met purposefully and often for-

---

[81] Cincinnati *Enquirer*, September 10, 21, and 25, 1841; *Cincinnati Post, and Anti-Abolitionist*, January 22–March 26, 1842; *Emancipator*, July 14, 1842.

mally, and they coordinated their actions several days in advance. Frequently they had either the support or the acquiescence of the dominant forces in the community. Sometimes they represented the Establishment. More frequently they *were* the Establishment.

5

What Manner of Men Were They?

Anti-abolition mobs were often led by prominent citizens such as
congressmen, attorneys general, judges, doctors, and mill owners.
Such information may be enlightening, but it tells us little about
the social composition of the mobs. A detailed analysis of the leadership of all anti-abolition mobs undoubtedly would reveal that
the mobs were usually led or engineered by the scions of old and
socially dominant Northeastern families. It may be informative—
and, to some historians, even amusing—that several mob leaders
claimed to have *Mayflower* ancestors, and that dozens traced their
lineage to the Massachusetts Bay Colony. Yet such data is incon-
clusive and perhaps misleading in regard to the anatomy of anti-
abolition mobs.[1]

We need to probe deeper. We need to concern ourselves not
only with the leaders but also with the ordinary rioters. Who were

[1] For the pitfalls inherent in simply analyzing leadership groups, compare
Richard Hofstadter, *The Age of Reform* (New York, 1960), Chapter 4, with
Richard B. Sherman, "The Status Revolution and Massachusetts Progressive
Leadership," *Political Science Quarterly* 78 (March 1963), 59–65; and David
Donald, "Toward a Reconsideration of the Abolitionists," in *Lincoln Recon-
sidered* (New York, 1956), 19–36, with R. A. Skotheim, "A Note on Histori-
cal Method," *Journal of Southern History* 25 (1959), 356–65.

the rioters? What kind of men composed the rank and file of the "typical" anti-abolition mob? How did they differ from their anti-slavery adversaries? How did they differ from the rank and file of the "atypical" lower-class anti-abolition mob? These are some of the questions we need to answer.

Contemporary observers provide us with a few clues. Nearly all agreed, for example, that the common phrase "gentlemen of property and standing" was more than a cliché; to some extent it reflected the composition of the mobs. Since anti-abolitionists obviously enjoyed portraying themselves as solid citizens, as men of means and influence, as patriots defending the polity against disorder and disunion, we might doubt and perhaps disregard their self-image. But the abolitionists also portrayed the rioters as men of property and standing. They, too, insisted that the rioters wore velvet and broadcloth as often as fustian and rags.

Essentially the abolitionists saw their adversaries in terms of three social groups. The first group was what they called "the tail of society." The tail, according to antislavery men, included "the sweepings of society, the reprobates from every good thing, men who drink deeply to revenge themselves upon the temperance reformation." Such "rabble" never started mobs, but they participated in the New York City mob of 1834, and in other mobs as well. They had no interest in the issues; their only motivation was "hatred of moral obligation." The second group was what abolitionists called "the bone and muscle of society." This group included farmers, but the phrase was mainly used in regard to the "honest, hard-handed, clear-headed, free laborers, and mechanics of the North." Such men were sometimes indifferent, but they neither started nor participated in mobs. Once they heard the "truth," antislavery men claimed, these men would become the backbone of the antislavery movement. The third group was called "the head of society." The head included "the aristocracy of the North"—the lawyers, politicians, clergymen, merchants, and bankers whose careers were associated with the mercantile economy of preindustrial America. Invariably, said the abolitionists, the Northern aristocracy instigated and participated in the mobs.[2]

2 "Hints on Anti-Abolition Mobs," *The Anti-Slavery Record* II (July

Abolitionists thus insisted that the rioters came largely from "the head and tail of society." Of these two groups, by far the more important was the head. Why did the "old élite" riot? Why did "purse-proud aristocrats" encourage "penniless profligates" to attack abolitionists? Abolitionists answered these questions in two ways. On the one hand, they insisted that many of the merchants, bankers, lawyers, politicians, and clergymen who composed the old élite sold their souls to the slave owners for Southern patronage, Southern votes, or Southern hospitality. On the other hand, antislavery men claimed that "the aristocracy of the North" regarded organized antislavery as a threat to their élite status. Northern anti-abolitionists, reported Elizur Wright, were men who paid homage only to "wealth and power and place." Their respect and reverence for a man depended more on the coat he wore than on his character. Such men were "always 'high church'—conservatists of forms, powers, creeds, usages." They deeply feared majoritarian democracy and never freely accorded "their fellow-men the right of thinking as they please on any subject." To be sure, they gave lip service to majority rule, but only when it served their interests. Educated for conservative leadership, "entrenched in offices of church or state, or wielding the power of old established presses," these men feared the prevalence of antislavery principles "not so much from their hostile bearing upon southern slavery, as lest they should undermine their own power and influence." Expecting to lead and fearing displacement, the old élite thus reacted vehemently to systematic agitation, engineered mobs, broke up antislavery meetings, destroyed presses, and demanded protective legislation against organized antislavery.[3]

1836), 73–82; American Anti-Slavery Society, *Third Annual Report* (New York, 1836), 81; American Anti-Slavery Society, *Fourth Annual Report* (New York, 1837), 57ff.; William Goodell, *Slavery and Anti-Slavery* (New York, 1852), Chapter XXXIII; Lydia Maria Child to the Reverend Convers Francis, December 19, 1835, *Letters of Lydia Maria Child* (Boston, 1883), 17–18; Bayard Tuckerman, *William Jay and the Constitutional Movement for the Abolition of Slavery* (New York, 1893), 80–81; Lovejoy, *Memoirs,* 188, 190, 210–11.

[3] American Anti-Slavery Society, *Fourth Annual Report,* 59–60 and *passim;* Lovejoy, *Memoir,* 210–11; Goodell, *Slavery and Anti-Slavery,* 402f. See also the sources listed in footnote 2.

Such was the abolitionists' image of their opponents. Perhaps some of this imagery was strained or fanciful. But how much? To what extent were the mobs composed of men of property and standing? To what extent were the rioters "high church"? To what extent did "riffraff" and "scum" participate in the mobs? How much weight, in short, are we to attribute to the assessments of the abolitionists? Certainly they had sufficient opportunities to develop expertise about the mobs. But have they left us sound and meaningful appraisals?

To test the significance of these appraisals and to gain further insight into the rioters, I assembled data on the membership of the Utica mob of 1835, the Cincinnati mob of 1836, and the New York City mob of 1834. I chose these mobs for several reasons. First, the names of a significant number of instigators and participants were available. For Utica I found seventy-eight names; for Cincinnati, forty-nine; and for New York City; ninety-four.[4] Second, I wanted panels for both the conventional and the unconventional types of mob. Utica and Cincinnati, as we saw in the last chapter, were more or less typical anti-abolition mobs; New York was atypical. Finally, I wanted one panel from an area where antislavery was unusually vigorous and Southern influence was minimal, and another panel from an area where Southern influence was strong. I reasoned that if the same kinds of men rioted in such distinct communities, then the findings would have greater significance for the North as a whole. If the rioters differed significantly from one community to the other, then we could at least make some judgments about the influence of community opinion or the impact of the Southern trade. Utica, which had negligible contacts with the South, was one of the chief hotbeds of abolition and reform sentiment; Cincinnati probably depended more on Southern patronage than any other Northern city.

II

Let us consider first the rioters in Utica and Cincinnati. For contrast and counterpoint, I compared these men with abolitionists in

[4] Lists of names and sources for the data are found in appendices A and B.

the same cities. It was relatively easy to construct a panel of abolitionists for Utica, as both the abolitionists and the anti-abolitionists published a list of either all or nearly all the rioters.[5] Thus I could use the names of all Uticans who attended the antislavery convention at Utica and Gerrit Smith's estate without biasing my sample. Cincinnati, unfortunately, necessitated some selectivity. Probably about ninety or one hundred men had a hand in either instigating the mob or destroying Birney's press. But only forty-nine names turn up in the newspaper accounts and the two trial reports. Most of these men were either leaders or very active rioters. My panel therefore is not a random sample. It does not include a fair proportion of the obscure and halfhearted rioters who threw only a few stones or simply cheered on their compatriots. To minimize this bias in my sample, I used only the leaders and the active nucleus of the Cincinnati Anti-Slavery Society—a total of twenty-six men—for my panel of local abolitionists.[6]

In identifying both the rioters and the abolitionists, I used biographical directories, city directories, manuscript census returns, church registers, and similar sources. Of the 242 men in both the Utica and the Cincinnati samples, I identified 239. The amount of information I was able to gather about these men varied greatly from category to category. I obtained, for example, the occupational and religious identification of over 90 per cent of the men, but discovered the political affiliation of less than 50 per cent.[7]

Data from these sources confirm the generalized belief of both

[5] At best there were no more than one hundred rioters. The various listings include either seventy-seven or seventy-eight men. Although there are many deviations in spelling various names, the major difference between the listings is that some include both Barent Bleecker Lansing and Richard Ray Lansing, and others include only one or the other. After some digging, I concluded that both of the Lansings participated.

[6] Distinguishing between "active" and "inactive" abolitionists may seem to call for a great deal of subjectivity. Actually it calls for very little. The active abolitionists in Cincinnati were very active; the inactive abolitionists, in reality, were only sympathizers.

[7] By this statement, I do not mean to imply that 90 per cent of the men were church members; I only mean to imply that I have identified at least 90 per cent of the church members. Only about two-thirds of the men appear in church registries.

abolitionists and anti-abolitionists that a disproportionate number of commercial and professional men rioted. About three-fourths of the men in both mobs were either professionals, merchants, bankers, shopkeepers, or clerks. The disparity is particularly striking in the case of Utica; there, as the following chart indicates, the percentage of rioters in these pursuits was twice that of local abolitionists:

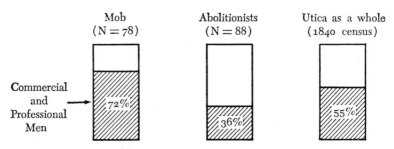

In Cincinnati the disparity between the mob and abolitionists is less striking; nevertheless, there is some disparity:

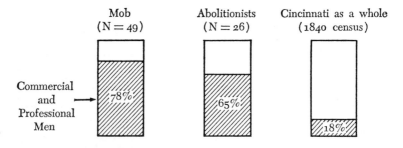

The Cincinnati chart may indicate that a large number of men in both groups had similar occupations. Closer examination of the data, however, reveals that the rioters generally followed pursuits with higher status. Consider, for example, the professionals. Of the eleven professionals in the Cincinnati Anti-Slavery Society, eight were schoolteachers, and five of the eight taught in Negro schools. Schoolteaching was respectable enough for a young man who was working his way through college or professional training, but as a lifetime profession it had little status, and teaching in Negro schools was undoubtedly a stigma. On the other hand, twelve of nineteen professionals who engineered or participated in the mob were lawyers. Unlike teaching, the law had high status as a lifetime profession, and by almost any standard lawyers ranked near the top of Cincinnati's social and occupational hierarchy.[8]

We gain additional insight into this matter if we push the analysis of our data a step further. Sidney Aronson, after considerable research into the problem of ranking various occupations, developed a twofold classification of high-ranking and middle-ranking occupations. His high-ranking category includes such occupations as landed gentry, merchant, banker, bank cashier, college president, professor, lawyer, minister, and doctor. His middle-ranking category includes occupations such as clerk, editor, shopkeeper, tavernkeeper, and teacher.[9] If we apply Aronson's classifications to our data, then the dissimilarity between abolitionists' and rioters' occupations becomes clearer. As the following chart indicates, a much higher percentage of high-ranking professional and commercial men rioted in both Cincinnati and Utica:

	Utica		Cincinnati	
	Mob (N = 78)	Abolitionists (N = 88)	Mob (N = 49)	Abolitionists (N = 26)
High-ranking Commercial and Professional Men	37%	20%	45%	23%

Using occupation as the major index of status undoubtedly has some drawbacks. Some lawyers have power and prestige; others

[8] In 1838, for example, only 7 per cent of Cincinnati's taxpayers had property evaluated at $5,000 or more. Nine of the twelve lawyers who rioted belonged to this select group.

[9] *Status and Kinship in the Higher Civil Service* (Cambridge, Massachusetts, 1964).

are regarded as shysters or thieves. Similarly, some merchants are rich and influential; others are improvident. Nevertheless, occupation was the means by which Uticans and Cincinnatians usually identified and placed one another. Other evidence, moreover, indicates that Aronson's occupation index does not enhance the status and prestige of the rioters. It may, however, enhance the position of the abolitionists.

Consider again the case of Cincinnati. Daniel Aaron, after an intensive study of the city from 1818 to 1838, compiled a list of 161 men who dominated the city's economic, political, social, and cultural life. None of the abolitionists, but twenty-six of the rioters —or 53 per cent of my sample—appear among this select group.[10] The 1838 tax list reveals that 7 per cent of some 2,500 taxpayers held 50 per cent of the city's real estate value. Among this group of rich Cincinnatians were fifteen rioters (31 per cent of the sample), as compared to two abolitionists (8 per cent).[11] In Cincinnati, then, the contemporary phrase "gentlemen of property and standing" was indeed more than a cliché; it reflected to a significant extent the composition of the mob.

Consider also the case of Utica. For that city we have neither a tax list nor a subjective evaluation by a prominent historian. But we do have a complete list of the men who held city-wide offices from 1817 to 1840. This list includes such esteemed positions as mayor, city treasurer, overseer of the poor, city attorney, trustee, alderman, and supervisor. Twenty-four rioters (31 per cent of the sample) held one or more of these offices, as compared to six abolitionists (7 per cent).[12] In Utica, then, the phrase "gentlemen of property and standing" also reflected reality.

[10] "Cincinnati, 1818–1838: A Study of Attitudes in the Urban West" (Unpub. Ph.D. dissertation, Harvard, 1942), appendix.

[11] In making this computation, I included Joseph Graham, who led the mob, and Christian and William Donaldson, merchants who financed the Cincinnati Anti-Slavery Society. Their holdings, however, do not appear as individual entries in the tax list; rather, they appear as corporate or combined entries. But since these combined holdings were substantial and these men dominated their combinations, I placed them in the élite category.

[12] Computed from data in *Charter and Ordinances of the City of Utica* (Utica, 1902), vi–xviii.

In both mobs, moreover, the high-ranking men were closely identified with the mercantile economy of Jeffersonian and early Jacksonian America. They were generally lawyers, bankers, financiers, or merchants, rather than doctors or ministers. In their biographical sketches certain standard phrases recur: "an old-style merchant," "a merchant in the best New England tradition," "a merchant of the old school," "a gentleman-merchant." High-ranking abolitionists, on the other hand, frequently were doctors or ministers; many were merchants; but only three were lawyers, and none was a banker or a financier. For Utica the occupational differences between the two groups are clear:

	Mob	Abolitionists
Lawyer	12	2
Banker, Financier	4	—
Merchant	10	7
Doctor	1	2
Minister	—	7

In Cincinnati two ministers sided with the mob; otherwise the pattern is similar:

	Mob	Abolitionists
Lawyer	12	1
Banker, Financier	2	—
Merchant	6	3
Doctor	—	2
Minister	2	—

Strong ties with the old-style mercantile economy may even have divided individual families. Consider, for example, the case of Oliver and Edmund Wetmore. Born and reared in New England, they claimed to be descendants of both Henry Brewster and Jonathan Edwards; both were staunch Presbyterians and "Puritans of the strictest type"; both were regarded as "kind-hearted, but tenacious and inflexible." Yet the Reverend Oliver Wetmore became a zealous abolitionist and the corresponding secretary of the Utica

Anti-Slavery Society. And his thirty-seven-year-old son, Edmund, whose law career was tied closely to the mercantile and banking interests, became one of the most active members of the Utica mob.[13] Whether Edmund Wetmore's occupational ties and interests had any direct bearing upon his riotous behavior is uncertain. But it is clear that men like him who had enduring ties with the old-style market economy were more likely to become rioters than abolitionists.

Such men, however, were less likely to have any identification with skilled labor or nascent industrialism. Many abolitionists were manufacturers, and many more were artisans such as chairmakers, coppersmiths, glassmakers, printers, harnessmakers, blacksmiths, carpenters, and joiners. Some rioters were artisans, but only three were manufacturers. The following chart for Utica illustrates vividly why some abolitionists had so much faith in "the bone and muscle of society":

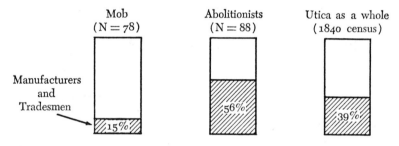

In the Cincinnati Anti-Slavery Society there were many skilled craftsmen and tradesmen. But not many of these men were among the leadership or active nucleus. Thus the following chart for Cincinnati probably minimizes the occupational differences between the rioters and the abolitionists; nevertheless, there is still some

[13] Moses M. Bagg, *Pioneers of Utica* (Utica, 1877), 532–35, 157–60; Henry J. Cookingham, *History of Oneida County* (2 vols.; Chicago, 1912), Vol. I, p. 520; *Utica City Directory, 1833–1834*, 176; First Presbyterian Church, Miscellaneous Papers, Uticana Collection, Utica Historical Society; *Brief History of the First Presbyterian Church & Society in Utica* (Utica, 1829); *Catalogue of the Resident Members of the First Presbyterian Church, Utica* (Utica, 1841); Manuscript Census Returns—Utica, 1840 and 1850, National Archives.

disparity between the two, and there is enormous disparity between the rioters and their fellow Cincinnatians:

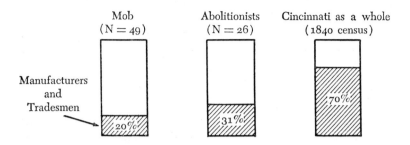

The rioters, then, lived in an age of growing industrialization, yet they had less attachment to manufacturing than did either the abolitionists or their fellow townsmen. Their biographical sketches indicate that some of the wealthier rioters eventually adjusted to the new economy, but that many—probably a majority—never quite adapted to a society that was beginning to be dominated by manufacturing as well as trade.

If the rioters were frequently prominent men of trade or of the bar, it is scarcely astonishing to find that many of them were in their thirties or forties. At the time of the disturbances, the median age for the men in both mobs was thirty-seven. The median age of the Utica abolitionists was forty-one; of the Cincinnati abolitionists, thirty-six. Thus both anti-abolitionist violence and antislavery were responses of mature men.

It is also hardly astonishing to find that many of the rioters were descendants of old and distinguished families. To be sure, the shopkeepers and clerks who rioted generally came from very ordinary families; most of their fathers were substantial citizens—farmers or small businessmen—but neither wealthy nor influential. In the biographical sketches of twenty-nine rioters, however, it was pointed out that the father in each case was a man of considerable wealth and importance. Six fathers were bankers or merchants; four were landed gentry; four were United States senators or congressmen; a few were ministers or doctors, and several were simply described as "rich" or "very wealthy." One of the "very wealthy" fathers left his son $400,000, and another lost nearly $100,000 during the Panic of 1837.

The ancestors of the abolitionists, on the other hand, were generally less distinguished. Only eight fathers of antislavery men were described as men of prominence, and only one had ever held a major public office. As far as I can tell, the fathers of the abolitionists generally worked with their hands. Only two were day laborers, but many were farmers, and many more were artisans. The antislavery artisans, as one would expect, were generally sons of artisans. But several of the antislavery merchants and professionals were also sons of artisans. These sons of craftsmen may have been anxious about the declining status of skilled labor and craftsmanship in an age of growing industrialization and sweatshop oppression, but it would be far-fetched to suggest that they belonged to a "displaced social élite" who wished to re-exert its former social dominance in Northern society. The fathers of the abolitionists could never have lost positions of community leadership and social dominance to the *nouveaux riche;* they could never have been elbowed aside as leaders by money-grubbing merchants or manufacturing tycoons. Too few of them had ever had positions of social dominance; too few of them had ever had esteemed positions to lose to the *nouveaux riche.* Many of the fathers, in fact, either never set foot in the United States or were first-generation immigrants.

While about 85 per cent of the rioters could trace their American ancestry back at least three generations, one-third of the abolitionists in both Utica and Cincinnati were born abroad. One abolitionist was born in Jamaica; another, in Catholic Ireland; but the rest were born in Protestant Britain. The foreign-born Uticans were usually Welshmen, and the foreign-born Cincinnatians were usually Englishmen. As the following chart indicates, four times as many Utica abolitionists were foreign-born; eight times as many Cincinnati abolitionists: [14]

[14] The statistics for Utica should not be taken too literally; I found the country of birth for only 74 per cent of my sample. Cincinnati is a different story; there I found the country of birth for all but one member of my

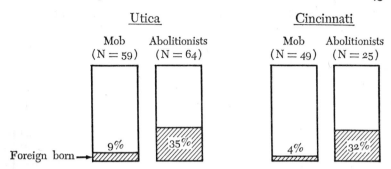

Utica

Cincinnati

Mob (N = 59)   Abolitionists (N = 64)   Mob (N = 49)   Abolitionists (N = 25)

Foreign born → 9%   35%   4%   32%

Violent anti-abolitionists thus were much more likely to be, as they put it, "of good American stock." This fact, in turn, partly explains why they constantly harped on the theme that organized antislavery was an alien movement, a foreign conspiracy, a British plot.

If we push our analysis of the data a step further, we gain an additional insight about the possible influences of British versus American upbringing. Once we distinguish between occupational categories such as "manufacturers and tradesmen" and "commercial men and professionals," it appears that antislavery artisans and manufacturers were more likely to be British-born than were professionals and businessmen. The following chart for Cincinnati illustrates this tendency:

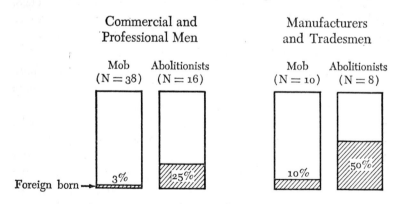

Commercial and Professional Men

Manufacturers and Tradesmen

Mob (N = 38)   Abolitionists (N = 16)   Mob (N = 10)   Abolitionists (N = 8)

Foreign born → 3%   25%   10%   50%

sample. (The Cincinnati directories of 1825 and 1839–1840 listed the country of birth for each citizen.)

Data for Utica give us a stronger illustration of this tendency:

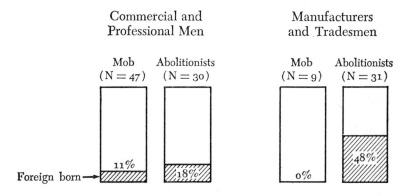

The abolitionists, then, included among their ranks a greater percentage not only of manufacturers and tradesmen but also of British-born manufacturers and tradesmen. The rioters, on the other hand, were more likely to be high-ranking commercial and professional men of old American stock, deeply aware of their place in society. These men felt a deeper kinship and responsibility than did most abolitionists for the older mercantile America. It was primarily their America, rather than the abolitionists' America, that was being jarred and disrupted by the rising industrialism and the bustling democracy of the 1830's. It was mainly their class, rather than the abolitionists' class, that faced the possibility of becoming an élite without a following.

These well-established men of old American stock were born and reared primarily in the Northeastern states. In Utica, where the population was overwhelmingly Yankee and Yorker, this fact is hardly startling. But in Cincinnati, where the population included a substantial number of Southerners, this fact has some significance. In 1839 the origin of 15 per cent of some 10,000 men listed in the city directory was Southern; 18 per cent of the men in the 1836 mob came from Southern states, as compared to 8 per cent of the local abolitionists. In contrast, 33 per cent of the men in the directory came from one of the Northeastern states; 73 per cent of the rioters came from these states, as compared to 56 per cent of the abolitionists.[15] Thus the Cincinnati mob was scarcely composed of demented Southerners.

These rioting descendants of old Northeastern families were generally "high church." They were not, of course, always "high church" as antislavery men insisted, but they did tend to be "conservatists of forms, powers, creeds, usages" in church matters. In Utica, where the great evangelist Charles Grandison Finney had had unusual impact, most of the churches in the 1830's were evangelical. As far as I can tell, only the Episcopal Church can safely be described as "high church." But even if we concern ourselves only with Episcopalians and non-Episcopalians, the division between the rioters and the abolitionists is clear. Twenty-nine rioters (37 per cent of the sample) were Episcopalians, but only two abolitionists were (2 per cent). But perhaps "high church" was merely a reflection of high social status. If we hold high-ranking and middle-ranking occupations constant, we find this very improbable.

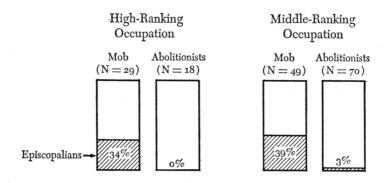

Similarly, if we hold occupational categories constant, we also find that "high church" affected riotous behavior:

---

15 *Cincinnati Directory for 1840* (Cincinnati, 1839), 484; data for the Northeastern states break down as follows:

	Cincinnati	Mob	Abolitionists
New England states	9%	26%	16%
Middle Atlantic states	24%	47%	40%

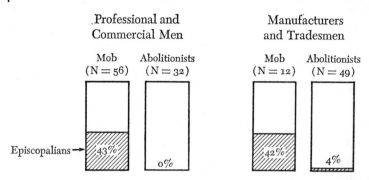

The affect of "high church" is particularly striking in the case of the foreign-born. All four of the British-born rioters were Episcopalians, but none of the twenty-two abolitionists was a member of his native country's established church.[16]

In Cincinnati the division between "high" and "low" churchmen was less pronounced. By abolitionist standards, however, at least two of the city's Protestant churches can safely be described as "high." One was the Episcopal Church, and the other was Joshua Lacy Wilson's First Presbyterian Church. Like its strong-willed and domineering pastor of nearly thirty years, First Church was Old School Presbyterian to the core; of the city's Protestant churches only the Episcopal placed more emphasis on formality and ritual in religious observance, and none placed more stress on ministerial authority. Thus to most of the city's would-be abolitionists, Wilson's church was anathema years before he denounced them from his pulpit.[17] In the mid-1830's one abolitionist was a

[16] The foreign-born abolitionists were Baptists, Methodists, and Presbyterians. My analysis, incidentally, confirms the traditional identification of antislavery with New Light Presbyterianism. Forty-three abolitionists (49 per cent of the sample) were Presbyterians, as compared with twelve rioters (15 per cent). But I have no evidence to support the hypothesis that the abolitionists were Finney converts. Almost all of them, to be sure, were members of evangelical Presbyterian churches—but long before Finney came to Utica.

[17] For Wilson and his church, see R. L. Hightower, *Joshua L. Wilson, Frontier Controversialist* (Chicago, 1934); *One Hundred and Fifty Years of Presbyterianism in the Ohio Valley, 1790–1940* (Cincinnati, 1940); Edward D. Mansfield, *Personal Memories* (Cincinnati, 1879), 150–51. Some of the would-be abolitionists became members of Lyman Beecher's Second Presby-

member of First Church, and one English-born antislavery man was an Episcopalian. Six rioters, on the other hand, were members of First Church, and six were Episcopalians. Thus twelve anti-abolitionists were "high church" men (24 per cent of the sample), as compared with two abolitionists (8 per cent).

In both Cincinnati and Utica, most of the riotous believers were zealous churchmen. A few, to be sure, may have been merely pew-warmers. But at one time or another, one Episcopalian rioter was a church organist, and nineteen others were either wardens or vestrymen. These men thus had more than a casual commitment to "high church" creeds, forms, and usages; they were among their city's staunchest "high church" men.

While most rioters and abolitionists apparently followed the faith of their fathers, about a dozen men in each group wandered from one church to another seeking a spiritual home. The paths that these pilgrims followed are particularly noteworthy. The rioters always moved toward churches that stressed the importance of ministerial authority, sacraments, and ritual. The abolitionists, on the other hand, always moved in the opposite direction; they moved toward churches that emphasized the conversion experience and evangelical doctrine. Typical was the case of the Snyder brothers. Both Snyders, sons of a Dutch immigrant, were about forty-five years old at the time of the Utica mob. Jacob manufactured chairs, while Rudolph manufactured and sold cabinetware. Both were prosperous, and both were staunch churchmen. Thirty years before, both had been members of the Methodist Episcopal Church. But by 1835, Jacob, an abolitionist, had turned his home into a haven for traveling evangelists and had become a "free" Methodist. And Rudolph, who was largely responsible for the mob that covered brother Jacob "with the filth of misbegotten fowls,"

terian Church; others were instrumental in forming the Sixth Presbyterian Church in 1831. For insight into the tone and structure of these churches, see *Act of Incorporation of the "Second Presbyterian Church"* (Cincinnati, 1829); Vine Street Congregational Church [formerly Sixth Presbyterian Church], Minutes of the Board of Trustees and Manuscript Record Book—both in the Cincinnati Historical Society.

had become a warden in the Trinity Episcopal Church.[18] Thus in
the bustling world of Jacksonian America, violent anti-abolitionists
tended to favor churches where one's position was ascribed and
certain—rather than dependent on such uncertainties as a conversion experience or the indwelling of the Holy Spirit.

While I have found plenty of information about the religious af-
filiations of both the rioters and the abolitionists, I have discovered
the political identification of only 59 per cent of the rioters and 28
per cent of the abolitionists. From the information I have, however, two facts seem clear. One is that political affiliation was
probably *not* an independent variable. In Utica, where impression-
istic evidence strongly indicates that merchants, bankers, and Episcopalians were predominantly Jacksonian, I estimate that at least
60 per cent of the rioters were Jacksonian.[19] But in Cincinnati,
where Daniel Aaron's analysis indicates that prominent men were
generally Whig, I estimate that at least 60 per cent of the rioters
were Whig.[20]

The second fact is that the rioters, regardless of their political
persuasion, had a much stronger commitment than the abolitionists to one of the existing parties. In their biographical sketches,
phrases such as "staunch Whig," "unwavering Democrat," "zealous
Van Buren man" constantly recur. Abolitionists, on the other hand,
are frequently designated as politically indifferent: several were
"probably Whig in principle"; many "leaned" toward one party or
the other; some "once had been" Adams men, Clay men, or Jackson men; and a few switched parties "frequently." Out of the entire group, I found only seven antislavery men whose political
identification was regarded as "strong," "staunch," "zealous," or
"firm." [21]

---

[18] Bagg, *Pioneers of Utica*, 226–27, 252–53, 257; *Utica City Directory for
1833–1834*, 165; The Reverend John Harding, ed., *One Hundred Years of
Trinity Church* (Utica, 1898), 137.

[19] I have the political preference for thirty-nine rioters; twenty-seven (69
per cent) were Jacksonian.

[20] Aaron, "Cincinnati," Appendix and *passim;* I have the political preference for thirty-six rioters; twenty-four (67 per cent) were Whig.

[21] Four were Whig; three, Jacksonian. On the basis of the limited information that I have, I estimate that about 60 per cent of the abolitionists in both

It is hardly astonishing, then, to find that the rioters were much more likely than the abolitionists to be members of the local political establishment. About half the rioters in both cities belonged to the courthouse clique. At least thirty-two men in the Utica mob (41 per cent of the sample) held one or more city, county, state, or federal officers during the 1830's, while at least seventeen men in the Cincinnati mob (35 per cent) held one or more similar offices. In contrast, the Utica abolitionists included in their ranks three city aldermen, and the Cincinnati abolitionists, one magistrate.

Thus the typical anti-abolition mob consisted largely of "gentlemen of property and standing"—lawyers, politicians, merchants, shopkeepers, and bankers whose careers were identified not only with the mercantile economy of preindustrial America, but also with the local political establishment. This fact, in turn, partly explains why anti-abolitionists harped on the theme that the Union, the Republic, and all American institutions were in grave danger. Organized antislavery, as countless historians have pointed out, obviously threatened the constitutional compromise with slavery and the institutions that were built upon it. The national party system, for example, undoubtedly rested on a tacit agreement to foreclose discussion of the slavery question. If the antislavery movement obviously threatened this understanding, as most men claimed, then the élites who ran the system certainly would have been among those who felt most threatened.

Indeed, viewed in the light of their personal characteristics, these thirty- and forty-year-old men were not improbable rioters. Who else had stronger motives for engineering mobs, for destroying presses, or for breaking up antislavery meetings? If men feared that organized antislavery undermined traditional patterns of power and influence, that it systematically bypassed local élites and appealed directly to all men, women, and children, that it threatened customary forms of deference, then these men—more than others—were ripe for violent anti-abolitionism. Reared for traditional leadership, attracted to "high church" forms and usages, entrenched in local offices, these men faced an obvious threat to

cities "leaned" toward Whiggism. Of the thirty-two abolitionists whose political preference I have identified, eighteen (56 per cent) were Whig.

both their leadership and their traditional values. Not only did the abolitionists, with their centralized organization and systematic agitation, threaten to disrupt the polity and to transfer leadership to the "wrong" groups in society, but by their effective use of revivalistic and mass-media techniques they personified the very forces that anti-abolitionists thought were most threatening in Northern society. Basically, then, the typical anti-abolitionist mob should be regarded as an attempt by an aggrieved class to protect its social dominance and to reinforce its traditional values.

III

Let us turn now from typical anti-abolitionist mobs to the atypical New York City mob of 1834. Who participated in the July riot? What manner of men demolished churches and razed the Negro quarters? Abolitionists, we may recall, insisted that William Leete Stone of the *Commercial Advertiser* and James Watson Webb of the *Courier and Enquirer* were responsible for stirring up this mob. But they also maintained that "the sweepings of society," rather than Northern "aristocrats" or hard-handed mechanics and workingmen, did the dirty work. As we have just seen, their appraisals about the composition of respectable mobs were basically sound. But have they left us with equally sound assessments of lower-class mobs?

To gain insight about the composition of the New York City mob, I compiled a list of ninety-four rioters—largely, but not entirely, from records of arrests, reports of judicial proceedings, and similar sources. Although the authorities generally recorded at least the occupations and the residences of those whom they arrested, I found it necessary in numerous instances to ascertain such information either from Thomas Longworth's *New York City Directory* or from newspaper accounts. Usually I was unable to find accurate information about age or birthplace.

Drawing conclusions from such data is undoubtedly far better, as Rudé insists, than relying on the usual imprecise identifications of mobs as "rabble" or "scum." Nevertheless, records of arrests and judicial accounts obviously present their own problems of bias. Who was deliberately ignored by the police? And who was arrested, but not booked? It is probably indicative, for example, that newsmen frequently maintained that a well-known civic official was arrested for rioting at Ludlow's church, but that the police booked no one who was connected with the local administration. It also seems strange that none of the men who posted bail ever stood trial, and that the men who received stiff sentences were either well-known thieves practicing their trade under ideal circumstances or sailors without a fixed residence. There are ample grounds, therefore, for believing that status and influence played their usual roles in determining whose name got on the police blotter. Accordingly, the statistics that I present should not be taken too literally; men of property and standing may be underrepresented.

Although the police may have systematically overlooked the "better sort" of rioter, there is little reason to believe that they systematically neglected the thieves, vagrants, pimps, and dregs of New York society. It is noteworthy, therefore, that only four of the rioters were known to the police, and only two were paupers. The press paid undue attention to these men, but it is clear that the "dangerous classes" played only a minor part in the riot.

The abolitionists, as well as most of New York's newspapers, badly misjudged the composition of the mob. To be sure, only one high-ranking professional and only a handful of small businessmen and clerks were among those arrested. But for every unskilled and semiskilled laborer arrested, almost twice as many skilled laborers were arrested. The common laborer, or day laborer, was unquestionably at the bottom of the white occupational hierarchy. He was at the mercy of the casual labor market; he had to take his chances daily in the competition for temporary employment; and more than any other white workingman he had to compete with the Negro for work. Yet surprisingly few common laborers were arrested. The typical arrestee stood far above the common laborer in the occupational hierarchy. He had a special skill; he had a vocation, rather than a mere job; frequently he was either a shoemaker, a mason, a carpenter, a tailor, a brassfounder, a baker, a blacksmith, or a printer. He had little reason to fear black competition, for precious few Negroes followed any of these vocations.[22] Yet, as the following table indicates, skilled laborers and their sons outnumbered both semiskilled and unskilled laborers combined: [23]

Professional and Commercial Men		17% of sample
Skilled Laborers and Tradesmen		45%
Men	36%	
Sons	9%	
Semiskilled and Unskilled		24%
Paupers and Criminals		4%
Unknowns		10%

Why did such men riot? One essential reason is that they lived within easy walking distance of the principal targets. If we pinpoint the residences of arrestees on a map, we find that very few rioters journeyed across town either to attack "amalgamationist" churches or to torment Negroes. Most of the principal targets were in the Fifth, Sixth, and Eighth wards. Half the arrestees lived in one of these three wards: 11 per cent lived in the Fifth Ward; 16 per cent in the Sixth; and 21 per cent in the Eighth. The only other ward to have a substantial percentage of arrestees—15 per

[22] It was probably easier, as Frederick Douglass claimed, for a Negro to find employment for his son in a lawyer's office than in a blacksmith's shop. Cf. Douglass, *The Life and Times of Frederick Douglass* (Hartford, Connecticut, 1884), 259–63; Philip Foner, ed., *The Life and Writings of Frederick Douglass* (4 vols.; New York, 1950–1955), Vol. I, p. 24; Vol. II, p. 234; American Union for the Relief and Improvement of the Colored Race, *Report of the Executive Committee* (Boston, 1836), 17 and *passim;* Leo H. Hirsch, Jr., "The Negro and New York, 1783–1865," *Journal of Negro History* 16 (October 1931), 434 ff.; Litwack, *North of Slavery,* Chapter V.

[23] The skilled labor category includes 6 shoemakers, 6 masons or stonecutters, 4 carpenters, 4 tailors, 3 bakers, 2 blacksmiths, 2 printers, 2 brassfounders, 1 machinist, 1 cardmaker, 1 cooper, 1 hatter, 1 plasterer, 1 sailmaker, 1 harnessmaker, 1 blindmaker, 1 dyer, 1 horseshoemaker, 1 dockmaster, 1 confectioner, and 1 master mariner. The semiskilled and unskilled category includes 13 sailors, 2 carters, 2 day laborers, 2 dock laborers, 1 boatman, 1 drayman, 1 cook, 1 stevedore. I suspect that the "unknowns" were mainly youths. Some of the "men" were in their late teens or early twenties.

cent—was the Tenth; it bordered the riot zone. Thus, as the map below illustrates, Negroes and abolitionists suffered primarily from unfriendly neighbors.[24]

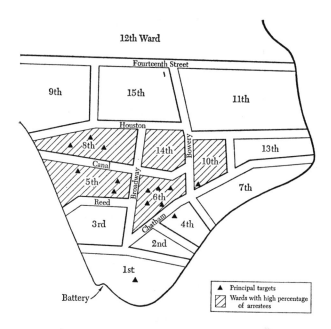

These unfriendly wards—with the notable exception of the Tenth—had much in common. Although the assessed valuation of both real and personal property indicates that the Tenth Ward's per capita wealth was very low, the per capita wealth of the three other wards was neither very low nor very high; it ranged from middle to lower-middle ranking.[25] Despite this middle-class char-

[24] In pinpointing the residences of the rioters, I relied on a ward and street map drawn by D. H. Burr for *New York As It Is, in 1835* (New York, 1835). Then (as now) the street numbers followed no conceivable plan and had no relation to block intersections. Fortunately, Longworth's *New York City Directory* included a table for locating street numbers.

[25] The assessed valuation of neither real nor personal property, of course, can really be equated with income. Much of the real property in New York City belonged to absentee landlords like John Jacob Astor, and most of the skilled and unskilled laborers probably lived in rented dwellings; to some

acteristic, living space was at a premium; the city's population
nearly doubled between 1825 and 1835, and not only the impover-
ished Tenth Ward but also the moderately wealthy wards were
crowded and congested.[26]

Only one characteristic, however, really distinguished the riotous wards from the other congested but moderately prosperous
wards of Lower Manhattan: [27] most of the city's wards had only a
few black residents, but the four riotous wards contained over half
the black population. The median for the less violent wards was 4
per cent Negro, while the median for the riotous wards was over
10 per cent Negro. By our standards, of course, none of New
York's wards had a large black population, but by ante-bellum
New York standards the Fifth, Sixth, and Eighth wards seemed
overrun with blacks. The very poor Tenth Ward, which was only 5
per cent Negro, differed little from the city's norm; but the other
three wards, which ranged between 10 and 11 per cent Negro, had
the highest percentage of blacks in the city.[28]

Thus in the midst of large numbers of middle and lower-middle
class whites, some 6,500 blacks huddled together in poverty and
desperation. In the light of this fact, it is easy to understand why

extent, however, property values probably determined rent and thus can be
considered as one indication of income and social class. A better index is
probably the assessed valuation of personal property. The median valuation of personal property in the less riotous wards was $179 per capita;
in the more violent wards, $165 per capita. Computed from data, Edwin
Williams, *New York Annual Register* (New York, 1836), 315, 320.

[26] Cf. Williams, *New York Annual Register* (New York, 1834), 276, with
Williams, *New York Annual Register* (New York, 1835), 312–13.

[27] Over all, the differences between the riotous and the less riotous wards
are not particularly striking. In terms of medians, the differences are as
follows:

	Males Eligible to Vote	Male Aliens	Tammany Supporters
Riotous wards	33.0%	18.7%	52.2%
Other wards	33.8%	21.7%	53.0%

Computed from data, Williams, *New York Annual Register* (1834), 279;
Williams, *New York Annual Register* (1836), 320.

[28] Computed from data, Williams, *New York Annual Register* (1836), 320.

so many middle-ranking whites rioted. If the dread of amalgamation—rather than the fear of cheap Negro labor—was the central issue, if men believed that Arthur Tappan and his colleagues planned to "mulattoize our posterity," then these men were ripe for anti-Negro and anti-abolitionist violence. Given their immediate environment, it would probably be *their* posterity, rather than someone else's, who would be mulattoized. Given their immediate environment, it would probably be *their* womenfolk, rather than someone else's, who would bear the black man's children.

IV

Abolitionists thus erred in their appraisal of what epitomized the lower-class mob, but they were surprisingly accurate in their dissection of the more typical anti-abolitionist mob. We may regard the New York rioters as morally debauched, but they hardly represented "the sweepings of society," as antislavery men claimed. They were, on the average, very ordinary citizens who despised Negroes and dreaded the thought of miscegenation.

The more typical anti-abolition mob, whom the abolitionists seem to have known well, differed markedly from the lower-class mob. The rioters were rarely tradesmen or artisans; instead they were largely professional and commercial men. Many, as antislavery men insisted, were "gentlemen of property and standing" who regarded organized antislavery as a threat to their élite status. They were preservers of traditional forms, powers, and usages, and thus they deeply feared the invasion and development of mass media techniques, systematic agitation, and centralized organization and control. These forces, which organized antislavery so strongly personified, not only threatened their élite status and moral leadership but also undermined their values and traditions; these forces, said one anti-abolitionist spokesman after another, heralded the destruction of an older America.

6

Decline of Violence

Violent anti-abolitionism reached high tide between 1834 and 1837. After 1837, Northern anti-abolitionist mobs became less frequent. In May, 1838, a mob of well-dressed Philadelphians burned down Pennsylvania Hall and razed the city's Negro quarters, while thousands of citizens watched and enjoyed the spectacle. In December, 1839, a Connecticut mob "burnt to ashes" an antislavery meeting house in Wolcott. Other New Englanders frequently mobbed the most eccentric of all abolitionists, Stephen Symonds Foster, in the early 1840's. Hoosiers clubbed and severely injured the famous Negro abolitionist, Frederick Douglass, at Pendleton, Indiana, in 1843. In 1847 a Harrisburg audience listened attentively while Garrison spoke, but disrupted the meeting by throwing firecrackers, cayenne pepper, stones, garbage, and rotten eggs when Douglass began to speak. And in 1850 the notorious Isaiah Rynders and his Empire Club made a farce out of the annual meeting of the Garrisonians at New York. As a result of these and dozens of similar incidents, antislavery men received an enormous amount of publicity and sympathy.

Nevertheless the day of the anti-abolitionist mob had largely disappeared. Between January 1834 and December 1837, *Niles'*

Register reported thirty-one anti-abolition and racial incidents throughout the nation, but in the next twelve years it recorded only sixteen incidents.[1] Similarly, the three leading antislavery papers—the *Liberator*, the *Emancipator*, and the *Philanthropist*—reported 157 Northern mobs between 1834 and 1837, but only 48 mobs in the subsequent years. As the following table indicates, the ebbtide of Northern mobs came in 1838: [2]

1834	15 incidents reported
1835	37
1836	64
1837	41
1838	4
1839	4
1840	4

Why *then?* Why did violent anti-abolitionism subside so rapidly? Did Northerners, as Russel B. Nye argues, suddenly realize that mobs endangered "the traditional right of the citizen to express his opinion"? Did they come to regard abolitionists "as guardians of white liberties, as well as crusaders for those of blacks"? Was the threat of mob violence to free discussion "a significant factor in cementing support in the North for the antislavery movement"? [3] Or were there other causes for the ebbing of anti-abolitionist violence?

II

Basically, there were four causes for the ebbing of anti-abolitionist violence. The most important of these grew out of the difficulties that the American Anti-Slavery Society experienced during the Panic of 1837. As early as January, 1837, the New York associates had to limit severely their gratuitous distributions of antislavery pamphlets and newspapers. On May 1, the abolitionists lost one of

[1] Computed from data, *Niles' Register*, Vols. 44–75.
[2] Computed from data, *Liberator, Emancipator, Philanthropist.*
[3] Nye, *Fettered Freedom*, 218 and Chapter V.

their principal sources of revenue when Arthur Tappan and Company had to suspend payment. On May 17, the Agency Committee informed its agents that "in the present state of things, it will be impossible for the Committee to sustain their agencies, unless each agent collects an amount sufficient to pay his salary and expenses." As a result, the number of antislavery agents declined from sixty in the winter of 1836–1837 to nineteen the following winter. By May, 1838, the society was so hard pressed for money that it decided to keep only ten of its fifteen remaining agents. Thus the task of forming new auxiliaries and expanding the movement was turned over almost entirely to "local agents" who were untrained, but who were willing to give their spare time to the cause.[4]

To make matters worse, the state societies—led by Massachusetts and New York—took this opportunity to declare their independence. In May, 1838, the Massachusetts Society took over operations within its domain, pledging $10,000 to the national treasury. In August, the New York Society followed suit, also pledging $10,000. About the same time similar steps were also taken by the Vermont and Connecticut societies. The state societies, as one might expect, generally failed to fulfill their pledges during the lean years, and dissension and friction among abolitionists increased accordingly.[5] Thus languished the American Anti-Slavery Society, which had once personified centralized organization and concerted action.

Lack of money, of trained agents, and of unity affected adversely the drive to "organize Anti-Slavery Societies . . . in every city, town and village in our land." [6] In 1836–1837, the national

[4] American Anti-Slavery Society, Agency Committee Minutes, meetings of December 20, 1836–May 8, 1838; *Emancipator*, May 11, 18, October 19, 1837; John L. Myers, "The Agency System of the Anti-Slavery Movement, 1832, 1837, and its Antecedents in other Benevolent and Reform Societies" (Unpub. Ph.D. dissertation, University of Michigan, 1960), 665–67.

[5] *Liberator*, June 15, 1838; Utica *Friend of Man*, August 22, 1838; *Emancipator*, August 23, 1838. See also Henry B. Stanton to Amos Phelps, September 23, 1837; Elizur Wright to Phelps, October 29, 1837; William L. Chaplin to Phelps, March 13, 1838—Phelps Papers, Boston Public Library.

[6] "Declaration of Sentiments," in Louis Ruchames, ed., *The Abolitionists: A Collection of Their Writings* (New York, 1963), 82–83.

society and some 500 auxiliaries formed 479 new organizations;
but in 1837–1838, the combined efforts of the national society and
some 1,000 auxiliaries led to only 340 new units. The growth rate,
as the following table illustrates, decreased even more in
1838–1839: [7]

1835–1836	134% growth	(225 old auxiliaries/302 new)
1836–1837	91%	(527/479)
1837–1838	34%	(1,006/340)
1838–1839	24%	(1,346/304)

Organized antislavery's declining energy, plus the switch to "local
agents," also weakened all attempts to establish beachheads in
"new" localities. As a result, abolitionists tended to concentrate on
areas where organized antislavery was already established, at the
expense of vast areas where their movement was virtually un-
known. Thus many counties in Massachusetts and several in New
York and Ohio had more antislavery societies than many states.
Trumbull County, Ohio, for example, had more auxiliaries by
May, 1838, than the states of Rhode Island, New Jersey, Illinois,
Michigan, or Indiana.[8]

The curtailed expansion of antislavery societies is crucial to understanding why violent anti-abolitionism subsided after 1837. For
anti-abolition mobs, as we noted earlier, were largely responses to
intensive organizing—and particularly to intensive organizing in
its initial phase. Once antislavery agents stopped invading unorganized areas and thus stopped threatening established élites,
then the tension relaxed; "gentlemen of property and standing"
had little cause to form mobs, destroy presses, or break up anti-
slavery meetings.

The second reason for the decline of anti-abolitionist violence
holds mainly for townships and counties that often experienced in-

[7] Computed from data, American Anti-Slavery Society, *Second* through
Sixth Annual Reports.

[8] Computed from data, American Anti-Slavery Society, *Fifth Annual Report.* Of about 17,000 abolitionists in Ohio in 1839, Trumbull County had
2,249 enrolled members. See *Philanthropist,* May 7, 1839.

tensive organizing. Such counties and townships were rare, but in each case the pattern was similar. First the inhabitants became apprehensive; then some turned to violent opposition; and finally the opposition either acquiesced or became apathetic. Consider, for example, the pattern of challenge and response in Geauga County, Ohio. When Theodore Dwight Weld and John Watson Alvord invaded the Western Reserve in the fall and winter of 1835, they aroused suspicion and then hostility. In Geauga County the two men managed to form five societies, but only in the face of stiff and sometimes violent opposition. One mob, with tin horns, sleighbells, and drums, disrupted a ladies' meeting and threw eggs and garbage at the women. Another mob stoned a house in which Weld was staying. Still another mob repeatedly broke up Alvord's meetings, stoned him on his way to an inn, kidnaped him one night, took him to a tavern five miles away, and promised him a coat of tar and feathers if he ever came back. Yet the following winter, antislavery men again invaded the Reserve. They encountered violent opposition in neighboring Trumbull County, where their organizational drive was very intense, but they met only token opposition in forming eight societies in Geauga County.[9] Had organized antislavery remained energetic, had many counties become centers for sustained organizing, I suspect that this pattern of apprehension—resistance—exhaustion would have characterized much of the North.

The third explanation for the decline of violence is essentially Nye's. There are ample grounds for believing that many Northerners did become concerned about the traditional liberties of white men. Few, to be sure, reacted as strongly to mob rule as did William Jay, Gerrit Smith, William Ellery Channing, and Wendell Phillips. But many responded to the violent death of Lovejoy with anguish and concern. Newsmen across the North insisted repeat-

[9] *Emancipator,* October 20, 1835, January 1836; *Philanthropist,* March 18, 1836; Barnes and Dumond, *Weld-Grimké Letters,* Vol. I, pp. 237–39, 256–60; John L. Myers, "Antislavery Activities of Five Lane Seminary Boys in 1835–36," *Bulletin of the Historical and Philosophical Society of Ohio* 21 (April 1963), 99–100.

edly that freedom of discussion, freedom of assembly, and particularly freedom of the press were in grave danger. Lovejoy's murderers, as Thurlow Weed put it, had to be crushed or "this Republic will be convulsed to its center." [10]

This anguish and concern, as Nye argues, undoubtedly dampened the ardor of violent anti-abolitionists. Many rioters seemed to suffer from uneasy and divided consciences. Although they argued that organized antislavery was a menace to the Union and to social order, many readily agreed that slavery was either a sin, a great evil, or at least a black mark on a Christian and a democratic republic.[11] They insisted that organized antislavery had to be ground underfoot, yet most agreed that mobs were generally bad. Certainly Edmund Wetmore must have felt some guilt about being a member of a mob that attacked his father. And surely Rudolph Snyder must have had some qualms of conscience after his brother returned home so befouled. Such men, I suspect, never would have become rioters without the blessing of the dominant forces in their community. Once newspapers and civic leaders became concerned about traditional Anglo-Saxon liberties, men of this stamp not only lacked the necessary support to become rioters but also faced increasing pressure to remain peaceful.

It is a mistake, however, to assume that Northerners became concerned about the civil liberties of *all* white men. "The irruption of the disciples of Mormon into Missouri," as one reader reminded Weed, "produced violence. . . . But who thought of arousing the Union in defense of the rights of conscience?" Why was Lovejoy's murder "more than one hundred others" worthy of such alarm? [12] Forty or more Mormons died during the Mormon war of 1838;

---

[10] *Albany Evening Journal*, November 20, 1837, as quoted in "Selections from the Follett Papers, IV," *Quarterly Publication of the Historical and Philosophical Society of Ohio* 11 (January–March 1916), 11. See also Nye, *Fettered Freedom*, Chapter V.

[11] A psychologist might well argue that in some instances violent anti-abolitionism was a defense mechanism; some anti-abolitionists may have overreacted to organized antislavery to subdue guilt feelings about slavery.

[12] Oran Follett to Thurlow Weed, December 4, 1837, "Selections from the Follett Papers, IV," 13, 11–12.

dozens of men died during the nativist riots of the 1840's. Yet none of these blood baths produced one half as much anguish and concern as Lovejoy's murder. How do we account for this? Why did the word "martyr" come to be associated with the abolitionists?

There are undoubtedly several valid answers to this question, but perhaps a central one is the expertise of the abolitionists as communicators. They invariably turned the mobs to their own advantage and touched the guilt-laden consciences of many Northerners. Thus the Garrison mob, which in comparison to most nativist or anti-Mormon mobs was neither "major" nor "serious," has become legendary. Thus Lovejoy was scarcely dead before the New York associates commissioned his brothers to prepare a memoir. Antislavery men, insisted James Gordon Bennett (an expert in such matters), knew how to appeal to the public; they knew how to make the most of Lovejoy's death. "The details," said the New York editor, "cannot fail to be deeply interesting, and . . . with all the coloring and effect for which the scribes of the Abolitionists are so renowned," they will probably raise "an excitement superior to that of the Maria Monk affair." [13]

The fourth reason for the decline of violent anti-abolitionism was that the ground upon which one might hold antislavery views was tremendously broadened in the late 1830's and 1840's. Abolitionism became linked not only with freedom of the press and freedom of speech but also with other issues that had little to do with its own validity. One such issue was the right of petition. Antislavery petitions poured into the House of Representatives in such numbers that in 1836 a House resolution ordered that all such petitions be laid on the table without debate. As a result of this "gag," John Quincy Adams and many other men who were temperamentally too conservative to become abolitionists identified with the antislavery movement. One Virginian claimed that the battle against the gag rule made "more abolitionists in one year, by identifying the right of petition with the question of slavery, than the

13 New York *Herald*, March 29, 1838.

abolitionists would have made for themselves in twenty-five years." [14]

The broadest of all such issues was free soil. It involved antislavery, but its appeal was so widespread that by 1856 it could command political majorities in all but five of the Northern states. Free soil, in fact, attracted as diverse a following as did African colonization. Some men became free-soilers because they opposed slavery, or because they opposed its expansion. But others joined the free-soil ranks largely because they hated and feared Negroes. "Free soil," in the minds of such Northerners, meant "white only." Hatred of the Negro, argues Eugene Berwanger in a recent study, played a central role in the development of free-soilism in the Old Northwest, Iowa, California, Oregon, and Kansas. Racism, observes Eric Foner, permeated the Free Soil party far more than it did the earlier antislavery movement. By ante-bellum standards, to be sure, the racial attitudes of the Free-Soilers were advanced for their time, but by earlier antislavery standards the party's stance on the race question was retrogressive. Earlier antislavery programs always included an appeal for equal rights for free Negroes of the North; in the Free Soil platform, however, the equal-rights plank was conspicuously missing.[15] Antislavery thus became "respectable" partly at the expense of the free Negro.

It is hardly astonishing, then, to find that many vehement anti-abolitionists of the mid-1830's later became antislavery men. In 1835, for example, John Parker Hale of Dover, New Hampshire, disrupted a lecture series by the Reverend George Storrs. After the close of Storrs's third lecture, Hale rose "with manifest warmth,"

---

[14] Samuel Flagg Bemis, *John Quincy Adams and the Union* (New York, 1956), 326–83, 416–48; James M. McPherson, "The Fight Against the Gag Rule," *Journal of Negro History* 48 (July 1963), 177–95; Nye, *Fettered Freedom*, 32–53.

[15] Eugene H. Berwanger, *The Frontier Against Slavery* (Urbana, 1967); Eric Foner, "Racial Attitudes of the New York Free Soilers," *New York History* 46 (October 1965), 311–29; Foner, "Politics and Prejudice: The Free Soil Party and the Negro, 1849–1852," *Journal of Negro History* 50 (October 1965), 239–56.

insisted that antislavery newspapers and pamphlets were "insurrectionary," and concluded that Negro slaves "ARE BEASTS IN HUMAN SHAPE, AND NOT FIT TO LIVE." Then, after a short pause, he added in a barely audible voice: "free." So turbulent was the subsequent demonstration that Storrs canceled his concluding lecture. Years later, Hale admitted that he had acted "as Saint Paul did before his conversion"; but "when light did shine" upon him, he altered his views; he thus became the Liberty party's standard-bearer in 1847 and the Free Soil party's presidential candidate in 1852.[16] Similarly, Orsamus B. Matteson participated in the Utica mob of 1835; years later, he became one of the most radical of the Radical Republicans, a close political associate of Hale, Benjamin Wade, Joshua Giddings, and Thaddeus Stevens.[17]

The "light" even shown on James Watson Webb, the most vehement of all anti-abolitionists in the mid-1830's. Webb, who had demanded in 1835 that Arthur Tappan and his "modern haberdashers of murderous negro tracts" be crushed underfoot like "reptilian eggs," became a free-soiler in the early 1850's. He never pretended to change his opinion of the Negro; slavery, as far as he was concerned, was "a great blessing" to the Negro, but it was "a curse to the country where it exists, and utterly demoralizing to the people who tolerate it." Thus the "reckless slaveholder" who wished to extend this curse threatened the well-being of the Northern white man. Both slaves and Negroes, argued Webb, must be kept out of both the North and the territories, and the free Northern Negro should be deported—perhaps to Brazil or Latin America. Meanwhile, the "Slave Power" must be "crushed." How much longer "can we be bullied, whipped and 'kicked,' into any course or policy which they may please to dictate to us"? Will the North, "acting under the lash of the Slave Power," willingly submit to Southern impudence and bullying? Or will manly Northerners

[16] *Congressional Globe*, 31 Congress, 1 Session (1849–1850), Appendix, 798–803; Richard H. Sewell, *John P. Hale and the Politics of Abolition* (Cambridge, Massachusetts, 1965), 32.

[17] Cookingham, *History of Oneida County*, Vol. I, pp. 252–54; *Biographical Directory of the American Congress, 1774–1961* (Washington, D. C., 1961), 1276.

"vindicate their right to freedom of speech" and drive slavery back "into the fens and marshes where it properly belongs"? Time, as one cynic put it, had brought some "strange changes" to the anti-slavery movement.[18]

III

Anti-abolitionist violence thus passed. But mob violence raised its head again in the mid-1840's and then again in the mid-1850's. There were not, to be sure, as many mobs in the mid-1840's as there had been in the 1830's. But the daily newspapers repeatedly carried lurid and shocking accounts of the anti-rent wars in up-state New York, the nativist riots in Philadelphia, the bank riot in Cincinnati, and the Mormon wars in Illinois.

Whether these later mobs should be regarded as attempts to sustain or to re-exert the ideals and forms of an older America is uncertain. Whether these rioters saw their targets as the embodiment of forces that threatened an established way of life, has yet to be explored. It is clear, however, that the Northern anti-abolition mobs were a reaction not only to the Negro and his white friends, but also to larger forces that were drastically dislocating Northern society.

The anti-abolition mobs were, in part, an outgrowth of Northern racism. Hatred of the black man prevailed in Northern society long before Jacksonian Americans had heard of the *Liberator*, William Lloyd Garrison, or "immediate abolition." Among both the crude and the genteel, in fact, Negrophobia had been common for as long as anyone cared to remember. Thus, while Garrison's early condemnations of Southern slavery scarcely raised eyebrows in the North, his crusade to destroy the American Colonization Society generated violent responses. For the abolitionists' war against African colonization infuriated not only zealous colonizationists but Negrophobes as well. Men assumed that abolitionists, march-

[18] New York *Courier and Enquirer*, March 20, June 6, September 1, 5, 1835; Webb, *Slavery and Its Tendencies* (Washington, D. C., 1856), 2, 5, and *passim*.

ing under the banner of "immediate abolition without expatriation," intended to assimilate the black man into American society.
And that goal, feared anti-abolitionists, could be accomplished
only through amalgamation.

The idea of amalgamation was undoubtedly painful for many
white Americans. For most it meant miscegenation, the debase-
ment of their posterity, and the downfall of white America. For
"gentlemen of property and standing," however, it also symbolized
the breakdown of distinctions among white men, the blurring of
social divisions, and the general leveling process that they saw enveloping ante-bellum America. They dreaded becoming cogs in a
mass society.

For such men, however, the antislavery movement embodied
other, more pressing treats. In the beginning, would-be anti-
abolitionists could dismiss the antislavery movement as trifling. The
Garrisonians, to be sure, obviously challenged the moral legiti-
macy of the society run by "respectable" men; Garrison's pronouncements clearly challenged the constitutional compromise
with slavery, the cornerstone of both national unity and the existing polity. Yet the Garrisonians were weak and ineffectual; they
had neither the means nor the power to disrupt the established
order. With the revolution in communications and the creation of
mass media, however, organized antislavery suddenly appeared to
be a major "conspiracy" against the status quo. Almost overnight,
it seemed, the nature of organized antislavery had changed; by
some nefarious means, Arthur Tappan and his associates had
transformed a weak and ineffectual movement into a highly
efficient, well-organized propaganda machine.

Their exaggerated vision of a relentless, powerful "combination"
terrified anti-abolitionists. Tappan and his associates clearly represented a major threat to their élite status. The Tappan group
seemed to have both the means and the power to disrupt the compromise with slavery and to challenge effectively the moral legiti-
macy of the established order. The New York associates, moreover,
symbolized the very forces in Northern society that anti-abolition-

ists found most threatening. They represented, in exaggerated form, the rise of organized pressure groups over which established leaders had little or no control. They bypassed city fathers and appealed directly to young and old, to simple and profound, to blacks as well as whites. They sought to manipulate large segments of Northern society through centrally directed auxiliaries, free newspapers, cheap tracts, massive petitions, horrifying images and pictures, and even hornbooks and primers; in other words, they used techniques that threatened to make obsolete traditional modes of social control.

Anti-abolitionist anguish, then, cannot be fully understood simply with reference to the antislavery movement. It was partly the by-product of larger forces that were drastically dislocating Jacksonian America and reorganizing Northern society around impersonal, large-scale organizations. Jacksonian America, as many historians have pointed out, was a society in transition; the old, traditional, agrarian order that Thomas Jefferson idealized was just out of reach, and the new order of modern capitalism was just coming into being. To men of the Jacksonian generation, therefore, the ways of the traditional community were neither wholly relevant nor completely irrelevant.

"Gentlemen of property and standing" had been raised, by and large, according to the dictates of the old community. They had been reared for an economy where gentlemen merchants, operating out of small shops in Albany or New Haven or even Philadelphia, still dabbled in virtually everything and dealt with the world as wholesalers, retailers, agents, shippers, financiers, and insurance brokers. They had been trained for leadership in a society where local men of "character" and "respectability" still dominated *all* affairs—not only political affairs, but economic, social, and moral affairs as well—and where common people generally deferred to their "betters." National leaders, to be sure, made many of the most important decisions; as a rule, however, they never shortcircuited local élites by appealing directly to the masses; by and large, they appealed to the people only through established local gentry, and thus they reinforced the existing status system of the traditional community.[19]

When men of this background came of age, however, they encountered a society that was in transition. Since the War of 1812, many Americans had been turning more and more to relatively large-scale, well-coordinated organizations to solve specific problems. In every area of American life, specialized organizations sprang up after the Treaty of Ghent, quickly established themselves, and spread rapidly from city to city, state to state, region to region. Some men founded organizations to increase production, manufacturing, and shipping; others, to build roads and canals; and still others, to increase the number of ministers and Sunday schools, to spread Bibles and tracts, to stop drinking and war, and to save souls by the thousands. Such organizations soon had scores of cadres and hundreds of agents, and many had budgets approaching $100,000. By 1830, as Tocqueville noted, Americans seemed to have a penchant for organizing and reorganizing. To be sure, the texture of economic, political, social, and religious life was a mixture of old and new. But life in America was moving toward bigness, specialization, impersonality, administrative coordination, and a regional or national orientation.

By their very nature, these new activities infringed upon the traditional prerogatives of community leaders and established organizations. The new organizations differed in goals, but they all required a network of auxiliaries or agents. Their appearance and expansion necessitated the development of extensive lines of communication and facilitated the rise of specialists in organization, administration, communication, and manipulation. As a result, the new organizations invariably disrupted established forms of social control and social organization. They competed with both traditional leaders and other organizations for funds, for cadre, and for loyal followers. They cut across traditional boundaries of kinship and community, intruded upon the prerogatives of pastors and

[19] For a recent discussion of this point, see Lynn L. Marshall, "The Strange Stillbirth of the Whig Party," *American Historical Review* 72 (January 1967), 452–53.

local gentry, and drew members of the local community into their orbit. In varying degrees, then, all of the new organizations encroached upon the accustomed powers of established organizations and traditional leaders.

The new organizations differed markedly, however, in the way they operated. Some tried to work almost entirely within the context of the traditional order. The American Colonization Society, for example, talked about persuading the "public mind" and enlightening the "people," but the society's pamphlets and newspapers aimed at men of rank and renown. Colonizationists, moreover, filled their ranks with careful attention to existing social ranks. And like Federalist and Jeffersonian leaders before them, leading colonizationists rarely bypassed local élites by taking their cause straight to the people; as a rule, they appealed to the masses only through local leaders of their persuasion. Their mode of operations thus reinforced the existing status system.

Other organizations, however, were more likely to violate the prerogatives of local gentry. The Temperance Society, which initially enjoyed wide support among the "better sort," turned more and more to mass meetings, revivalistic methods, public pledges, and direct appeals to the grass roots to further its cause. As a result, temperance men frequently angered local leaders: not only were their pronouncements objectionable, but their methods usurped the leadership role of pastors and other local leaders, and thus undermined the existing status system. The American Anti-Slavery Society, in the eyes of "respectable" men, was the worst of a bad lot; it carried organized agitation and the techniques of "popular excitement" to an extreme, appealing directly not only to white women and children, but to blacks as well. With the mechanization of printing and the sudden outpouring of free literature, the fearful envisaged the outlines of a gargantuan power; Arthur Tappan and his associates seemed to have both the means and the power to destroy the old order, and they were in the vanguard of forces that threatened to change America into a centrally directed mass society.

Thus to "gentlemen of property and standing" the American

Anti-Slavery Society became a monster, representing an overt threat to their beloved Republic, epitomizing forms and powers hostile to their leadership, and symbolizing forces antagonistic to traditional distinctions between followers and leaders, common men and gentlemen, and—worst of all—perhaps even between blacks and whites. Many responded with words; some issued threats; and others aroused their townsmen to violence and sought their enemy in battle.

Several years later, the crisis posed by the rise of organized anti-slavery passed. Arthur Tappan and his associates never fulfilled the premonitions of Northern anti-abolitionists. White supremacy prevailed, and the free Negro remained in the gutter. The fever of the mid-1830's subsided, and violent anti-abolition became virtually a thing of the past. Many of the underlying tensions remained, however, to haunt a troubled people for a long time to come.

Appendix A:
List of Rioters and Abolitionists

I. UTICA

A. Mob

John Anson
Benjamin Ballou
Harvey Barnard
Ezra S. Barnum
Samuel Beardsley
Henry M. Benedict
Alvin Blakesly
Adam Bowman
Truman K. Butler
Joshua M. Church
Lewis W. Clark
Amos Cleaver
Thomas Colling
Elon Comstock
Benjamin Franklin Cooper
Augustine G. Dauby
Ezra Dean
John C. Devereaux
Samuel Doolittle
Joseph H. Dwight
John Egan
William H. Fellows

Thomas M. Francis
Theodore Sedgwick Gold
Timothy O. Grannis
Francis W. Guiteau
Ephraim Hart
Jarvis M. Hatch
Burton Hawley
Chester Hayden
Augustus Hickox
George J. Hopper
George W. Hubbard
Kellogg Hurlburt
Holmes Hutchinson
Alexander B. Johnson
Robert Jones
James H. Keeling
John F. Kittle
Barent Bleecker Lansing
Richard Ray Lansing
Robert S. Lattimore
Ebenezer Leach
John D. Leland

James M. Lewis
Van Vechten Livingston
Robert Mc Bride
James Mc Donough
Orsamus B. Matteson
Rutger Bleecker Miller
Daniel J. Morris
S. Germond Mott
Jesse Newell
Norman C. Newell
William Curtis Noyes
Milton D. Parker
John B. Pease
Daniel Penfield
Thomas Rockwell
Chauncey Rowe
Richard Sanger

Gerry Sanger
Horatio Seymour
——— Skinner
Hiram S. Smith
Nicholas Smith
Rudolph Snyder
Albert Southmayd
Julius A. Spencer
Isaiah Tiffany
William Tracy
David Wager
Nicholas N. Weaver
Edmund A. Wetmore
Abraham B. Williams
Henry Hunt Williams
James Watson Williams
Charles S. Wilson

B. Abolitionists

Samuel H. Addington
John Bailey
John S. Bailey
Moses S. Bailey
Erastus Barnes
Samuel Bayley
Elias R. Beadle
Samuel M. Beckwith
Arba Blair
George Brayton
Elisha Cadwell
Ezekiel Clark
E. P. Clark
James Clark
Oren Clark
Welcome Clark
Henry S. Cole
J. D. Corey
Abijah Crane
Thomas Davis
Robert Debnam
James C. De Long
George Luther Dickinson

Jesse W. Doolittle
George D. Foster
John Frost
Wells M. Gaylord
James C. Gilbert
W. Frederick Gould
William H. Gray
Beriah Green
James Griffeths
John P. Guest
William D. Hamlin
Edward D. Herrick
Amaziah Hotchkiss
Thomas James
Levi Kellogg
Levi Spencer Kellogg
Palmer Vose Kellogg
Spencer Kellogg
Orin Kendall
John S. Lattimore
George Lawson
Lewis Lawrence
Samuel Lightbody

Joseph T. Lyman
David Lynes
John Martin
Thomas M. Martyn
William G. Miller
Abijah Mosher
Henry Nash
Henry Newland
Job Parker
Stephen M. Perine
Leonard P. Rising
William G. Rodgers
Thomas Roundey
Amos Savage
James Sayre
Asaph Seymour
John B. Shaw
George Smith
Jacob Snyder
Frederick Southworth
Alvan Stewart

Thomas Stevenson
Shubael Storrs
Charles Stuart
John F. Temple
Briggs W. Thomas
Daniel Thomas
John Thomas
Richard C. Thomas
Thomas Thomas
Ira Thurber
Philip Thurber
Henry D. Tucker
Jacob Vanderheyden
Josiah J. Ward
Jared Eliot Warner
Alfred Wells
Oliver Wetmore
Noah White
Morris Wilcox
Oliver Norton Worden
Francis Wright

II. CINCINNATI

A. Mob

Thomas W. Bakewell
Joseph S. Bates
Joseph Benham
Wilson Brown
Robert Buchanan
William Burke
Jacob Burnet
John A. D. Burroughs
John O. Clark
James F. Conover
David T. Disney
John Foote
Charles Fox
Archibald Gordon
Joseph Graham
David Griffey
William Greene

William Groesbeck
Charles Hale
Archibald Irwin
Levi James
Edward Kinsey
Josiah Lawrence
Nicholas Longworth
David Loring
James Loring
Hamilton Lyon
Robert T. Lytle
Milton McLean
Julien Neville
Morgan Neville
George W. Neff
Nathaniel Greene Pendleton
Joseph Pierce

C. R. Ramsay
Nathaniel C. Read
Oliver M. Spencer
Jacob Strader
Peyton Symmes
Joseph Talbot
Samuel Talbot
Eben S. Thomas

William Tift
Benjamin Urner
Timothy Walker
Jesse Whitcomb
Allen Wilson
John H. Wood
John Crafts Wright

B. Abolitionists

Gamaliel Bailey
Amzi Barber
Benjamin Bassett
James Gillespie Birney
Emeline Bishop
Joseph C. Clopper
Isaac Colby
Christian Donaldson
William Donaldson
John Faulkner
William Holyoke
Augustus Hopkins
Albert Kellogg

Susan E. Lowe
James C. Ludlow
Phebe Matthews
Thomas Maylin
John Melindy
Edward Patterson
Rees E. Price
Achilles Pugh
Marius Robinson
F. A. Sayre
Winthrop B. Smith
William T. Truman
Augustus Wattles

III. NEW YORK CITY MOB

Joseph G. Allen
John Armstrong
Theodore N. Baldwin
Jacob Blackledge
William Brockington
George Brown
William Brunah
George W. Bull
James Burn
James Burrows
William Campbell
John Cappan
Henry Clarrot
Thomas Comb(s)
Alexander Crawford
Abraham Davis

William H. Day
Timothy Donovan
Thomas Dowd
John Doxey
Edgar Dozy
Nicholas Eaery
Adolphus Elliott
John Edwards
Daniel Fitzgerald
James Flinn
John Gateright
George Gaybright
Francis Gibson
Robert Gibson
John Gilbert
William Gilbert

Samuel Goodwin
Stephen Gordon
Charles Halliday
Benjamin C. Hallsted
Daniel Holden
Francis I. Hope
Francis Indelope
Edward James
Francis Kelly
Murtagh Kelly
Thomas Kelly
John Lang
Stephen Lane
Thomas Lee (alias Rogers)
William Lee
Henry Leipner
A. Levi
George Ludlow
John Marsh
James M'Dermott
John M'Govern
Horace Mazy
George Miller
James Moneypenny
James Mowry
Michael Nealen
John Nixon
John Oaks
George Parmlee
Arthur Pillsworth
Edward Pillsworth
James Quin

Joseph Reed
Patrick Riley
Samuel Robbins
William Rockingham
Henry G. Rose
Andrew Rourke
Isaac Skates
John Skinner
Isaac Soule
Henry Spencer
Horace Spencer
George Spream
Henry Stewart
(alias Woods)
William Sweeney
Levi Tabor
Ezekiel Thatcher
William Thompson
Henry Townshend
John Vanderbogart
John Van Loan
Peter Van Loon
Thomas Vultee
Robert D. Walker
Cornelius White
Luke Williams
Jacob Wilson
John Wilson
William Wilson
Thomas Wood
Jacob Young

Appendix B:
Sources for Career Lines

I used only the sources indicated in the text for constructing data on the New York City mob. Among New York's many newspapers, the *Sun* and the *Journal of Commerce* were particularly helpful. The *Sun* carried extensive accounts of the judicial proceedings following the riot; the official records of the Court of Special Sessions (the court that either tried or disposed of the rioters) apparently exist, but I was unable to locate anyone—either at the Hall of Records or at the Municipal Archives—who had the slightest idea where these records are stored.

In constructing the career lines on the men of Cincinnati and Utica, I used dozens of sources. It would be pointless to list every source that I used, but the following lists contain the principal items:

I. UTICA

A. Manuscripts and Other Unpublished Materials

Daughters of the American Revolution (Oneida Chapter), "Bible, Cemetery and Church Records," typescript, 13 vols., Utica, 1925–1950, Utica Public Library.

First Presbyterian Church, Miscellaneous Papers, Oneida Historical Society.

Literary Club—Minute Book, 1832–1834, Oneida Historical Society.

Manuscript Census Returns, National Archives.

Oneida County Bible Society, Record Book, Oneida Historical Society.

Oneida County Baptist Church Records, Oneida Historical Society.

Oneida County Cemetery Records, Oneida Historical Society.

Reformed Dutch Church Accounts, Oneida Historical Society.

Second Baptist Church—Record Book, 1820–1839, Oneida Historical Society.

Second Presbyterian Church—Roll Book, Oneida Historical Society.

Utica Temperance Society Records, Oneida Historical Society.

B. Printed Sources

Articles of Faith and Practice of the Second Baptist Church . . . , With a List of Its Members. Utica, 1835.

Bagg, Moses, ed. *Memorial History of Utica.* Syracuse, 1892.

———. *Pioneers of Utica.* Utica, 1877.

Bielby, Isaac P. *Sheriffs of Oneida County.* Utica, 1890.

Brief History of the First Presbyterian Church . . . Together with the Names of the Members of the Church. Utica, 1829.

Catalogue of the Resident Members of the First Presbyterian Church, Utica. Utica, 1841.

Cookingham, Henry J. *History of Oneida County.* 2 vols. Chicago, 1912.

———. *Recollections of the Oneida Bar.* Utica, 1903.

Corey, D. G. *A Quarter of Century.* Utica, 1867. [Contains a list of Baptist church members who died after 1842.]

[Durant, Samuel W.] *History of Oneida County.* Philadelphia, 1878.

Fowler, Philemon H. *Historical Sketch of Presbyterianism Within the Bounds of the Synod of Central New York.* Utica, 1877.

Harding, John R. *One Hundred Years of Trinity Church, Utica.* Utica, 1898.

Hurd, Edith S. *A Century in Westminster.* Utica, 1955.

Piper, John. *Thoughts at Random: On the Lights of Other Days of . . . Utica.* Utica, 1855.

Pouroy, J. *Annals of Oneida County.* Rome, New York, 1851.

Proceedings of the New York Anti-Slavery Convention, Held at Utica, October 21, and New York Anti-Slavery Society. Held at Peterboro', October 22, 1835. Utica, 1835.

Risley, Edwin H. *Historical Sketch of the (Second) Tabernacle Baptist Church.* Utica, 1919.

Souvenir of the Eightieth Anniversary of the Founding of the Reformed (Dutch) Church of Utica, 1830–1910. Utica, 1910.

Third Annual Report of the American British Tract Society . . . with a List of Life Members. Utica, 1829.

[Thomas, William.] *The Enemies of the Constitution Discovered . . . .* New York, 1835.

Wager, Daniel E. *Men, Events, Lawyers, Politics and Politicians of Early Rome.* Utica, 1879.

———. *Our County and Its People.* Boston, 1896.

Utica City Directory. Utica, 1833, 1834, 1836–1837.

II. CINCINNATI

A. Manuscripts and Other Unpublished Materials

Aaron, Daniel, "Cincinnati, 1818–1838: A Study of Attitudes in the Urban West," Unpub. Ph.D. dissertation, Harvard, 1942.

Central Christian Church (Disciples of Christ), Records, Cincinnati Historical Society.

First Unitarian Church of Cincinnati, Records, 1830–1917, Cincinnati Historical Society.

"Hickory Club," Subscription Lists, Cincinnati Historical Society.

Journal of David Kirkpatrick Este, Cincinnati Historical Society.

Kemper, Willis M., "History of the First Presbyterian Church on Walnut Hills, 1818–1878," typescript, Cincinnati, 1918, Cincinnati Historical Society.

Lists of Names of the Members of the Old Columbia (Baptist) Church, 1790–1911, Cincinnati Historical Society.

Manuscript Census Returns, National Archives.

Obituaries of Cincinnatians, newspaper clippings, Cincinnati Historical Society.

Records of Baptisms, Marriages and Deaths of the First New Jerusalem Society (Swedenborgian) of Cincinnati, 1809–1847, Cincinnati Historical Society.

Records of Infant Baptism, First Presbyterian Church, Cincinnati Historical Society.

Vine Street Congregational Church, Minutes of the Board of Trustees, 1831–1926, Cincinnati Historical Society.

Vine Street Congregational Church, Record Book, 1831–1868, Cincinnati Historical Society.

B. Printed Sources

Act of Incorporation of the "Second Presbyterian Church and Society in Ohio." Cincinnati, 1829.

Catalogue of the Members of the First Orthodox Congregational Church of Cincinnati. Cincinnati, 1847.

Cincinnati Almanac for 1840.

Cincinnati Almanac for 1846.

Cincinnati City Directory. Cincinnati, 1825, 1829, 1836, 1839.

Cist, Charles, *Sketches and Statistics of Cincinnati in 1851.* Cincinnati, 1851.

Constitution and Address of the Cincinnati Society for the Promotion of Knowledge. Cincinnati, 1848. [Episcopalian]

Dabney, Wendell Phillips. *Cincinnati's Colored Citizens.* Cincinnati, 1926.

Directory of the Seventh Presbyterian Church. Cincinnati, n. d.

Drake, B., and E. D. Mansfield, *Cincinnati in 1826.* Cincinnati, 1827.

Eisenlohr, Hugo G. *History of St. John's Unitarian Church.* Cincinnati, 1934.

Finley, James B. *Sketches of Western Methodism.* Cincinnati, 1854.

Ford, Henry A. and Kate B. *History of Cincinnati.* Cleveland, 1881.

History of the Ninth Street Baptist Church. Cincinnati, 1884.

Mansfield, Edward D. *Memoirs of the Life and Services of Daniel Drake . . . with Notices of the Early Settlement of Cincinnati.* Cincinnati, 1855.

———. *Personal Memories.* Cincinnati, 1879.

Manual of the First Orthodox Congregational Church. Cincinnati, 1856. [Includes membership list of the church from its founding.]

One Hundred and Fifty Years of Presbyterianism in the Ohio Valley, 1790–1940. Cincinnati, 1941.

Proceedings of the Ohio Anti-Slavery Convention . . . at Putnam. Cincinnati, 1835.

Proceedings of the Wardens and Vestry of Christ Church. Cincinnati, 1827.

Rule and Roll of Genl. Conference in Cincinnati. Cincinnati, 1836. [Includes names of local Methodists.]

Saga of the Welsh Congregational Church . . . 1840–1952. Cincinnati, 1952.

Semi-Centennial Celebration of the Vine Street Congregational Church. Cincinnati, 1881.

Taylor, William H. *A History of the Cincinnati Monthly Meeting of Friends.* Cincinnati, 1889.

Thayer, George Augustine. *The First Congregational Church (Unitarian) of Cincinnati: A Historical Sketch.* Cincinnati, 1917.

Bibliographical Essay

This essay is selective rather than exhaustive; it calls attention only to those works that I found to be especially valuable.

I. GENERAL AIDS

The handiest bibliographical guide to abolitionist history is Russel B. Nye, *Fettered Freedom* (East Lansing, Michigan, 1963). Good supplements are Louis Filler, *The Crusade Against Slavery* (New York, 1960); Dwight L. Dumond, *A Bibliography of Antislavery in America* (Ann Arbor, Michigan, 1961); James M. McPherson, *The Struggle for Equality: Abolitionists and the Negro in the Civil War and Reconstruction* (Princeton, 1964); and Eugene H. Berwanger, *The Frontier Against Slavery* (Urbana, Illinois, 1967).

The standard guide to Negro history is Monroe N. Work, *A Bibliography of the Negro in Africa and America* (New York, 1928). More recent, but less exhaustive, is Dorothy P. Porter, "Early American Negro Writings: A Bibliographical Study," *The Papers of the Bibliographical Society of America*, XXXIX (1945), 192–268. A convenient entry to the most important Negro materials is Leon Litwack, *North of Slavery* (Chicago, 1961).

There is no comprehensive guide to anti-abolitionist literature. Sometimes helpful, but occasionally misleading, are the footnotes and biblographies in Nye, Filler, and Dumond. More rewarding is Lorman Rather, *Powder Keg: Northern Opposition to the Antislavery Movement, 1831–1840* (New York, 1968).

On mob history, mob psychology, and methodology, the most convenient entry is George Rudé, *The Crowd in History* (New York, 1964). Relevant are R. W. Brown, "Mass Phenomena," in Gardner Lindzey, ed., *Handbook of Social Psychology* (Cambridge, Massachusetts, 1954); Allen Day Grimshaw, "A Study in Social Violence: Urban Race Riots in the United States" (Unpub. Ph.D. dissertation, University of Michigan, 1959); Neil J. Smelser, *Theory of Collective Behavior* (London, 1962); and Gordon S. Wood, "A Note on Mobs in the American Revolution," *William and Mary Quarterly*, 23 (October 1966), 635–42.

The handiest guide to the study of violence is "Patterns of Violence," *The Annals of the American Academy of Political and Social Science*, 364 (March 1966), entire issue. Also helpful are Elton B. McNeil, ed., *The Nature of Human Conflict* (Englewood Cliffs, New Jersey, 1965); Jules Masserman, ed., *Violence and War* (New York, 1963); Stanley E. Gunterman, "A Bibliography on Violence and Social Change," *Proceedings of the Academy of Political Science*, 29 (July 1968), 183–90; and Hugh Davis Graham and Ted Robert Gurr, eds., *Violence in America* (New York, 1969).

II. MOBS: PRINTED MATERIALS

Due to the public's appetite for facts and figures about mobs, most of the basic materials on anti-abolitionist mobs are in print. Curious about the workings of mobs, Hezekiah Niles reprinted many valuable "eye-witness" accounts and public documents in his *Weekly Register* (Baltimore, 1811–1849). Antislavery newspapers regularly reported mob activities and reprinted many pertinent articles—both hostile and friendly to the mobs—from other newspapers. Among the more useful abolitionist newspapers are the *Liberator* (Boston, 1831–1865), edited by William Lloyd Garrison; the *Emancipator* (New York and Boston, 1833–1850), edited mostly by Joshua Leavitt; and the *Philanthropist* (Cincinnati, 1835–1847), edited by James G. Birney and Gamaliel Bailey. Also helpful are *The Friend of Man* (Utica, New York, 1836–1842), edited by William Goodell; *Frederick Douglass' Paper* (1847–1863; title and place varies); the *Pennsylvania Freeman* (Philadelphia, 1838–1844), edited by John Greenleaf Whittier; and the *National Anti-Slavery Standard* (New York, 1840–1870), edited for some time by David and Lydia Child.

Indispensable for understanding violent anti-abolitionism is the New York *Courier and Enquirer*, edited by James Watson Webb from 1829 to 1861. Helpful for the 1850's is the most radical of all anti-abolitionist journals, the New York *Day Book*, edited by John Van Evrie and N. R. Stimson. Almost every newspaper in the North carried articles on the anti-abolitionist uproar of 1835–1837. Particularly useful are: Albany *Argus*, Albany *Evening Journal*, Alton *Spectator*, Alton *Telegraph*, Boston *Atlas*, Boston *Courier*, Cincinnati *Journal*, *Cincinnati Republican*, *Cincinnati Whig*, *Connecticut Journal*, *Hazard's Register of Pennsylvania*, New Haven *Register*, New York *Commercial Advertiser*, New York *Herald*, Oneida *Whig*, Philadelphia *Gazette*, Philadelphia *Morning Pennsylvanian*, Rochester *Daily Democrat*, and Utica *Observer*.

Valuable for colonizationist opinion on mobs is the *African Repository* (Washington, D. C., 1825–1844).

Often more valuable than newspaper accounts are the books, pamphlets, and articles by contemporaries and by later evaluators. An exhaustive bibliographical guide to the Lovejoy episode is John Gill, *Tide Without Turning* (Boston, 1958). The Alton riot can be followed profitably in Joseph and Owen Lovejoy, *Memoir of the Rev. Elijah P. Lovejoy* (New York, 1838), and in Edward Beecher, *Narrative of Riots at Alton* (Alton, 1838). More revealing are the "phonographic" reports of the trials of both those who defended the press and those who destroyed it, compiled by William S. Lincoln and published as *Alton Trials* (New York, 1838). Also useful are the reminiscences of Henry Tanner in *History of the Rise and Progress of the Alton Riots* (Buffalo, 1878) and in *The Martyrdom of Lovejoy* (Chicago, 1881). Disappointing are the memoirs of Lovejoy's most formidable opponent, Usher F. Linder; his *Reminiscences of the Early Bench and Bar of Illinois* (Chicago, 1879) understandably minimize his role in the events leading to the riot. More helpful is the account of George T. M. Davis, the lawyer for some of the leading rioters, in his *Autobiography* (New York, 1891). Also helpful is the eye-witness report of an "innocent bystander," which the Cincinnati *Journal* serialized in November, 1837.

Nearly every Garrisonian wrote about the Garrison mob. The fullest accounts include that of his children, Wendell P. and Francis J. Garrison, *William Lloyd Garrison* (4 vols.; Boston, 1885); Maria Weston Chapman, *Right and Wrong in Boston* (Boston, 1836); and *Proceedings of the Anti-Slavery Meeting Held in Stacy Hall, Boston, on the Twentieth Anniversary of the Mob of October 21, 1835* (Boston, 1855).

Theodore Lyman III, in defense of his father's actions, published Mayor Lyman's records in *Papers Relating to the Garrison Mob* (Cambridge, 1870). Other documents were published by Ellis Ames, "Garrison Mob," *Proceedings of the Massachusetts Historical Society*, 18 (February, 1881). The target of the mob, George Thompson, has been frequently ignored by historians; his experiences are partly covered in his *Letters and Addresses . . . During His Mission in the United States* (Boston, 1837); the only study of his life is Raymond English, "George Thompson and the Climax of Philanthropic Radicalism, 1830–1842" (Unpub. Ph.D. dissertation, Cambridge University, 1948).

Information on other New England mobs can be found in various abolitionist reminiscences and biographies. Particularly useful are the accounts of John Greenleaf Whittier, Henry Stanton, and Parker Pillsbury. A full abolitionist account of one small-town mob is Isaac Stearn, *Right and Wrong in Mansfield, Mass., or an Account of the Pro-Slavery Mob of October 10th, 1836* (Pawtucket, Massachusetts, 1837).

Less has been written about the New York City mobs. Most helpful is Edward S. Abdy, *Journal of a Residence and Tour in the United States* (3 vols.; London, 1835). John Neal's defense of his actions in his *Wandering Recollections of a Somewhat Busy Life* (Boston, 1869) does not square with his earlier account, which can be found among the papers of the American Colonization Society (Library of Congress). Supplemental are the biographies of Isaac T. Hopper, the Tappan brothers, and Elizur Wright, Jr. Also helpful as Henry Fowler, *The American Pulpit* (New York, 1856); Asher Taylor, *Recollections of the Seventh Regiment* (New York, 1868); and Gustave de Beaumont, *Marie: or Slavery in the United States* (Barbara Chapman translation; Stanford, 1958). The best recent account of the 1834 riot is Linda Kerber, "Abolitionists and Amalgamators: The New York City Race Riots of 1834," *New York History*, 48 (January 1967), 28–39.

A few upstate New York mobs are well covered. Important pamphlets are "Defensor" [William Thomas], *The Enemies of the Constitution Discovered, or, an Enquiry into the Origin and Tendency of Popular Violence* (Utica, 1835); *The Mob at Troy* (Troy, 1836); and *The Report of the Committee of Internal Affairs to the Assembly of New York: Dealing with Mobs* (Albany, 1838).

Particularly useful for Cincinnati and other Ohio mobs are Gilbert Hobbes Barnes and Dwight L. Dumond, eds., *The Letters of Theodore Dwight Weld and Sarah Grimké, 1822–1844* (2 vols.; American Historical Assn., 1934), and Dwight L. Dumond, ed., *Letters of James Gillespie Birney, 1831–1857* (2 vols.; American Historical Assn., 1938). More detailed are *Narrative of the Late Riotous Proceedings Against the Liberty of the Press in Cincinnati* (Cincinnati, 1836); William Birney, *James G. Birney and His Times* (New York, 1890); and Levi Coffin, *Reminiscences* (Cincinnati, 1880). The Granville riot of 1836 is covered in two articles by Robert Price, "The Ohio Anti-Slavery Convention of 1836," *Ohio Archaeological and Historical Quarterly*, 45 (April 1836), 173–188, and "Further Notes on Granville's Anti-Abolition Disturbances of 1836," *ibid.*, 45 (October 1836), 365–368. Helpful on the Cincinnati race riot of 1829 are "Public Warning to Cincinnati Negroes and Commentary on Their Reaction," *Journal of Negro History*, 8 (July 1923), 331–332, and Richard Wade, "The Negro in Cincinnati, 1800–1830," *ibid.*, 39 (January 1954), 43–57.

On the burning of Pennsylvania Hall, many of the pamphlets that appeared immediately after the event were subsequently collected and published as *The History of Pennsylvania Hall, Which Was Destroyed by a Mob* (Philadelphia, 1838). Supplemental are William Ellery Channing, *Remarks on the Slavery Question . . . to Jonathan Phillips, Esq.* (Boston, 1839), and James Trecothic Austin, *Review of the Rev. Dr. Channing's Letter to Jonathan Phillips* (Boston, 1839). Helpful on Philadelphia and Pennsylvania race riots are Edward R. Turner, *The Negro in Pennsylvania* (Washington, D. C., 1911); W. E. B. DuBois, *The Philadelphia Negro* (Philadelphia, 1899); Abdy, *Journal of a Residence and Tour in the United States;* and William F. Wormer, "The Columbia Race Riots," *Lancaster County Historical Society Papers*, 26 (1922), 175–87.

III. MANUSCRIPTS

Few rioters left any account of their participation in mobs. I did find, however, a few important letters of John Neal on the New York City mob of October, 1833, in the American Colonization Society Papers, and several very suggestive letters on the New York riot of July, 1834, in the Miscellaneous Papers of the New York Historical Society. In reaching an understanding about the workings of the American Anti-Slavery Society, I found the society's minutes particularly helpful. I also found the Samuel L. Gouverneur Papers to be most valuable for following the pamphlet campaign of 1835. Like every student of the antislavery question, I consulted with profit the manuscript collections of white abolitionists. Here is a list of manuscript collections in which I found significant information:

African Colonization Society Papers, Library of Congress
American Anti-Slavery Society Papers, Boston Public Library
Salmon P. Chase Papers, Library of Congress
Joseph Clopper Collection, Cincinnati Historical Society
William Lloyd Garrison Papers, Boston Public Library
Samuel L. Gouverneur Papers, New York Public Library
Andrew Jackson Papers, Library of Congress (microfilm)
William Learned Marcy Papers, Library of Congress
Joshua Leavitt Papers, Library of Congress
Samuel May, Jr., Papers, Boston Public Library
Robert Todd Lytle Correspondence, Cincinnati Historical Society
Miscellaneous Papers—Alabama, New York Historical Society
Miscellaneous Papers—Riots—1834, New York Historical Society
New England Anti-Slavery Society, Papers, Boston Public Library
Amos A. Phelps Papers, Boston Public Library
Gerrit Smith Papers, Syracuse University Library (microfilm)
Benjamin Tappan Papers, Library of Congress
Lewis Tappan Papers, Library of Congress
Martin Van Buren Papers, Library of Congress (microfilm)
Timothy Walker Papers, Cincinnati Historical Society
Elizur Wright, Jr., Papers, Library of Congress

IV. ANTI-ABOLITIONIST LITERATURE

Anti-abolitionists wrote extensively, both before and after the Civil War, to persuade their fellow Northerners of the correctness of their position. Two typical anti-abolitionist histories of the entire ante-bellum period are Felix de Fontaine, *The History of American Abolitionism* (New York, 1861), and George Lunt, *Origin of the Late War* (New York, 1866). More radical is R. G. Horton, *A Youth's History of the Great Civil War* (New York, 1868). An unbelievable, but once popular, racist polemic is John Van Evrie, *White Supremacy and Negro Subordination* (New York, 1868). Both Horton's and Van Evrie's books went through numerous editions. In addition to these four books, I found the following helpful:

Adams, Nehemiah, *The Sable Cloud*. Boston, 1861.
———. *A South-Side View of Slavery*. Boston, 1854.

Austin, James Trecothic. *Remarks on Dr. Channing's Slavery.* Boston, 1835.

———. *Remarks on Dr. Channing's Slavery* [with postscript]. Charleston, 1836.

———. *Review of the Rev. Dr. Channing's Letter to Jonathan Phillips, Esq. on the Slavery Question.* Boston, 1839.

Bacon, Leonard. *Slavery Discussed in Occasional Essays from 1833–1846.* New York, 1846.

Bird, Robert Montgomery. *Peter Pilgrim: Or, A Rambler's Recollections.* Philadelphia, 1838.

———. *Sheppard Lee.* New York, 1836.

Black, Jeremiah Sullivan. *The Doctrines of the Democratic and Abolition Parties Contrasted.* Philadelphia, 1864.

Bolokitten, Oliver [pseud.]. *A Sojourn in the City of Amalgamation in the Year of Our Lord 19—.* New York, 1835.

Burden, Jesse R. *Remarks . . . in the Senate of Pennsylvania, on the Abolition Question.* Philadelphia, 1838.

Campbell, John. *Negro-mania: Being an Examination of the Falsely Assumed Equality of the Various Races of Men.* Philadelphia, 1851.

Clough, Simon. *A Candid Appeal to the Citizens of the United States . . .* New York, 1834.

Colfax, Richard H. *Evidence Against the Views of the Abolitionists . . .* New York, 1833.

[Colton, Calvin] *Abolition a Sedition.* Philadelphia, 1839.

———. *The Americans by An American in London.* London, 1833.

———. *Colonization and Abolition Contrasted.* Philadelphia, 1839.

———. *Political Abolition.* New York, 1844.

———. *Thoughts on the Religious State of the Country.* London, 1837.

Cox, Samuel Sullivan. *Eight Years in Congress.* New York, 1865.

Debate on Modern Abolitionism in the General Conference of the Methodist Episcopal Church. Cincinnati, 1836.

Dewey, Orville. *A Discourse on Slavery and the Annexation of Texas.* New York, 1844.

Fitzgerald, W. P. N. *A Scriptural View of Slavery and Abolition.* Second Edition. New Haven, 1839.

Gannett, Ezra Stiles. *Relation of the North to Slavery.* Boston, 1854.

Hill, Isaac. *Speech . . . on the Motion of Mr. Calhoun that the Senate Refuse . . . the Petition.* Washington, D. C., 1836.

Hodge, Charles. *Abolitionism*. Princeton, New Jersey, 1845.

Hopkins, John Henry. *Bible View of Slavery*. New York, 1863.

———. *Slavery: Its Religious Sanction* . . . Buffalo, 1851.

Horton, R. G. *Life and Public Services of James Buchanan*. New York, 1856.

Ingersoll, Charles J. *African Slavery in America*. Philadelphia, 1856.

———. . . . *View of the Texas Question*. Washington, D. C., 1844 [?].

James, Henry Field. *Abolition Unveiled; Or, Its Origin, Progress, and Pernicious Tendency Fully Developed*. Cincinnati, 1856.

Junkin, George. *The Integrity of Our National Union Vs. Abolitionism*. Cincinnati, 1843.

[Lord, Nathan.] *A Letter of Inquiry to Ministers* . . . *on Slavery*. Boston, 1850.

———. . . . *Second Letter to Ministers* . . . *on Slavery*. New York, 1855.

Morse, Samuel F. B. *An Argument on the Ethical Position of Slavery* . . . . New York, 1863.

———. *The Present Attempt to Dissolve the American Union, a British Aristocratic Plot*. New York, 1862.

Morse, Sidney Edwards. *The Bible and Slavery*. New York, 1855.

———. *Premium Questions on Slavery* . . . . New York, 1860.

Parker, Joel. *Papers and Slavery, Rebellion, etc., 1856–67*. 8 vols. Cambridge, 1867.

Paulding, James Kirke. *Slavery in the United States*. New York, 1836.

Priest, Josiah. *Slavery, As It Relates to the Negro* . . . *with Strictures on Abolitionism*. Albany, New York, 1843.

Reese, David Meredith. *A Brief Review of the "First Annual Report of the American Anti-Slavery Society* . . . ." New York, 1834.

———. *Humbugs of New York*. New York, 1838.

———. *Letters to the Honorable William Jay*. New York, 1835.

Rice, Nathan L. *A Debate on Slavery*. Cincinnati, 1846.

———. *Lectures on Slavery, Delivered in the First Presbyterian Church, Cincinnati*. Cincinnati, 1845.

———. *Lectures on Slavery: Delivered in the North Presbyterian Church, Chicago*, Chicago, 1860.

———. *The Pulpit: Its Relation to Our National Crisis*. New York, 1862.

———. *Ten Letters on the Subject of Slavery*. St. Louis, 1856.

Sawyer, William. *Negroes in Ohio* . . . . Washington, D. C., 1848.

Seabury, Samuel. *American Slavery Distinguished from the Slavery of English Theorists* . . . . New York, 1861.

Selections from the Speeches and Writings of Prominent Men in the United States, on the Subject of Abolition and Agitation . . . . New York, 1851.

Sleigh, William Willcocks. *Abolitionism Exposed!* Philadelphia, 1838.

Smith, Delazon. *Oberlin Unmasked.* Cleveland, 1837.

South Vindicated from the Treason and Fanaticism of the Northern Abolitionists. Philadelphia, 1836.

Spring, Gardiner. *The Danger and Hope of the American People* . . . . New York, 1843.

Stuart, Moses. *Conscience and the Constitution.* New York, 1850.

Sullivan, Thomas Russell. *Letters Against the Immediate Abolitionists* . . . . Boston, 1835.

————. *The Limits of Responsibility in Reforms.* Boston, 1861.

Tracy, Joseph. *Colonization and Missions* . . . . Boston, 1844.

————. *Natural Equality.* Windsor, Vermont, 1833.

Tyson, Job Roberts. *A Discourse Before the Young Men's Colonization Society of Pennsylvania* . . . . Philadelphia, 1834.

————. *Speech . . . on the Alleged Assault by Mr. Brooks on Senator Sumner* . . . . Washington, D. C., 1856.

————. *Speech . . . on the Fugitive Slave Laws* . . . . Washington, D. C., 1857.

Tyson, J. Washington. *The Doctrines of the "Abolitionists" Refuted.* Philadelphia, 1840.

Van Dyke, Henry. *The Character and Influence of Abolitionism!* New York, 1860.

Van Evrie, John H. *Negroes and Negro Slavery: The First, An Inferior Race—The Latter, Its Normal Condition.* Baltimore, 1853.

Wall, Garret Dorset. *Speech . . . on the Memorial . . . for the Abolition of Slavery . . . in D. C.* Washington, D. C., 1836.

Wayland, Francis. *The Limitations of Human Responsibility.* Boston, 1838.

Wayland, Francis, and Richard Fuller. *Domestic Slavery Considered as a Scriptural Institution* . . . . New York, 1845.

Woods, Leonard. *The Works of Leonard Woods.* 5 vols. Andover, 1850–1857.

Index

Aaron, Daniel, 138, 148

Abolitionists: fear of, 10, 15-19; and violence, 10, 15-19; as "incendiaries," 52-54; on their opponents, 132-33, 151, 155; social characteristics of, 134-50; as communications experts, 162

Adams, John Quincy, 162

African colonization: plan of, 21-22; attacked by Garrison, 21-26; endorsed by New York mob of 1833, 26-30; endorsed by other mobs, 30, 37, 118; supported by James Watson Webb, 31-32; and Northern racism, 31-32, 33, 34, 165-66; endorsed by James Hall, 41-42; as alternative to amalgamation and race war, 44-46; debated in Utica, 86. *See also* American Colonization Society.

African Repository, 24, 25

Albany *Argus*, 87

Allport, Floyd H., 83

Alton, Illinois: mob in, 3, 92-93, 100-11; colonizationists in, 30, 106; defended in Boston, 69; compared with Utica and Cincinnati, 92-93, 100-1; compared with Eastern cities, 110-11. *See also* Lovejoy, Elijah.

Alton *Observer*, 102-7 *passim*

Alvord, John Watson, 160

Amalgamation: defined, 16n; fear of, 30, 31-32, 40-46, 94-95, 114-15, 122, 166; and New York mob of 1833, 30, 31; and James Watson

Webb, 31-32; and New Haven, 38; and Cincinnati, 40-43, 94-95, 122; and New York riot of 1834, 43, 114-15, 120-22, 155; and Philadelphia riot of 1838, 43; answer to race problem, 43-46; and blurring of social distinctions, 45, 166; part of British conspiracy, 66, 71; disclaimed by abolitionists, 121, 122; and Cincinnati riot of 1841, 122-23

American Anti-Slavery Society: fear of, 10, 15-19, 47-49, 56-58, 58-59, 169-70; and violence, 10, 15-19; personnel indicted, 17; organization and power, 47-49, 52, 56-58, 58-59, 70, 71-72, 157-59, 169; organized, 49; becomes notorious, 50-51; and pamphlet campaign, 52, 53-54; use of pictures, 53-54; on its opposition, 54, 55; use of petitions, 57-58; and British antislavery movement, 62-63; and British "plot," 62-63, 70, 116; and printing revolution, 72-73; growth of, 75n; disavows amalgamation, 121; decline of, 157-59; and organized pressure groups, 169; and status system, 169

American Colonization Society: organized, 21; opposed by free blacks, 22; attacked by Garrison, 21-26, 165-66; denounced by Arthur Tappan, 25; attacked by British abolitionists, 25-26, 68; internal weaknesses of, 26, 30; and

190